T0330411

A Research Agenda for Tourism and Wellbeing

Elgar Research Agendas outline the future of research in a given area. Leading scholars are given the space to explore their subject in provocative ways, and map out the potential directions of travel. They are relevant but also visionary.

Forward-looking and innovative, Elgar Research Agendas are an essential resource for PhD students, scholars and anybody who wants to be at the forefront of research.

For a full list of Edward Elgar published titles, including the titles in this series, visit our website at www.e-elgar.com.

A Research Agenda for Tourism and Wellbeing

Edited by

HENNA KONU

Associate Professor of Tourism Business, Business School, University of Eastern Finland, Finland

MELANIE KAY SMITH

Associate Professor in Tourism Management, Budapest Metropolitan University, Hungary, Visiting Lecturer, University of Tartu, Pärnu College, Estonia and Research Associate at the Department of Historical and Heritage Studies, Faculty of Humanities, University of Pretoria, South Africa

Elgar Research Agendas

Cheltenham, UK • Northampton, MA, USA

Published by
Edward Elgar Publishing Limited
The Lypiatts
15 Lansdown Road
Cheltenham
Glos GL50 2JA
UK

Edward Elgar Publishing, Inc.
William Pratt House
9 Dewey Court
Northampton
Massachusetts 01060
USA

A catalogue record for this book
is available from the British Library

Library of Congress Control Number: 2023948406

This book is available electronically in the **Elgar**online
Geography, Planning and Tourism subject collection
http://dx.doi.org/10.4337/9781803924342

ISBN 978 1 80392 433 5 (cased)
ISBN 978 1 80392 434 2 (eBook)
Printed and bound by CPI Group (UK) Ltd, Croydon, CR0 4YY

Contents

Figures

Tables

Contributors

Fanny Aapio is a Master of Science (Faculty of Biological and Environmental Sciences) who emphasizes the importance of sustainable lifestyles. She focuses on consumer citizens and sustainability transitions, and sustainable eating. She works as a doctoral and project researcher at the University of Turku in the Academy of Finland's funded research project Biodiversity-Respectful Leadership (BIODIFUL) with a focus on sustainable food consumption.

Marcel Bastiaansen is a full Professor of Leisure and Tourism Experience at Breda University of Applied Sciences (BUas). At Tilburg University, he is affiliated with the department of Cognitive Neuropsychology of the School of Social and Behavioural Sciences. At BUas, Marcel is the co-founder and director of BUas's Experience Lab which houses a range of innovative research facilities for objective, biologically based measurements of visitor experiences and emotions. Marcel is also a member of the management team of BUas's Academy for Leisure and Events.

Jerram Bateman, PhD, is a Research Fellow within the Department of Social and Preventive Medicine at the University of Otago. His current research is focused on supportive care in cancer treatment and inequity in supportive care. His other research interests include tobacco control; HIV/AIDS; health and wellbeing in diaspora tourism; and resilience and development in rural communities.

Adiyukh Berbekova is an Assistant Professor of Tourism Management in the School of Travel Industry Management, Shidler College of Business, University of Hawaii at Mānoa. Her research interests include quality of life and destination performance, and crisis management in tourism. Email: aberbekova@umass.edu (corresponding author of a chapter).

J. A. (Tony) Binns has been Ron Lister Professor of Geography in the University of Otago, New Zealand since October 2004. He has worked in the field of Geography and Development Studies for over 40 years, and has a long-standing interest in post-conflict reconstruction, food production systems, food security and community-based development. Much of his field-based research has been undertaken in sub-Saharan Africa.

Daumantas Bočkus is Doctoral Researcher at the University of Eastern Finland, Lecturer and Project Researcher at Klaipeda University, and Associate Professor at the Lithuanian Business University of Applied Sciences. His research interests include wellness tourism development, destination marketing and competitiveness, tourist experience, entrepreneurship and cultural differences. He participates in the implementation of different international projects related to sustainable tourism development of the Baltic Sea region. Email: daumantas_b@yahoo.com (corresponding author of a chapter).

Larry Dwyer publishes widely in the areas of tourism economics, management, policy and planning. Larry is a Fellow and past President of the International Academy for Study of Tourism. He is past President of the International Association for Tourism Economics, and currently serves on its International Advisory Board. Email: larry.dwyer@uts.edu.au (corresponding author of a chapter).

Jelena Farkić is a Lecturer at the Breda University of Applied Sciences. Her academic interest lies in explorations of sociological and philosophical dimensions of being in the outdoors and other wild, derelict or abandoned places, with particular focus on existential concepts such as impermanence, comfort, wellbeing and ontological security. Email: farkic.j@buas.nl (corresponding author of a chapter).

Sebastian Filep, PhD, is Associate Professor and Assistant Dean at the School of Hotel and Tourism Management of the Hong Kong Polytechnic University, Hong Kong. Dr Filep has published widely on various topics related to tourist behaviour, health and wellbeing. He has global expertise on positive psychology and tourism, serving as an editor and author of three books on this topic. Filep is on editorial boards of multiple, major tourism journals.

Susan E. Gordon is an Associate Professor in the White Lodging-J.W. Marriott, Jr. School of Hospitality & Tourism Management at Purdue University. Her research focuses on employee wellbeing in the hospitality industry and how organizations can improve employee wellbeing through increasing supervisor and organizational support. Prior to entering academia, Dr Gordon worked for over ten years in the hospitality industry holding various management positions with Walt Disney World, Starwood Hotels & Resorts, and Marriott International. Email: gordon31@purdue.edu (corresponding author of a chapter).

Miia Grénman is a Postdoctoral Researcher focusing on a good and meaningful life. She is specialised in the transformative consumer research, positive psychology, wellness tourism and consumption, eudaimonic wellbeing, flourishing, and Gen Z. She works at the Jyväskylä University School of Business and Economics in the Academy of Finland's funded research project Biodiversity-Respectful Leadership (BIODIFUL) with a focus on biodiversity-respectful flourishing life and Gen Z as future consumers and leaders. Email: miia.grenman@utu.fi (corresponding author of a chapter).

Gorana Isailović is the President of the Medical SPA Association of Serbia and Vice-President of Forest Therapy Sout Eastern Europe. She is an ANFT-certified forest therapy guide and INFOM certified Forest medical specialist. She conducts research in the field of forest medicine, Rx nature, mental wellbeing, art in nature, and certification of forest trails, and takes an individual approach to health tourism and forest SPA clients.

Catherine Kelly, Dr., is a Geographer working in the tourism discipline within the School of Business and Law at the University of Brighton, UK. Her research interests include wellbeing tourism, blue spaces, and sustainability. She is the author of the bestselling public audience book *Blue Spaces: How and Why Water Can Make You Feel Better*. She sits on the UK government Environment Agency's national Blue Spaces Forum and works in policy advocacy to support the use of water for wellbeing. She also runs her own wellbeing and coastal environmental education enterprises. Email: C.kelly5@brighton.ac.uk (corresponding author of a chapter).

Raija Komppula is Professor Emeritus at University of Eastern Finland Business School. Her research focuses on tourist experiences, experience design and marketing.

Henna Konu, PhD, is working as an Associate Professor at University of Eastern Finland Business School focusing on examining nature-based tourism business. Her current research interests are designing experiential tourism services, customer engagement, nature connectedness, nature-based and wellbeing tourism, and transformative and regenerative travel. Email: henna.konu@uef.fi.

Xinran Lehto is a Professor in the White Lodging-J.W. Marriott, Jr. School of Hospitality & Tourism Management at Purdue University. Her area of expertise is experience design, management, and marketing in tourism and hospitality. Her research addresses how destinations and businesses can effectively plan and market experience-based products and programmes to consumers. Dr. Lehto considers wellness-centred design a strategic advantage for businesses and a social responsibility. Prior to her academic appointments, Dr. Lehto was a practitioner in the tourism industry.

Xavier Matteucci, PhD, is an Independent Researcher based in Vienna, Austria. He specialises in tourist experiences, wellbeing, cultural tourism, and qualitative research methodologies. Matteucci is particularly interested in the power of some leisure and tourism spaces in fostering transformative and emancipatory experiences. Email: xmatteucci@gmx.net (corresponding author of a chapter).

Scott McCabe is Professor of Marketing at Birmingham Business School, University of Birmingham, Edgbaston, Birmingham, UK, and Professor of Tourism Marketing and Management at the University of Eastern Finland Business School. His research focuses on tourist experience, behaviour and marketing, particularly disadvantaged consumers.

Ondrej Mitas is interested in the psychology of tourist and leisure experiences with a focus on emotions and well-being and quality of life outcomes. Specifically, he examines positive emotions in leisure and tourism experiences over time and the mechanisms of enjoyment, positivity, and flow in tourism and leisure experiences, and innovative research methods using longitudinal, visual and mixed-method approaches.

Dušan Perić is appointed as a Professor at the Faculty of Sport and Psychology in Novi Sad, Serbia. He was the president of the Expert Council of the Association for Recreation and Fitness of Serbia. He conducts research on Physiotherapy and Clinical Immunology and is the author of several textbooks and scientific monographs, as well as numerous scientific articles published in leading world journals. He is a member of the editorial board and reviewer of several international scientific journals in the field of sports and sports medicine.

Emma Pope (PhD, BA) is a nature-based Tourism Researcher interested in how experiences outdoors can create connection with self, nature and place. Her PhD explored the transformational potential of adventure tourism experiences, focusing on nature connection, wellbeing, and pro-environmental behaviour. She continues to explore these areas through her platform *Root Waymarking*. Email: e-pope@live.co.uk (corresponding author of a chapter).

Juulia Räikkönen is an Adjunct Professor and university researcher at the Biodiversity Unit of the University of Turku. Her research addresses sustainable tourism and recreation, experience design and management, and experience value in various tourism contexts, such as nature-based science tourism and tourism beyond humans. She coordinates the Academy of Finland's funded research project Biodiversity-Respectful Leadership (BIODIFUL) and leads the work package biodiversity and consumer transformation.

Melanie Kay Smith, PhD, is an Associate Professor and Researcher at Budapest Metropolitan University, Hungary and University of Tartu, Pärnu College, Estonia, as well as a Research Associate at the Department of Historical and Heritage Studies, Faculty of Humanities, University of Pretoria, South Africa. She has worked for over 20 years on issues relating to health tourism, spas, wellness and wellbeing. She has lectured extensively on these subjects in several countries and has published many books, journal articles and chapters. She has been a Consultant for ETC/UNWTO and an invited Keynote Speaker at numerous international health tourism and wellness conferences worldwide. Email: msmith@metropolitan.hu.

Muzaffer Uysal is a Professor and Chair of the Department of Hospitality and Tourism Management, Isenberg School of Management at the University of Massachusetts, Amherst. His current research interests centre on tourism demand/supply interaction, impact and tourism development, and quality of life research in tourism and hospitality.

Elli Vento is a Postdoctoral Researcher at the University of Eastern Finland Business School. She has been exploring the effects of social tourism in the Finnish context. Email: elli.vento@uef.fi (corresponding author of a chapter).

1 Progress in tourism and wellbeing research

Melanie Kay Smith and Henna Konu

1.1 Preface

The rationale for writing and editing this book came from a perceived need to revisit the relationship between tourism and wellbeing in a post-COVID era, considering the significant and sometimes devastating impact that the pandemic had on both travel and health. Authors almost immediately started to note an increasing interest in health and wellness tourism in the post-COVID era (Jiang & Wen, 2020). It was suggested that wellbeing and wellness could become attractive factors for tourists, providing an impetus for developing new activities and products in tourism destinations, as well as dealing with crisis and adversity (Pocinho et al., 2022). It is important to note, of course, that travel became impossible at some stages during the pandemic. As a result, authors started to question the benefits of short breaks or excursions close to home compared to long distance or international travel (Packer, 2022), but the results of the studies were somewhat inconclusive (Lin et al., 2021). What emerged from the post-COVID literature was that tourism and travel were greatly missed by the travelling public and many were willing to take the risks involved to benefit from relaxation, social connectedness and personal growth (Aebeli et al., 2021). However, many tourists, as well as industry professionals, are also mindful of the need to pay greater attention to sustainability, avoiding the previous mistakes which led to overtourism in many popular destinations.

1.2 Introduction

The relationship between tourism and wellbeing has been explored for many decades already, especially those studies that also measured the (relative) importance of travel for quality of life and life satisfaction (e.g., Bushell & Sheldon, 2009; Smith & Puczkó, 2017). In recent years, interest in the relationship between the topics has grown exponentially, but it has been suggested that research in this area is fragmented (Vada et al., 2020). The field of tourism and wellbeing studies spans several fields and disciplines from philosophy to positive psychology to policy and product development. In their systematic review of tourism and wellbeing studies in the field of positive psychology, Vada et al. (2020) state that the main variables, which are measured in current research are happiness, wellbeing, emotions and life satisfaction. While the PERMA model (Positive emotions, Engagement, Relationships, Meaning and Achievement) has been applied quite often using these five building blocks of wellbeing and happiness (Seligman, 2004), certain emotions have not been covered in as much detail as others, for example, kindness and gratitude (Filep et al., 2017). Vada et al. (2020) also highlight the relative lack of studies on residents, host communities and tourism workers. It is only recently that studies are turning their attention to the wellbeing of residents (Godovykh et al., 2023).

The extent to which tourism can contribute to happiness or subjective wellbeing has been researched fairly extensively in recent years (McCabe & Johnson, 2013; Chen et al., 2013; Nawijn & Filep, 2016; de Bloom et al., 2017; Pyke et al., 2016; Kwon and Lee, 2020), with several studies aiming to ascertain how far tourism contributes to longer term wellbeing (Chen et al., 2013; Nawijn et al., 2013; Kirillova et al., 2017; Mitas et al., 2017). It was noted that more research is needed to determine how behavioural choices affect tourists' subjective wellbeing, including timing, choice of destination or activities, as well as influencing factors like age, life-stage or cultural background (Mitas et al., 2016). The need to research the role of relationships in tourism and wellbeing has also been noted, for example, regarding social connections and connections with nature (Filep et al., 2022).

The link between tourism, nature and wellbeing has been researched for several decades, but it has been re-examined more intensively since the pandemic (Santos et al., 2020). One systematic review of tourism, nature and wellbeing dates interest in the field back to 1989 (Font-Barnet & Andreu, 2023). A perceived need for forms of 'healing tourism' were propounded, arguing that social wellbeing can be improved by spending time in outdoor locations (Ma et al., 2020). Some researchers have returned to the concept of 'attention restoration theory' (Kaplan & Kaplan, 1989), which explores the restorative effects of being in natural landscapes (Lehto & Lehto, 2019; Buckley & Westaway, 2020; Packer, 2021). References to so-called 'therapeutic landscapes' or 'healing places', which can include green spaces, seasides, deserts and even thermal bathing sites, have appeared frequently (Gesler, 1992). Abraham et al.'s (2010) work is quite often cited because of its reference to the mental, physical and social wellbeing benefits of landscapes. Little (2015) also referred to the transformational wellbeing benefits of nature. There has been a consensus in comparative natural landscape studies that seasides afford the most therapeutic benefits (Gascon et al., 2017; Ram & Smith, 2019) and that deserts are the most spiritual spaces (Moufakkir & Selmi, 2018). However, there has been a growing number of studies on green spaces which promote the benefits of spending time in nature-based and protected areas such as national parks (Smith & Puczkó, 2017; Azara et al., 2018). The interest in forest therapy has also been growing because of its proven health benefits (Ohe et al., 2017), with some researchers exploring the wellbeing benefits of forest therapy experiences for tourists (Konu, 2015; Komppula & Konu, 2017).

The role of spirituality within wellbeing is a more elusive subject, which has sometimes been connected to nature-based experiences (Sharpley & Jepson, 2011), in addition to religious ones. One recent study showed that definitions of spirituality for Millennials and Generation Z are mostly linked to connections to self as well as nature (Smith et al., 2021). Even when tourists are spending time in spiritual buildings such as temples, the surrounding natural landscape is of great importance too (Jiang et al., 2018). Smith (2022) shows that spiritual tourists tend to engage with other spiritual beliefs and traditions in different geographical contexts but concludes that the inner journey is more important than the physical location. Several studies of spiritual tourism have focused on self-discovery through challenging experiences relating to pilgrimage (Kato & Progano, 2017) or adventure (Cheer et al., 2017). Visiting retreats, ashrams, temples, meditation centres and doing yoga feature quite prominently in tourism and wellbeing research, which is often centred around personal healing (Norman & Pokorny, 2017). Many studies have started to explore eudaimonic paths to wellbeing through forms of tourism that involve spiritual as well as transformational activities. This might refer to desire to connect with a 'true' or 'authentic' self (Kelly & Smith, 2017) or to transform into a 'better' person (Reisinger, 2013; Sheldon, 2020; Smith, 2023).

The differentiation between hedonic and eudaimonic wellbeing has become a prominent theme in both philosophical and psychological studies of tourism and wellbeing since the early 2010s (Filep, Moyle & Skavronskaya 2022). However, Vada et al. (2020) suggested that there has been a lack of studies on eudaimonic wellbeing, especially with regard to self-development and transformation (Sirgy & Uysal, 2016). There are a few exceptions, for example, studies of women, self-discovery and transformation through travel (Kelly & Smith, 2017; Laing & Frost, 2017), especially in retreat centres (Heintzman, 2013; Fu et al., 2015; Smith, 2018; Smith, 2023). Attention has also been paid to hedonic and eudaimonic concepts in the field of wellness tourism (Voigt, 2017). A growing area of interest are theories of embodiment and the senses (Filep et al., 2022; Matteucci, 2021), a theme that has recently been explored in more depth by Agapito (2023), who concludes that multisensory experiences can contribute to both hedonic and eudaimonic experiences. Although hedonic pleasure-seeking activities can provide instant wellbeing, eudaimonic effects often manifest themselves in delayed positive benefits from situations that were challenging at the time (Knobloch et al., 2016). It has been argued that 'existential authenticity' is integral to wellbeing, but the quest can be challenging (Kirillova & Lehto, 2015) and involves confronting one's fears or negative experiences too. For example, Nawijn and Filep (2016) suggest that even dark tourism can be meaningful in the context of wellbeing and Heintzmann (2013) documents how holistic retreat participants confront and work through negative life events. Overall, it has been argued that hedonic experiences in tourism may serve only to 'tranquilize' existential anxiety in the short-term (Kirillova & Lehto, 2015), whereas eudaimonic forms of tourism create longer-term impacts connecting to existential authenticity, self-realisation or transformation (Reisinger, 2013). In addition to philosophical and psychological studies of tourism and wellbeing, it is also important to consider the practical implications of research. Tourists' choice of destinations might be affected by marketing that draws on positive psychological variables and their experiences can be enhanced beyond mere satisfaction to include more eudaimonic benefits such as personal growth and achievement (Vada et al., 2020). Better understandings of the relationship between tourism and wellbeing can contribute to policy development and communication. For example, researchers have investigated the extent to which wellbeing principles can be integrated into public health policy in sustainable tourism destination management incorporating the needs of tourists, businesses, residents and other stakeholders. Wellbeing can be used as a business opportunity and contribute to economic growth (Pyke et al., 2016). Research on residents should be shifted from economic factors to wellbeing and it has been noted that the wellbeing of communities in tourism destinations can be enhanced by creating high-quality tourist facilities. Indeed, policy for destination management should aim to harmonise the wellbeing needs of the destination and its residents with the tourist experience (Hartwell et al., 2016). More recent studies have focused specifically on the wellbeing of local residents taking into consideration both short- and long-term impacts, as well as hedonic and eudaimonic forms of tourism (Godovykh et al., 2023).

With some of these research gaps in mind and the identified need to elaborate on themes and debates of growing importance, this book was conceived. The authors were invited to participate due to their ongoing dedication to the subject area, their past research and publications. They were asked to identify areas of interest that they had been working on in recent years which they felt would be especially pertinent to current debates about tourism and wellbeing. The editors guided the process only insofar as they selected and invited the participants and provided guidelines that their work should be cutting edge, theoretically and empirically robust, relevant to current academic debates, as well as ideally contributing to industry practice.

The book is structured around several important themes ranging from international and government policy, to measurements and indicators of wellbeing, to product and service development, to motivation and segmentation. All the authors provide definitions and discussions of wellbeing and its relationship to quality of life, happiness, wellbeing or life satisfaction. It is argued in more than one chapter that wellbeing should be centralized in government policies. Attention is paid to the way in which wellbeing can or could be measured, including identifying indicators and methods. A multidisciplinary framework stresses the need to go beyond economic or utilitarian indicators towards a sustainable living systems approach which also prioritizes social wellbeing. For example, resident wellbeing is an important focus of the chapters by Larry Dwyer, as well as Adiyukh Berbekova and Muzaffer Uysal.

The wellbeing benefits of tourism are a central theme in most of the research, including the impacts of being in different environments or therapeutic landscapes (e.g., forests or blue spaces) and the importance of social connections (e.g., within a social tourism or diasporic tourism context). Social dimensions of wellbeing can focus on host communities and especially employees from tourism and hospitality. This can include impacts and benefits of tourism, but it can also relate to the need to create more comprehensive work-based wellness programs. Motivations for or 'pathways' to wellbeing are also explored in more depth with a focus on specific segments or groups, for example, different nationalities or age groups. This is especially important in the post-COVID era where many people's priorities shifted to include more wellness or nature-based activities, as well as craving social contact and connections again. Such explorations are also useful for products and service development and experience creation, for example, when creating forest therapy packages or developing blue space destinations.

Some authors also explore the social trends and pressures that create the need to focus more on the wellbeing benefits of leisure and tourism, for example, workaholism and the cult of speed. This may vary according to people's age, gender, nationality or life stage. For this reason, it is important to consider socio-cultural and economic contexts when trying to create or develop wellbeing policy, packages and benefits. Experiences in the destination should ideally be memorable as well as affording some eudaimonic benefits in the long term, otherwise the fadeout effect can be quite fast and even painful. This may be especially true of social tourism, which may not be repeated often for many participants. The type and length of trips also must be considered to ascertain what creates the optimum experience and minimize fadeout.

The book does not claim to answer all these questions or to be fully comprehensive, but it provides a revisitation of some of the most complex and challenging issues in tourism and wellbeing studies.

1.3   Conceptual Definitions and Measurement of Wellbeing

The editors of this book made a conscious decision to use the term 'wellbeing' rather than 'wellness'. This was related to the richness and diversity of wellbeing studies and research compared to the more industry-focused and academically superficial coverage of wellness, a research area that is still in its relative infancy. Differentiating between wellbeing and wellness can be quite challenging. Some authors have argued that quality of life represents the general wellbeing of both individuals and society and that wellness represents the process of trying to improve those aspects of life that contribute to wellbeing or quality of life and especially health (Oliver et al., 2018). Wellness has been described as a personal and individual 'path to wellbeing' (Nahrstedt, 2004; Smith & Diekmann, 2017) which relies on making informed choices about lifestyle behaviours and actions. These might relate to health awareness and self-care (Stoewen, 2017; Damijanić, 2019) to achieve physical fitness, social connectedness, emotional stability, financial security and spiritual growth (Oliver et al., 2018). Some studies have suggested that spirituality is of less importance or interest than other domains of wellbeing (e.g., health, social connection, safety, work, economic stability), including as a motivation for travel (Smith et al., 2022). However, other authors have argued that spiritual health is as important as physical health (Ghiya, 2019).

Wellbeing has a much wider application than wellness and tends to focus on objective and subjective domains of life including economics, politics, social and environmental issues. There are no unanimous definitions of wellbeing (Carlisle et al., 2009), but philosophers argue that wellbeing is related to what is non-instrumentally good for a person (Crisp, 2016). This means that it goes beyond notions of hedonic happiness, which may be short-term and pleasure-orientated and has wider implications for society. This connects wellbeing to utilitarian approaches to tourism development which should aim to create the maximum benefits for the greatest number of people. This incorporates both sustainability and resilience, especially in the wake of numerous economic, environmental and health crises.

Wellbeing can be conceptualized and measured in several different ways. There are numerous academic and research-based studies which have attempted to define and measure wellbeing and differentiate it from quality of life, life satisfaction, happiness and other indicators of a good life. Wellbeing and quality of life are sometimes used synonymously, as they incorporate a diverse number of factors. These can be objective, for example, relating to external political, economic or environmental factors or subjective, which relate to life satisfaction and desire fulfilment (Armenta et al., 2015).

The first two chapters in this book argue that societal wellbeing needs to be reconceptualised and measured differently from how it was in the past, moving away from purely economic measures. Recent studies have suggested that people's wellbeing, health and quality of life are more important values in human life and tourism development than income, revenues, and other monetary outcomes (Godovykh et al., 2023). Happiness economists are becoming more aware of the importance of including broader indicators of wellbeing such as health, social life and environmental quality. The latter is especially important for debates about sustainability which need to look to the future.

Larry Dwyer argues that wellbeing outcomes need to play a central role in policy, especially resident wellbeing outcomes in the context of tourism. Subjective and objective dimensions of wellbeing should be considered simultaneously, but appropriate measures need to be employed differently depending on context and location. Generic indicators may provide a framework for measuring wellbeing but contextual indicators are needed for both individual communities. Dwyer argues that a Better Life wellbeing framework can provide the most promising option for sustainable tourism based on the preservation of economic, human, social and natural 'stocks' that support resident wellbeing over time. Such frameworks should integrate intergenerational wellbeing into destination competitiveness indices.

Adiyukh Berbekova and Muzaffer Uysal also focus on the measurement of the relationship between wellbeing, resident quality of life and tourism. Like Dwyer, they argue that objective and subjective measures are needed in a tourism context, but also argue against standard indicators in favour of the consideration of the stage and level of (tourism) development as well as the socio-cultural fabric of the location. The interaction between demand and supply is important in tourism contexts and the nature and quality of interaction between tourists and residents. Emotional wellbeing is highlighted as an important focus, including both cognitive and affective factors. It is argued that tourism experiences can be designed to improve wellbeing or quality of life and service-dominant logic is used to examine the relationship between tangible and intangible resources in the creation of value or the operand and operant (supply and demand). Overall, their work provides a review of existing constructs from the perspective of demand and supply interaction and offers several recommendations and future research directions relating to measurement tools for wellbeing and quality of life in tourism.

1.4   Individual Wellbeing in Tourism

Although wellbeing often refers to society as a whole and consists of numerous objective and subjective domains, it is also important to recognise the role of the individual. This could include tourists, local residents or employees working within the sector. Broader political, economic or social structures are critical in the creation of wellbeing policy for destination management and addressing, for example, sustainability goals. However, individuals are frequently concerned about their subjective wellbeing, which includes personal travel and wellness experiences. Significant themes might include occupational wellbeing, the benefits of taking time off work, work-life balance and stress management. Recent global studies have shown that in the post-COVID era, the world's workers are less engaged at work, stress has reached an all-time high, employee exhaustion is growing and many workers even want to quit their jobs (World Economic Forum, 2021; Gallup, 2022).

One of the chapters in this book addresses this topical subject. Susan Gordon and Xinran Lehto focus on employee wellbeing, especially within irregular working conditions that require intensive emotional labour like the hospitality sector, which was badly affected by COVID. It can be difficult to maintain the same level of wellbeing in jobs where the nature of the work varies significantly day by day and where no one day is the same. When differentiating between wellness and wellbeing in this context, wellness is often defined narrowly to include only physical health (especially in work-based wellness programs), whereas wellbeing refers to the whole person. For this reason, work-based wellness programs may not be incorporating mental and emotional factors and the focus is mainly short-term. It is noted that there are close links between employee wellbeing and satisfaction, productivity and quality of life. Research shows that employees perceive wellbeing differently and life stage plays a role (e.g., having children at home or being close to retirement). The situation is also different according to whether jobs are active or sedentary or require constant contact with clients or customers. It is advocated that a culture of well-ness or wellness as a business philosophy can and should be cultivated which reframes working life to think about work-life balance, working 'smarter' and a 'feeling well-serving well' approach.

Work-related stress may lead to tourists making different choices on holiday, for example, slowing down, visiting natural environments to counterbalance urban living or seeking personal wellness experiences. In this book, Jelena Farkić, Gorana Isailovic and Dušan Perić discuss an important paradigm shift from a culture of overwork to the enhancement of wellbeing through slowing down. They argue that too much pride and satisfaction exist in boasting of being 'overworked' and position idleness as a traditionally noble value in con-trast to workaholism. So-called idleness can be essential for contemplation and creativity, as well as regaining much-needed balance and control over our lives to counter-balance the cult of speed. Slow travel is posited as the relinquish-ment of (ubiquitous) busyness and the constant striving for the achievement of goals. However, research participants tended to view laziness as a negative characteristic and resting and relaxation are not prioritized due to demands, commitments and the need to be productive most of the time. On the other hand, they expressed their enjoyment of having time to contemplate in natural settings, experiencing simplicity, disconnecting from technology, resting and sleeping. Overall, this chapter advocates modalities of holidays that encour-age simplified, slower, immersive experiences, which celebrate mindfulness, slowness and stillness. This approach paves new avenues for understanding and thinking about idleness as an equally creative, rewarding, rejuvenating and fulfilling holiday pursuit, which not only enhances people's wellbeing and quality of life but also contributes to sustainable destination development.

It is interesting to consider what the optimum travel experience should consist of. Filep (2012) used Seligman's (2002) authentic happiness model (pleasant life, good life, meaningful life) to suggest that the ideal wellbeing-enhancing tourism experiences should revolve around pleasure, altruistic activities and meaningful experiences. Using a similar framework, Smith and Diekmann (2017) advocate holidays which provide a combination of pleasure and hedon-ism (i.e., having fun), altruistic activities (e.g., being environmentally friendly or benefitting local communities), and meaningful experiences (e.g., educa-tion, self-development). Such discussions relate to the extent to which tourism contributes to eudaimonic as opposed to hedonic experiences, the latter being mainly short-term and pleasure-orientated, the former providing more opportunities for long-term self-development and fulfilment. It is increasingly accepted in the social sciences that hedonia and eudaimonia are not mutually exclusive and are complementary psychological functions (Huta, 2015).

In this book, Miia Grénman, Juulia Räikkönen and Fanny Aapio address questions related to hedonic and eudaimonic wellbeing, nature-connectedness, happiness and meaning. Happiness and meaning were closely connected for their respondents, including relationships and human contact. However, happiness was linked more closely to positive affect and enjoyable activities like hobbies, adventure and travelling, whereas meaning was linked to self-development, education or achieving goals. Nature connection was important and connected to healing, recreation and spirituality, as well as sustainability and transformation. It is suggested that future tourism experiences should be as meaningful, transformational and eudaimonic as possible.

1.5   Facilitating Wellbeing Experiences in Tourism

This section focuses on tourism destinations and resources as well as the development of individual services. Authors explore how to use destination resources such as natural landscapes or wellness facilities to provide wellbeing-enhancing experiences for tourists. This includes an analysis of the motivations and service preferences of tourists by age, gender or nationality, for example, as well as analysing the need for stakeholder collaboration in destinations and the development of appropriate marketing strategies. As stated earlier, much of the emphasis in tourism and wellbeing studies has been on therapeutic landscapes and connections to nature. Natural landscapes often provide important settings or locations for wellbeing or wellness activities (Konu et al., 2010). In transformational destination experience creation, it has been advocated that a focus on the wellbeing of the resident community is essential, incorporating local culture and traditions, as well as connections with nature (Sheldon, 2020).

In this section, Emma Pope and Henna Konu discuss the transformative potential of nature building on previous studies that focused on therapeutic landscapes from several disciplinary perspectives. The main theoretical contribution of the chapter lies in exploring Lumber et al.'s (2017) pathways to nature connectedness in tourism research. Questions are asked about the nature of therapeutic landscape-based experiences, especially in terms of hedonic and eudaimonic benefits, which can be complementary, integrative or synergistic. Ideally, experiences should be cultivated that are meaningful, memorable and long term and it is noted that the way in which time is spent (quality) is more important than the length of time spent (quantity). The research explores possibilities to facilitate nature-based wellbeing experiences through pathways to nature connection and biophilia. They use examples of forest therapy, which are linked to beauty, meaning, sensory engagement, emotions, compassion and care towards nature. Contact, beauty and emotion were the most important pathways, and it is suggested that eudaimonia could be connected to empowerment through nature, the facilitation of mindfulness, as well as rest, relaxation and reflection. Overall, this chapter furthers the understanding of how eudaimonia is researched and created through tourism experiences, particularly in the context of nature-based tourism.

Catherine Kelly provides in-depth analysis of a therapeutic landscape focusing on the wellbeing benefits of blue spaces and how to centralise them in product, service and destination marketing. Although seaside locations have been promoted in studies of the 'healthy coast', the chapter refers to all water-based experiences. The study explores the physical and psychological benefits, including the aesthetic, kinetic, immersive, contemplative, social and symbolic (e.g., sense of place or identity). The work also examines the relationship between landscapes, emotional geographies and place attachment. It is recommended that stakeholder collaboration and co-production are desirable when managing blue-space-centred destinations and experiences. It is important to maintain links to sustainability and to cultivate stewardship or custodianship of the natural landscape.

In addition to natural landscapes, it is also important to recognise the significance of other wellness settings and activities which provide the opportunity for rest, relaxation, pampering and other physical, as well as mental benefits. The wellness tourism sector has been linked to several products and services that aim to help improve physical health (e.g., thermal baths, spas, fitness programmes), as well as emotional and spiritual growth (e.g., retreats offering yoga, meditation and mindfulness) (Dini & Pencarelli, 2021). Recent studies have noted the importance of the physical body in wellness tourism, including both exercise and nutrition, but the increasing interest in mental wellness activities leading to growth and transformation has also been emphasised (Dilette et al., 2021). The design of experiences can play an important role in optimising wellness or wellbeing. Several factors will be significant from service quality to interior design to hygiene and safety. Sensory dimensions are especially crucial within a wellness or spa setting (Buxton, 2018) and the whole customer journey should be taken into consideration to create a seamless experience (Smith, 2021; Smith & Wallace, 2020). In this section, Daumantas Bockus, Elli Vento and Raija Komppula focus on destinations and the relationship between perceptions of wellness on the part of customers and supply elements of destinations. They show how different national groups differ in their preferences for products, services and activities. As discussed earlier, wellness can be defined more closely in accordance with individual preferences and choices than wellbeing, which is defined as a broader societal concept. They argue that wellbeing is the result of wellness practices rather than an action in itself and wellness is seen as a process which includes proactive activities and consumption choices connected to exercise, healthy nutrition, meditation, and so forth. It can also include natural and resource-based therapies. Motivations for wellness tourism can range from the desire to escape, relax, to be pampered or beautified, achieve physical health improvements or healing, spiritual growth or the novelty of trying new things. Overall, it is noted that wellness tourism customers are quite heterogenic in their motivations but that specific preferences can be identified among different nationality segments, for example.

1.6 Effects of Tourism on Wellbeing

This final section focuses on the relatively underresearched area of social wellbeing and tourism (Filep et al., 2022). Emphasis is placed on subjective wellbeing as well as wider social relationships between communities, families and other tourists. Authors revisit the role that tourism plays in subjective wellbeing, as well as satisfaction with leisure life, emphasising the importance of social tourism, diasporic tourism and visiting friends and relatives, in addition to the inevitable fadeout effects of tourism. As stated earlier, the benefits of tourism have been clearly recognised by numerous researchers and especially since the pandemic, the need for social contact has been reemphasised. Yet, tourism tends to be the privilege of wealthier members of society, hence the need for systems that support and facilitate social tourism. In this section, Elli Vento, Scott McCabe and Raija Komppula examine wellbeing outcomes of social tourism. The continued support of social tourism by many governments indicates the value and importance of tourism for wellbeing. However, it is often challenging to measure those benefits to justify funding, but research should also be used to help enhance experiences which may be rare and precious for participants. One of the identified gaps in the research is social inclusion, which results in feelings of belonging, membership, meaning and purpose, as well as family bonding and creating happy childhood memories. The research shows the importance of escapism, socializing, physical activities, as well as children having fun and parents resting and relaxing. Although it is difficult to measure social inclusion directly, social tourists can clearly share in discussions about leisure and travel as well as enjoying its benefits.

Many diasporic tourists are unable to travel regularly to visit friends and relatives, which negatively affects their subjective wellbeing. Xavier Matteucci,

Sebastian Filep, Jerram Bateman and Tony Binns explore diasporic tourism and the benefits it can bring to both diasporic tourists and the host community back home, often consisting partly of family and friends. Host communities can benefit economically from financial donations, gifts and local spending in terms of utilitarian function. From the perspective of the diasporic tourists themselves, socio-psychological benefits are emphasized, which can include pride, belonging and shared heritage associated with being 'at home'. This can lead to the reconnecting to one's sense of self, essence or identity through the 'autobiographical past'. This is particularly important for diasporic individuals who miss positive aspects of their home culture and report a homesickness or malaise. Reference is made to certain cultural practices that are common in the home country, experiences of loneliness and missing physical and emotional warmth, as well as nostalgia and reminiscence or sensory cues connected to landscape and nature. Ultimately, these visits and reconnections enhance eudaimonic wellbeing dimensions such as meaning and purpose in life. Overall, this chapter contributes to the scant research on diaspora tourism, providing a chance for an overlooked community who struggle with their identity and daily life to report on travel experiences that contributed to their sense of wellbeing.

Even those tourists who are lucky enough to travel regularly will suffer from the inevitable fadeout effect. Ondrej Mitas and Marcel Bastiaansen contribute the only known experimental intervention aimed at mitigating the fadeout effect of vacationing. They examine vacation fadeout effect, reiterating the importance of vacations and their contribution to health, longevity, social cohesion and quality of life generally. This includes recovery from work demands and improved physical health, as well as improvements in shorter-term mood and longer-term life satisfaction. The contribution to eudaimonic wellbeing can include relationship quality. Tourism experiences elevate wellbeing levels above the typical daily levels with the middle of a vacation representing the peak of positive emotion. The frequency of vacations also contributes to wellbeing year by year. Unfortunately, however, it is thought that the fadeout effect of vacation experiences lasts only a few days returning to baseline emotions within two weeks. The intervention in this chapter is based on perfume and examines ways to prolong the 'holiday feeling' by finding ways to trigger memory through sensory experiments using smell. Smell has long been connected to reminiscence and the elicitation of olfactory-evoked memories. Although the experiment was not conclusive in its results, it is recommended that further research should examine the impacts of altering the duration, type or timing of vacations as well as exploring how the fadeout effect differs between individuals with different types of occupations. Overall, tourism-related businesses should consider the period after a vacation as an important part of the tourism product they deliver.

References

Abraham, A., Sommerhalder, K., & Abel, T. (2010). Landscape and well-being: A scoping study on the health-promoting impact of outdoor environments, *International Journal of Public Health, 55*, 59–69.

Agapito, D. (2023). Tourism, senses and well-being. In Vaz, E. (ed), *Geography of happiness. Contributions to regional science* (161–176). Cham: Springer. https://doi.org/10.1007/978-3-031-19871.

Armenta, C. N., Ruberton, P. M., & Lyubomirsky, S. (2015). Subjective wellbeing, psychology of. In J. D. Wright (ed), *International encyclopedia of the social & behavioral sciences* (pp. 648–653), 2nd edition, Vol 23. Oxford: Elsevier.

Azara, I., Michopoulou, E., Niccolini, F., Taff, B. D., & Clarke, A. (eds) (2018). *Tourism, health and wellbeing in Protected Areas.* Oxford: CABI.

Buckley, R., & Westaway, D. (2020). Mental health rescue effects of women's outdoor tourism: A role in COVID-19 recovery. *Annals of Tourism Research, 85*, 103041. https://doi.org/10.1016/j.annals.2020.103041.

Bushell, R., & Sheldon, P. J. (2009). *Wellness and tourism: Mind, body, spirit, place.* New York, NY: Cognizant Communication.

Buxton, L. (2018). Destination spas and the creation of memorable guest experiences. *International Journal of Spa and Wellness, 1*(2), 133–138. https://doi.org/10.1080/24721735.2018.1493778.

Carlisle, S., Henderson, G., & Hanlon, P. W. (2009). Wellbeing: A collateral casualty of modernity? *Social Science and Medicine, 69*, 1556–1560.

Cheer, J. M., Belhassen, Y., & Kujawa, J. (2017). The search for spirituality in tourism: Toward a conceptual framework for spiritual tourism. *Tourism Management Perspectives, 24*, 252–256. https://doi.org/10.1016/j.tmp.2017.07.018.

Chen, Y., Lehto, Y., & Cai, L. (2013). Vacation and well-being: A study of Chinese tourists. *Annals of Tourism Research, 42*, 284–310. https://doi.org/10.1016/j.annals.2013.02.003.

Crisp, R. (2021). Well-being. In E. N. Zelta (ed), *The Stanford encyclopedia of philosophy,* https://plato.stanford.edu/archives/win2021/entries/well-being (accessed 16 February 2023).

Damijanić, A. T. (2019). Wellness and healthy lifestyle in tourism settings. *Tourism Review, 74*(4), 978–89. https://doi.org/10.1108/TR-02-2019-0046.

Dini, M., & Pencarelli, T. (2021). Wellness tourism and the components of its offer system: A holistic perspective. *Tourism Review, 77*(2), 394–412. https://doi.org/10.1108/TR-08-2020-0373.

Filep, S. (2012). Positive psychology and tourism. In M. Uysal, R. Perdue & M. J. Sirgay (eds), *Handbook of tourism and quality of life research* (pp. 31–50), Dordrecht: Springer. https://doi.org/10.1007/978-94-007-2288-0_3.

Filep, S., Macnaughton, J., & Glover, T. (2017). Tourism and gratitude: Valuing acts of kindness. *Annals of Tourism Research, 66*, 26–36. https://doi.org/10.1016/j.annals.2017.05.015.

Filep, S., Moyle, B. D., & Skavronskaya, L. (2022). Tourist wellbeing: Re-thinking hedonic and eudaimonic dimensions. *Journal of Hospitality and Tourism Research*. https://doi.org/10.1177/10963480221087964.

Font-Barnet, A., & Andreu, M. N. (2023). Research on tourism, wellbeing, and nature: A bibliometric analysis. *Anatolia*, *34*(2), 163–175. https://doi.org/10.1080/13032917.2021.2002699.

Fu, X., Tanyatanaboon, M., & Lehto, X. Y. (2015). Conceptualizing transformative guest experience at retreat centres. *International Journal of Hospitality Management*, *49*, 83–92. https://doi.org/10.1016/j.ijhm.2015.06.004.

Gallup. (2022). State of the global workplace: 2022 report. https://www.gallup.com/workplace/349484/state-of-the-global-workplace-2022-report.aspx (accessed 27 January 2023).

Gascon, M., Zijlema, W., Vert, C., White, M. P., & Nieuwenhuijsen, M. J. (2017). Outdoor blue spaces, human health and well-being: A systematic review of quantitative studies. *International Journal of Hygiene and Environmental Health*, *220*(8). 1207–1221. https://doi.org/10.1016/j.ijheh.2017.08.004.

Gesler, W. (1992). Therapeutic landscapes: Medical geographic research in light of the new cultural geography. *Social Science & Medicine*, *34*(7), 735–746. https://doi.org/10.1016/0277-9536(92)90360-3.

Ghiya, G. D. (2019). Promoting spiritual health and holistic wellness. *Journal of Health Management*, *21*(2), 230–233. https://doi.org/10.1177/0972063419835104.

Godovykh, M., Ridderstaat, J., & Fyall, A. (2023). The well-being impacts of tourism: Long-term and short-term effects of tourism development on residents' happiness. *Tourism Economics*, *29*(1), https//doi.org/10.1177/13548166211041227.

Hartwell, H., Fyall, A., Willis, C., Page, S., Ladkin, A., & Hemingway, A. (2016). Progress in tourism and destination wellbeing research. *Current Issues in Tourism*, *21*(16), 1830–1892. https://doi.org/10.1080/13683500.2016.1223609.

Heintzman, P. (2013). Retreat tourism as a form of transformational tourism. In Y. Reisinger (ed), *Transformational tourism: Tourist perspectives* (pp. 68–81), Oxford: CABI.

Huta, V. (2015). The complementary roles of eudaimonia and hedonia and how they can be pursued in practice. In S. Joseph (ed), *Positive psychology in practice: Promoting human flourishing in work, health, education, and everyday life* (2nd edn., pp. 59–182), New York: John Wiley & Sons. https://doi.org/10.1002/9781118996874.

Jiang, T., Ryan, C., & Zhang, C. (2018). The spiritual or secular tourist? The experience of Zen meditation in Chinese temples. *Tourism Management*, *65*, 187–199. https://doi.org/10.1016/j.tourman.2017.10.008.

Jiang, Y., & Wen, J. (2020). Effects of COVID-19 on hotel marketing and management: A perspective article. *International Journal of Contemporary Hospitality Management*, *32*, 2563–2573. https://doi.org/10.1108/IJCHM-03-2020-0237.

Kaplan, R., & Kaplan, S. (1989). The experience of nature: A psychological perspective. Cambridge: Cambridge University Press.

Kato, K., & Progano, R. N. (2017). Spiritual (walking) tourism as a foundation for sustainable destination development: Kumano-kodo pilgrimage, Wakayama, Japan. *Tourism Management Perspectives*, *24*, 243–251. https://doi.org/10.1016/j.tmp.2017.07.017.

Kelly, C., & Smith, M. K. (2017). Journeys of the self: the need to retreat. In M. K. Smith & L. Puczkó (eds), *The Routledge handbook of health tourism* (pp. 138–151). Abingdon: Routledge.

Kirillova, K., & Lehto, X. (2015). An existential conceptualization of the vacation cycle. *Annals of Tourism Research, 55*, 110–123.

Kirillova, K., Lehto, X., & Cai, L. (2017). Tourism and existential transformation: An empirical investigation. *Journal of Travel Research, 56*(5), 638–650. https://doi/10.1177/0047287516650277.

Knobloch, U., Robertson, K., & Aitken, R. (2016). Experience, emotion and eudaimonia: A consideration of tourist experiences and well-being. *Journal of Travel Research, 56*(5), 651–662. https://doi.org/10.1177/0047287516650937.

Konu, H., Tuohino, A., & Komppula, R. (2010). Lake wellness – a practical example of a new service development (NSD) concept in tourism. *Journal of Vacation Marketing, 16*(2), 125–139.

Konu, H. (2015). Developing a forest-based wellbeing tourism product together with customers – an ethnographic approach. *Tourism Management, 49*, 1–16. https://doi.org/10.1016/j.tourman.2015.02.006.

Komppula, R., & Konu, H. (2017). Designing forest-based wellbeing tourism services for Japanese customers – a case study from Finland. In N. K. Prebensen, J. S. Chen & M. S. Uysal (eds), *Co-creation in tourism experiences* (pp. 50–63). Abingdon: Routledge.

Kwon, J., & Lee, H. (2020). Why travel prolongs happiness: Longitudinal analysis using a latent growth model. *Tourism Management, 76*, 103944. https://doi.org/10.1016/j.tourman.2019.06.019.

Laing, J. H., & Frost, W. (2017). Journeys of well-being: Women's travel narratives of transformation and self-discovery in Italy. *Tourism Management, 62*, 110–119. https://doi.org/10.1016/j.tourman.2017.04.004.

Lehto, X. Y., & Lehto, M.R. (2019). Vacation as a public health resource: Toward a wellness-centered tourism design approach. *Journal of Hospitality and Tourism Research, 43*(7), 935–960. https://doi.org/10.1177/1096348019849684.

Lin, Z., Wong, I. A., Kou, I. E., & Zhen, X. (2021). Inducing wellbeing through staycation programs in the midst of the COVID-19 crisis. *Tourism Management Perspectives, 40*. https://doi.org/10.1016/j.tmp.2021.100907.

Little, J. (2015). Nature, wellbeing and the transformational self. *Geographical Journal, 181*(2), 121–128.

Lumber, R., Richardson, M., & Sheffield, D. (2017). Beyond knowing nature: Contact, emotion, compassion, meaning, and beauty are pathways to nature connection. *PloS One, 12*(5), e0177186.

Ma, S., Zhao, X., Gong, Y., & Wengel, Y. (2021). Proposing "healing tourism" as a post-COVID-19 tourism product. *Anatolia, 32*(1), 136–139. https://doi.org/10.1080/13032917.2020.1808490.

McCabe, S., & Johnson, S. (2013). The happiness factor in tourism: Subjective well-being and social tourism. *Annals of Tourism Research, 41*, 42–65. https://doi.org/10.1016/j.annals.2012.12.001.

Matteucci, X. (2021). Existential hapax as tourist embodied transformation. *Tourism Recreation Research, 47*(5–6), 631–635. https://doi.org/10.1080/02508281.2021.1934330.

Mitas, O., Nawijn, J., & Jongsmaa, B. (2017). Between tourists: Tourism and happiness. In M. K. Smith and L. Puczkó (eds), *Routledge handbook of health tourism* (pp. 47–64), Abingdon: Routledge.

Moufakkir, O., & Selmi, N. (2018). Examining the spirituality of spiritual tourists: A Sahara desert experience. *Annals of Tourism Research, 70*, 108–119. https://doi.org/10.1016/j.annals.2017.09.003.

Nahrstedt, W. (2004). Wellness im Kurort: Neue Qualität für den Gesundheitstourismus in Europa. *Spektrum Freizeit*, *26*(2), 37–52.

Nawijn, J., De Bloom, J., & Geurts, S. (2013). Pre-vacation time: Blessing or burden? *Leisure Sciences*, *35*(1), 33–44. https://doi.org/10.1080/01490400.2013.739875.

Nawijn, J., & Filep, S. (2016). Two directions for future tourism well-being research. *Annals of Tourism Research*, *61*, 221–223. https://doi.org/10.1016/j.annals.2016.07.007.

Norman, A., & Pokorny, J. J. (2017). Meditation retreats: Spiritual tourism and well-being interventions. *Tourism Management Perspectives*, *24*, 201–207. https://doi.org/10.1016/j.tmp.2017.07.012.

Ohe, Y., Ikei, H., Song, C., & Miyazaki, Y. (2017). Evaluating the relaxation effects of emerging forest-therapy tourism: A multidisciplinary approach. *Tourism Management*, *62*, 322–334. https://doi.org/10.1016/j.tourman.2017.04.010.

Oliver, M. D., Baldwin, D. R., & Datta, S. (2018). Health to wellness: A review of wellness models and transitioning back to health. *The International Journal of Health, Wellness and Society*, *9*(1), 41–56. https://doi.org/10.18848/2156–8960/CGP/v09i01/41–56.

Packer, J. (2022). Taking a break: Exploring the restorative benefits of short breaks and vacations. *Annals of Tourism Research Empirical Insights*, *2*(1), 100032. https://doi.org/10.1016/j.annale.2020.100006.

Pocinho, M., Garcês, S., & Neves de Jesus, S. (2022). Wellbeing and resilience in tourism: A systematic literature review during COVID-19. *Frontiers in Psychology*, *12*. https://doi.org/10.3389/fpsyg.2021.748947.

Pyke, S., Hartwell, H., Blake, A., & Hemingway, A. (2016). Exploring well-being as a tourism product resource. *Tourism Management*, *55*, 94–105. https://doi.org/10.1016/j.tourman.2016.02.004.

Ram, Y. and Smith, M. K. (2019). An assessment of visited landscapes using a Cultural Ecosystem Services framework, *Tourism Geographies*, *24*(4–5), 523–548. https://doi.org/10.1080/14616688.2018.1522545.

Reisinger, Y. (2013). *Transformational tourism: Tourist perspectives*. Wallingford: CABI.

Santos, A., Gonzalez, C., Haegeman, K., & Rainoldi, A. (2020). *Behavioural changes in tourism in times of COVID-19*, Luxembourg: Publications Office of the European Union.

Seligman, M. E. P. (2002). *Authentic happiness*. New York: Free Press.

Sharpley, R. and Jepson, D. (2011). Rural tourism: A spiritual experience? *Annals of Tourism Research*, *38*(1), 52–71. https://doi.org/10.1016/j.annals.2010.05.002.

Sheldon, P. J. (2020). Designing tourism experiences for inner transformation. *Annals of Tourism Research*, *83*, 102935. https://doi.org/10.1016/j.annals.2020.102935.

Sirgy, M. J., & Uysal, M. (2016). Developing a eudaimonia research agenda in travel and tourism. In J. M. Sirgy, & M. Uysal (eds), *Handbook of eudaimonic well-being* (pp. 485–495). Switzerland: Springer.

Smith, M. K. (2023). Retreating towards subjective well-being. In T. V. Singh, R. Butler & D. A. Fennell (eds), *Tourism as a pathway to hope and happiness* (pp. 135–151). Bristol: Channel View.

Smith, M. K. (2022). Religion, spirituality and wellness tourism. In D. Olsen & D. J. Timothy (eds), *The Routledge handbook of religious and spiritual tourism* (pp. 68–78). Abingdon: Routledge.

Smith, M. K. (2021). Creating wellness tourism experiences. In R. Sharpley (ed), *Routledge handbook of the tourist experience* (pp. 364–377). Abingdon: Routledge.

Smith, M. K. (2018). Wellness in the U-bend of life: Why the core market is middle-aged and female. *International Journal of Spa and Wellness*, *1*(1), 4–19. https://doi.org/10 .1080/24721735.2018.1438480.

Smith, M. K., & Diekmann, A. (2017). Tourism and wellbeing. *Annals of Tourism Research*, *66*, 1–13. https://doi.org/10.1016/j.annals.2017.05.006.

Smith, M. K., Kiss, R., & Chan, I. Y. F. (2022). Millennials' perceptions of spirituality, wellness and travel. In S. K. Walia & A. Jasrotia (eds), *Millennials, spirituality and tourism* (pp. 85–103). Abingdon: Routledge.

Smith, M. K., & Puczkó, L. (eds). (2017). *Routledge handbook of health tourism*. Abingdon: Routledge.

Smith, M. K., & Wallace, M. (2020). An analysis of key issues in spa management: Viewpoints from international industry professionals. *International Journal of Spa and Wellness*, *2*(3), 119–134, https://doi.org/10.1080/24721735.2020.1819706.

Stoewen, D. L. (2017). Dimensions of wellness: Change your habits, change your life. *The Canadian Veterinary Journal*, *58*(8), 861–862. https://www.ncbi.nlm.nih.gov/ pmc/articles/PMC5508938.

Vada, S., Prentice, C., Scott, N., & Hsiao, A. (2020). Positive psychology and tourist well-being: A systematic literature review. *Tourism Management Perspectives*, *33*, 100631. https://doi.org/10.1016/j.tmp.2019.100631.

Voigt, C. (2017). Employing hedonia and eudaimonia to explore differences between three groups of wellness tourists on the experiential, the motivational and the global level. In S. Filep, J. Laing, & M. Csikszentmihalyi (eds), *Positive tourism* (pp. 105–121). Abingdon: Routledge.

World Economic Forum. (2021). The global risks report, 16th edition, https://www3 .weforum .org/ docs/ WEF _The _Global _Risks _Report _2021 .pdf, accessed 27th January 2023.

PART I

ECONOMICS AND MEASUREMENT OF WELLBEING IN TOURISM

2   Addressing the wellbeing gap in tourism economics

Larry Dwyer

2.1   Introduction

Gross domestic product (GDP), the value of the goods and services produced in an economy in a given year, has long been the preferred measure for assessing progress in human development (Aitken, 2019). Although it was never created for this purpose, growth in GDP is now central to neoliberalism and an important objective sought by destinations worldwide. Over the past decade, however, a growing number of researchers have identified substantial problems associated with use of this concept to estimate quality of life or wellbeing (Bleys, 2012; Fleurbaey & Blanchet, 2013). As a consequence, a broad movement, known as the *Beyond GDP* approach, has emerged to develop broader measures of social progress to either replace, adjust or complement GDP (Stiglitz et al., 2018a, b).

There is growing recognition among researchers and policy makers that economic growth and higher personal income are not synonymous with societal advancement and human development and that the measurement of societal wellbeing must go beyond traditional economic measures (Verma, 2017). The notion of wellbeing has been receiving increased attention in social science research, measurement and policy. In 2011, resolution 65/309, adopted by the UN General Assembly, called upon all member countries to formulate wellbeing measures other than GDP. While GDP remains the critical indicator of a destination's macroeconomic condition, and the yardstick by which countries compare their performance, the *Beyond GDP* approach, attracting researchers across all disciplines, emphasises the need for a shift of emphasis from a production-oriented economic measurement system to one focused on the wellbeing of current and future generations (Durand, 2015). Several prominent tourism economists now explicitly affirm that the primary purpose of economics to contribute to enhanced wellbeing of persons (Dalziel et al., 2018; Fioramonti et al., 2019; Costanza et al., 2020).

Attention to wellbeing in tourism research typically involves four types of stakeholders: residents, tourists, industry employees and public agencies. Taking the *Beyond GDP* approach seriously implies a rethinking of societal goals, refocusing measures of progress, and according wellbeing outcomes a central place in policy analysis. Curiously, the essential ideas driving the approach have had little impact on tourism economics research. In much of economics research effort, resident wellbeing is typically either neglected entirely or else given an overly narrow meaning that limits its relevance to concept development and tourism policy.

Following a brief discussion of the nature of wellbeing and the ideal criteria for developing a framework to assess resident wellbeing outcomes associated with tourism related activity, the chapter identifies several important areas of tourism economics that have yet to respond appropriately to the challenges posed by the *Beyond GDP* approach. It will be argued that the neglect of wellbeing considerations has diminished the relevance of the tourism economics research effort and its policy significance in areas such as tourism and economic growth, destination competitiveness, event evaluation, sustainable development, and tourism participation in the 2030 SDG agenda. Recognising that wellbeing is a primary policy objective, tourism economics must incorporate resident wellbeing outcomes into conceptual analysis, empirical findings and policy assessment in a more inclusive way. The chapter concludes with a discussion of wellbeing as a tourism policy objective, identifying some challenges that must be met if resident wellbeing outcomes are to play a key role in tourism planning, development and policy assessment.

2.2   The Nature of Wellbeing

Wellbeing studies share important objectives: examining the sources of wellbeing, identifying a range of indicators that provide measures of wellbeing and determining how better measures of wellbeing and progress can inform public policy (Adler & Seligman, 2016; Tov, 2018). Despite some differences of emphasis, wellbeing is widely agreed to be a multidimensional concept that embraces the things that people value, incorporating notions of material comforts, life satisfaction, happiness, individual freedoms, opportunities, flourishing, mental states and capabilities (Adler & Seligman, 2016; Smith & Diekmann, 2017; Helliwell et al., 2020). This conceptualization of wellbeing implies that individuals should have the freedom to make choices in life according to their awareness and aspirations, and the resources to realize their aspirations (Croes, 2016).

The bulk of wellbeing study undertaken by tourism researchers has concerned tourist wellbeing (Uysal et al., 2012). This is somewhat curious since the tourism industry in any destination is developed primarily for the benefit of residents, not for outsiders. Of course, the more satisfied tourists are with the destination offerings, the more likely they are to respond to informed marketing strategies, to contribute economically to the destination and to promote it further (by positive word of mouth and/or repeat visitation), but from the destination viewpoint, the benefits to tourists have instrumental rather than ultimate value, compared to resident benefits.

The question arises as to which set of indicators can best inform economic analysis and policy to help estimate resident wellbeing outcomes associated with tourism activity and development. To answer this question, we must understand the criteria for constructing an 'ideal' wellbeing framework. Essential criteria include (i) inclusion of both subjective and objective sources of wellbeing; (ii) distinction between current and future wellbeing outcomes, allowing sustainability considerations to be embedded into the framework; (iii) theoretically sound but flexible enough to include additional dimensions and indicators, as these are required to embrace resident values; and (iv) policy relevance (Durand, 2015, 2020). We discuss each in turn, emphasizing the relevance for tourism economics.

2.2.1   Sources of Wellbeing: Subjective and Objective Dimensions

Subjective wellbeing (SWB) embraces individuals' emotional and cognitive evaluations of their lives, and their conceptualization of happiness, peace, need fulfilment, and life satisfaction (Diener et al., 2018). It comprises three elements: *Life evaluation, Experiential* and *Eudaimonia* (Tov, 2018). Each of these elements is itself complex with several interactive components (Stone & Krueger, 2018). SWB indicators measure wellbeing outcomes directly, by asking individuals to report on these different aspects of their wellbeing.

In contrast, objective measures of wellbeing are the actual or reported levels of externally verifiable potential contributors to, or components of, wellbeing. Objective sources of wellbeing include material living standards (income, consumption, wealth, quality of housing), alongside variables such as equity and fairness in the distribution of goods and services, mental and physical health, nutrition, education, workplace features, work-life balance, social relationships, community vitality, personal and financial security, environmental quality and opportunities for civic engagement (Iriarte & Musikanski, 2017; OECD, 2020).

While recognising the relevance of objective measures of wellbeing to policy making, tourism research in general has tended to employ subjective measures of wellbeing, employing relatively easily collected survey-based data on 'perceptions' and 'attitudes' of tourists and residents (Uysal et al., 2012; Hartwell et al., 2018; Uysal & Sirgy, 2019). Within the SWB focus, measures of resident 'life satisfaction' tend to be emphasised (Woo et al., 2018), ignoring the fact that the different elements of SWB capture different concepts, and the most appropriate measure to be employed will depend on context. Tourism economists, in particular, focus on SWB measures in their analyses. Economic modelling in tourism still tends to be based on utility maximisation rather than addressing real world determinants of societal wellbeing associated with tourism development (Fleurbaey & Blanchet, 2013). However, the economic concepts of 'utility' or 'welfare' cannot be equated with the broader multi-dimensional conception of 'wellbeing' advocated in the wider social science literature (Tov, 2018; OECD, 2020).

In recent years, a broader notion of wellbeing, beyond the neoclassical 'welfarist' conception, has received increasing attention in economic wellbeing research, measurement and policy (Adler & Seligman, 2016; Durand & Exton, 2019). Developments in behavioural economics, challenging the assumptions of the revealed preference approach, have led to a renewed interest in 'Happiness Economics' (Frijters et al., 2020; Nikolova & Graham, 2020). Happiness research has been applied to a range of issues within the field of tourism economics (Croes, 2012; Rivera et al., 2016; Ridderstaat et al., 2016; Chattopadhyay et al., 2021). Happiness economists do not seek to replace income-based measures of welfare, but instead to complement them with broader measures of wellbeing. Micro-econometric happiness equations have the standard form: $W_{it} = a + bx_{it} + e_{it}$, where W is the reported wellbeing of individual i at time t, X is a vector of known variables, including socio-demographic and socio-economic characteristics such as marital status, income, health, employment status, social life, environmental quality and so on. The error term accounts for other, uncaptured causes of SWB.

While happiness economics has provided new insights into our understanding of human experience and behaviour (Nikolova & Graham, 2020), emphasis on SWB reflects an 'instrumentalist' view that valued attributes of life such as good health, material security, fulfilling social relationships and so on, are merely causal contributors to the ultimate goal of a pleasurable subjective state (Austin, 2016). Indeed, the assumption that narrow welfare effects equate to personal or social wellbeing has greatly restricted the real-world relevance of the type of economic modelling undertaken in the study of sustainable development generally (Costanza et al., 2020; Dwyer, 2021). Subjective measures also risk insufficient attention being given to the structural causes of wellbeing. Not only are individuals often poor judges of their own future wellbeing, they tend to give intergenerational wellbeing outcomes relatively little weight in decision making compared to current wellbeing. A focus on happiness is thus likely to ignore conditions that affect the sustainability of wellbeing outcomes (Dwyer, 2021). Taken on its own, SWB is not a reliable public policy yardstick. While happiness or satisfaction surveys can serve as important complementary indicators for public policy making (Nikolova & Graham, 2020), more robust measures of wellbeing, beyond resident perceptions, are necessary if resident attitudes or perceptions are to link with the different drivers of wellbeing.

Both subjective and objective dimensions of resident wellbeing are essential components of any wellbeing framework to measure social progress and should be considered simultaneously (Iriarte & Musikanski, 2019; OECD, 2020; Fuchs et al., 2020). A multidimensional approach with mix of subjective and objective sources of wellbeing comprising a broad dashboard of wellbeing indicators, provides a sounder basis for analysis and for the design and appraisal of public policy than does a focus on a single source (Austin, 2016; Durand, 2020). Tourism researchers should devote more effort to include objective dimensions of wellbeing in the assessment exercise, and to analysing the links between the subjective and objective dimensions of wellbeing (Berbekova et al., 2021).

2.2.2   Current and Future Wellbeing

Current wellbeing relates to that of the present generation within or outside of a particular destination. Intragenerational studies address the distribution of wellbeing between different groups in society (Alvaredo et al., 2018). Future or intergenerational wellbeing refers to levels of resident wellbeing that (potentially) could exist in the future as a result of development activity.

An important question is whether a proposed policy improves wellbeing *now* or in the *future*? Distinguishing the sources of current and future wellbeing allows sustainability considerations to be embedded into tourism study (Dwyer, 2021). Resident wellbeing is affected by changes in economic capital, through provision of infrastructure and finance for investment; human capital through education, health, productivity and capacity for innovation; social capital through networking, collaboration and institutional trust; and natural capital through provision of destination stock of renewable and nonrenewable natural resources and ecosystem services. Changes in each type of capital stock affect resident future wellbeing, as well as present wellbeing (Dwyer, 2021).

The main focus of studies of resident (and tourist) wellbeing has concerned wellbeing of the current generation with less attention to intergenerational wellbeing (Asmelash & Kumar, 2019). However, it cannot be assumed that a tourism development policy that achieves current wellbeing objectives will necessarily have the positive future wellbeing outcomes required to achieve or maintain sustainable development. The essential role of future wellbeing estimation, essential to determining whether or not a destination is progressing along a sustainable development path, has largely been neglected in tourism research.

2.2.3   Theoretical Soundness and Flexibility

Given the need for wellbeing estimates to inform tourism analysis and policy, the measures used by tourism researchers must be credible with a sound basis in theory. To the extent that different variables and measures are used to assess resident wellbeing, the various findings regarding the effects of tourism activity on resident wellbeing lack comparability.

An ideal wellbeing framework will comprise both 'generic' indicators based on credible frameworks and 'contextual' indicators relating to particular resident values within the destination (Dwyer, 2022b). Ideally, the framework should allow individuals and communities to set their own weights on the importance of each of the different dimensions of wellbeing. A dashboard approach to indicator development, rather than a composite index, also has the advantage of presenting separate information for each wellbeing dimension, making it possible to identify the different sources of resident wellbeing outcomes associated with development activity (Durand, 2020).

Selected according to international principles such as political significance of data, quality of data, comparability, and frequency of data collection, wellbeing measures now provide credibility and consistency to wellbeing study (Exton & Shinwell, 2018). In a series of recent articles, Dwyer (2020, 2021, 2022a, b, c) has supported use of the *Better Life* wellbeing framework in tourism study, arguably the most highly regarded conceptual framework for understanding and measuring wellbeing and societal progress, consistent with the *Beyond GDP* agenda (Durand, 2015; Durand & Exton, 2019; OECD, 2020; Durand, 2020). The range of wellbeing indicators associated with *Better Life* is substantially greater than indexes such as Human Development Index (HDI) that are employed by tourism researchers (Croes & Kubickova, 2013; Kubickova et al., 2017; Croes et al., 2020). At the same time, the framework is flexible enough to include additional dimensions and indicators of wellbeing as these are developed, including those that may be specifically tourism related (Dwyer, 2020).

The quality of data and the empirical robustness of wellbeing measures may be expected to progress over time as indicators are developed by researchers and statistical agencies that better capture conditions reflecting various dimensions of people's value systems (De Smedt et al., 2018; Diener & Biswas-Diener, 2019). Theory-based indicator selection ensures that their development is strategic and promotes consistency of use in different studies.

2.2.4   Policy Relevance

A wellbeing framework relevant to destination development should inform debate on the most relevant dimensions of wellbeing among destination residents and also guide policies that improve resident wellbeing. Wellbeing assessment is progressively moving towards the development of internationally comparable measures to better understand people's lives at the individual, household and community level (Exton & Shinwell, 2018; Fuchs et al., 2020). An advantage of indicators developed in consultation with international statistical agencies is their consistency with destination Systems of National Accounts, SNA (Stiglitz et al., 2018a, b; OECD, 2020), providing a credible basis for benchmarking and policy making (Adler & Seligman, 2016). Unless tourism researchers adopt or develop the types of new wellbeing measures employed by policy makers, their findings will have little relevance to the wider public debates on appropriate resource allocation to enhance social wellbeing.

In view of the above, a wellbeing framework suitable for use in economic analysis and policy ideally should contain a mix of subjective and objective dimensions of wellbeing, indicators of current and future wellbeing, flexibility to adopt new indicators as relevant to the context, theoretically sound and having policy relevance. The following section identifies some of the benefits to analysis and policy in selected areas of tourism economics.

2.3   How Study of Resident Wellbeing Outcomes can Advance Tourism Economic Analysis and Policy

Resident wellbeing considerations have either been ignored or marginalised in several important areas of tourism economics (Dwyer, 2022d). We now examine these different areas of tourism economics to illustrate how the neglect of resident wellbeing outcomes has restricted the scope of economic analysis and the policy significance of study findings.

2.3.1   Tourism and Economic Growth

Tourism economists continue to debate the issue of tourism- led economic growth versus economic growth- led tourism, while ignoring the resident wellbeing outcomes of each process (Dwyer, 2020). Increased GDP does not improve long-term societal wellbeing once a comfortable standard of living has been reached (Easterlin & O'Connor, 2020). An explanation for this is that human aspirations increase along with income, and after basic needs are met, wellbeing depends on relative rather than absolute levels of income (Nikolova & Graham, 2020). The two-way relationship found between tourism growth and resident wellbeing (Ridderstaat et al., 2016; Kubickova et al., 2017; Lee et al., 2021) suggests that tourism development policies should give increasing importance to non-economic aspects of life beyond a certain income level, rather than focusing almost exclusively on economic growth.

These findings receive support from recent studies showing that productivity growth can generate wider outcomes beyond material wellbeing (Llena-Nozal et al., 2019; Dwyer, 2022c). Rather than focusing solely on economic growth as measured by growth in GDP, tourism economists should estimate the ultimate outcome – human wellbeing (Dwyer, 2018), identifying types of productivity-enhancing development strategies that can improve social wellbeing (Dwyer, 2022c) Attention to resident wellbeing outcomes associated with tourism growth can provide policy makers with valuable insights into important questions such as how tourism growth translates into improved living standards and societal progress according to community values and how the fundamental drivers of wellbeing can act as drivers of sustainable tourism growth.

2.3.2   Sustainability

Wellbeing considerations play an essential role in enabling the sustainability of tourism development. Sustainable development depends on the simultaneous preservation or increase in quantities and qualities of several 'stocks' – economic, human, social and natural that support resident wellbeing over time. To provide a comprehensive account of changes in resident wellbeing associated with sustainable development, indicators of current wellbeing must be complemented by indicators of future wellbeing (Stiglitz et al., 2018a; Costanza et al., 2020).

On the so-called 'capitals approach' to sustainable development, the condition for sustainable development is that the present generation must leave the next generation a stock of productive capacity that is capable of sustaining wellbeing per capita at a level no less than that enjoyed by the present generation (Arrow et al., 2012). Capital stocks act as a transmission mechanism for supporting intergenerational wellbeing, an essential condition for destination development to be sustainable. The 'capitals approach' helps to prioritise alternative development paths, informing decision makers about the substitution possibilities between capital stocks and permissible trade-offs that may be made between them (Qasim & Grimes, 2018).

The role of changes in capital stocks as a transmission mechanism for supporting intergenerational wellbeing, an essential condition for development to be sustainable, has been underresearched in tourism economics (Dwyer, 2021). If tourism research on sustainability is to be theoretically grounded, the role of changing capital stocks and the associated resident wellbeing outcomes must be acknowledged as essential to sustainability assessment (Dwyer, 2021). From a policy making perspective, it is important to recognise the complex interrelationships between the different types of capital and outcomes for resident wellbeing both intra- and intergenerationally (Ekins et al., 2008; Arrow et al., 2012). The essential dynamic dimension of sustainable development, and the roles of changing capital stocks, are unable to be captured within static models of the type typically constructed by tourism researchers. Recognition of the dynamic nature of the sustainability concept flags the need for tourism researchers to develop more future-directed sustainability indicators. This is essential if tourism research is to become more relevant to, and consistent with, advances in sustainability theory and practice in the wider research literature.

If the capitals approach is to adequately inform sustainable tourism development, in a way that is more practically relevant, its scope needs to be extended beyond restrictive utility-based 'welfarist' models to capture the multidimensional complexity of the wellbeing concept (Dwyer, 2021). Tourism economists can play an important leading role in exploring the relevance of the capitals approach to advance our understanding of the conditions for achieving sustainable tourism development. New metrics are under development that incorporate current knowledge of how manufactured, human, social and natural capital assets interact to contribute to sustainable resident wellbeing (De Smedt et al., 2018). Greater effort is needed to determine the nature of the capital stocks supporting sustainable tourism development, how they are to be valued in the different contexts of tourism development, and their links with resident wellbeing. Tourism researchers must confront some important measurement challenges in the effort to develop frameworks of analysis that truly integrate current and future resident wellbeing. Economists can play an important role in this effort. The challenge of valuing capital stocks has by and large been neglected by tourism scholars. Tourism economics is well-suited to this task but has made little contribution to date (Dwyer, 2021).

2.3.3   Destination Competitiveness

Determining appropriate strategies to achieve destination competitiveness is central to tourism policy debate. The past decade has seen a growing awareness among tourism stakeholders that the ultimate rationale for achieving a competitive tourism industry is to contribute to the 'wellbeing' or 'quality of life' of residents (Crouch & Ritchie, 2012; Boley & Perdue, 2012; Croes & Kubikova, 2013; Bimonte & Faralla, 2016; Croes et al., 2020). Despite this acknowledgement, wellbeing indicators remain conspicuously absent from the indicator sets developed to assess destination competitiveness. Indeed, none of the major frameworks include wellbeing measures in any explicit way within their identified indicator sets (WEF, 2020; Dwyer, 2022b). Rather, resident wellbeing and quality of life considerations are typically addressed as 'add-ons', with little or no attempt to provide a theoretical basis for indicator development or for integrating wellbeing outcomes into the established destination competitiveness frameworks. Since the 'competitiveness' of the host destination must embody tourism's potential to enhance resident wellbeing, omission of wellbeing indicators limits their policy significance. Consequently, the established destination competitiveness frameworks do not provide the basis for tourism policy that they may be expected to have (Dwyer, 2022b).

A further argument for incorporating resident wellbeing outcomes into destination competitiveness analysis is that resident wellbeing directly and indirectly affects a range of variables associated with destination performance (Ridderstaat et al., 2016; Kubickova et al., 2017; Woo et al., 2018). Studies show that enhanced resident wellbeing is associated with features such as better health, educational attainment, productivity growth, entrepreneurship, resident support for tourism development and hospitality afforded to visitors (Helliwell et al., 2020), each of which supports destination competitiveness (Crouch & Ritchie, 2012). Understanding the connectedness between destination competitiveness and wellbeing is critical to advancing destination competitiveness theory and practice (Croes & Semrad, 2018). Tourism economists can make an important contribution to this research effort.

New indicators and new measures will be required to assess destination competitiveness in addition to the standard destination performance indicators. Detailed research needs to be undertaken, both at a conceptual and empirical level, to truly integrate resident wellbeing outcomes into destination competitiveness research (Dwyer, 2022b).

2.3.4   Festival and Event Evaluation

Historically, festival and special event evaluation has been dominated by economic impact analysis (EIA) or cost-benefit analysis CBA (Dwyer & Forsyth, 2019). There is increasing awareness, however, that festivals and events provide opportunities for enhancing a variety of experiences, social interactions and relationships that promote resident wellbeing (Yu et al., 2022). These outcomes are not captured by standard EIA, which estimates economic outcomes, nor by CBA, which is firmly based in neoclassical economic theory, conceiving of human wellbeing in terms of consumer willingness to pay for and opportunity cost of goods and services (Dwyer & Forsyth, 2019).

Growing numbers of researchers are now exploring the SWB associated with participant and resident experience of special events (Yu et al, 2022). The inadequacy of SWB as the sole primary input to inform policy making has been addressed above. Taking human wellbeing to be the overarching objective of event development, researchers should acknowledge the crucial relevance of the wider economic, social and environmental impacts essential to an overall 'holistic' assessment of event wellbeing outcomes. Estimation tools required to measure community wellbeing effects associated with festivals and special events need more detailed attention from researchers.

Growth in the events sector, fuelled by global competition, implies that DMO focus should be on developing on managing a portfolio of events to best enhance human wellbeing. The capitals approach has the potential to provide the conceptually appropriate basis to analyse the legacy effects of events, and future research should reflect this, since it is the changing quantity and quality of capital stocks with their associated wellbeing outcomes that will determine the legacy effects of festivals and special events (Dwyer & Forsyth, 2019). This requires that wellbeing assessment be employed proactively as an adaptive management tool to achieve better resident outcomes from holding special events.

2.3.5   Tourism Participation in SDG 2030 Agenda

An understanding of resident wellbeing outcomes and associated indicators is necessary to determine the success of the global tourism industry in meeting the Sustainable Development Goals (SDG) 2030 Agenda (UNWTO, 2018). In much of the research literature, positive wellbeing outcomes are simply assumed to follow upon progress towards achieving each SDG. This (false) assumption has resulted in the relative neglect by tourism researchers as to how wellbeing outcomes can be incorporated into development of comprehensive indicators of SDG achievement. Assessment of tourism's progress towards achievement of the SDGs is incomplete without a full accounting of the outcomes of tourism development on current and future wellbeing (Dwyer, 2022a).

Estimation of resident wellbeing outcomes can inform tourism policy making to achieve sustainability objectives consistent with the 2030 SDG agenda. Determining the trade-offs between the wellbeing outcomes of different policies, and the possibility of multiple wellbeing objectives, introduces a new level of complexity beyond the standard 'goal prioritising' challenge that has occupied researchers of the SDG 2030 agenda. Different destinations should emphasise particular SDGs over others depending on their expected outcomes for resident wellbeing (Costanza et al., 2016; Dwyer, 2022a). Trade-offs must also be made between wellbeing outcomes achievable at the present time and those of future generations. Complementary studies are also needed of the effects of changing capital stocks on both current and future wellbeing, and the links with the different SDGs, a relatively neglected research area to date (Dwyer, 2022a).

2.4   Wellbeing as a Tourism Policy Objective

Given that the primary objective of tourism industry activity is to enhance resident wellbeing, a major concern of policy analysis is to identify the specific wellbeing outcomes associated with tourism development. If measures of resident wellbeing are to make a real difference to people's lives, they must be explicitly employed in the tourism policy making and assessment process. To date, impact analyses have focused on the economic, social and environmental effects of tourism development while ignoring wellbeing outcomes. By incorporating resident wellbeing as the primary tourism industry performance variable, tourism economists can help other researchers to take a more holistic, people-centered, perspective to assess the relative importance of the different tourism development strategies.

There are two main ways in which resident wellbeing outcomes can be incorporated into tourism analysis and policy making. One option is to select particular wellbeing indicators to sit alongside standard indicators of destination performance. On this strategy, a selection of wellbeing measures would be added to the performance indicators used to measure tourism impacts (Croes & Kubikova, 2013; Uysal & Sirgy, 2019; Berbekova et al., 2021). A second option is to employ a broad set of wellbeing indicators to act as a 'lens' or 'filter' through which tourism development outcomes must pass in order for their effects on resident wellbeing to be identified and measured (Dwyer, 2021) This option takes seriously the claim that the primary policy objective of tourism development is to enhance human wellbeing, and that wellbeing outcomes do not merely *complement* key performance indicators but form the ultimate assessment criteria for estimating the level of progress associated with tourism development.

Adopting the capitals approach to assessing sustainable tourism development supports good public policy focused on enhancing the capacity of different types of capital to improve wellbeing for destination residents (Dwyer, 2021). Preliminary attempts have been made to demonstrate how a wellbeing lens may be employed in tourism wellbeing research to inform policy efforts to enhance resident wellbeing outcomes and to measure societal progress (Dwyer, 2021, 2022a, b, c, d, 2023a). The wellbeing lens can act as a 'filter' or 'prism' to identify potential current and future wellbeing outcomes associated with tourism impacts. It can inform public and private sector strategies of 'designing for wellbeing' (Uysal et al., 2020), involving investments that expand residents' capabilities for creating and sustaining wellbeing (Dalziel et al., 2020). Public and private sector organisations can invest in types of built, human, social and natural capital that will best enhance wellbeing outcomes given the resources employed. The wellbeing lens can be used *ex ante* (policy formulation) or *ex post* (policy evaluation), and can be adapted and improved over time as better statistics become available and as the links between tourism impacts and resident wellbeing outcomes are better understood. Managing a portfolio of different capital stocks must now be regarded as a central task of DMO policy for achieving and maintaining sustainable destination development. While various conceptual and empirical challenges still need resolution, the recommended wellbeing lens can represent an essential component of policy making (Dwyer, 2023b).

A growing number of countries (e.g. Bhutan, New Zealand, United Kingdom, France, Scotland, Sweden, Ecuador, Italy) are using wellbeing metrics to guide decision-making and inform budgetary processes (Exton & Shinwell, 2018; Llena-Nozal, et al., 2019; Durand & Exton, 2019). However, putting resident wellbeing as central to tourism policy making requires not just better measures and data but also embedding wellbeing into the culture and machinery of government decision making (Durand & Exton 2019). In this way, policy goals defined in terms of well- being outcomes are systematically reflected in decision-making across the economy. In the view of a growing number of critics, to install wellbeing in its appropriate place in sustainable development, a major transformation in stakeholder values and practice will be needed at all levels of decision making (Dwyer, 2018, 2020, 2023b).

2.5   Conclusion

The influence of the *Beyond GDP* approach has been less obvious in tourism economics research than in other social sciences. Since economic measures do not embrace important aspects of quality of life, broader measures of social progress that go beyond measures of income, wealth and consumption to incorporate nonmaterial sources of wellbeing have an essential role to play in tourism economics research and practice. It was argued that the neglect of wellbeing considerations has diminished the relevance of the tourism economics research effort and its policy significance in several areas. Recognising that wellbeing is a primary policy objective, tourism economics will need to incorporate resident wellbeing outcomes into conceptual analysis, empirical findings and policy assessment in a more inclusive way than has been the practice to date. To this end, it is recommended that wellbeing indicators be employed as a lens, providing more comprehensive evaluations of the outcomes of specific tourism policies on the lives of residents, than standard performance indicators. Several areas of tourism research were identified where determination of wellbeing outcomes can enrich economic analysis and its input into policy making. Use of a wellbeing lens allows the research effort in tourism economics to convert tourism development impacts into resident wellbeing outcomes, and better align with the broader *Beyond GDP* research agenda to measure societal progress. Meeting these challenges will require new concepts and new systems of measurement to support tourism policy making with tourism economists expected to play an important role in the research effort.

References

Adler, A., & M. Seligman (2016). Using wellbeing for public policy: theory, measurement, and recommendations, *International Journal of Wellbeing*, 6(1), 1–35.

Aitken, A. (2019). Measuring welfare beyond GDP. *National Institute Economic Review*, 249(1), R3–R16.

Alvaredo, F., Chancel, L., Piketty, T., Saez, E., & Zucman, G. (2018). Distributional national accounts. In J. E. Stiglitz, J.-P. Fitoussi, & M. Durand (eds), *For good measure: Advancing research on wellbeing metrics beyond GDP* (pp. 143–162). OECD Publishing. https://doi.org/10.1787/9789264307278-en.

Arrow, K. J., Dasgupta, P., Goulder, L., Mumford, K., & Oleson, K. (2012). Sustainability and the measurement of wealth, *Environment and development economics, 17*(3), 317–353.

Asmelash, A. G., & Kumar, S. (2019). Assessing progress of tourism sustainability: Developing and validating sustainability indicators. *Tourism Management, 71*, 67–83.

Austin, A. (2016). On wellbeing and public policy: Are we capable of questioning the hegemony of happiness? *Social Indicators Research, 127*(1), 123–138.

Berbekova, A., Uysal, M., & Assaf, A. (2021). Toward an assessment of quality of life indicators as measures of destination performance. *Journal of Travel Research, 61*(6), 1424–1436. https://doi.org/10.1177/00472875211026755.

Bimonte, S., & Faralla, V. (2016). Does residents' perceived life satisfaction vary with tourist season? A two-step survey in a Mediterranean destination. *Tourism Management, 55*, 199–208.

Bleys, B. (2012). Beyond GDP: Classifying alternative measures for progress. *Social Indicators Research, 109*(3), 355–376.

Boley, B. B., & Perdue, R. R. (2012). Destination management, competitiveness, and quality of-life: A review of literature and research agenda. In M. Uysal, R. Perdue & J. M. Sirgy (eds) *Handbook of tourism and quality-of-life research* (pp. 515–528). Dordrecht: Springer.

Chattopadhyay, M., Kumar, A., Ali, S., & Mitra, S. K. (2021). Human development and tourism growth's relationship across countries: a panel threshold analysis. *Journal of Sustainable Tourism, 30*(6), 1384–1402.

Costanza, R., Fioramonti, L., & Kubiszewski, I. (2016). The UN sustainable development goals and the dynamics of wellbeing. *Frontiers in Ecology and the Environment, 14*(2), 20–22.

Costanza, R., Erickson, J. D., Farley, J., & Kubiszewski, I. (eds) (2020) *Sustainable wellbeing futures: A research and action agenda for ecological economics*. Cheltenham: Edward Elgar Publishing.

Croes, R. (2016). Connecting tourism development with small island destinations and with the wellbeing of the island residents. *Journal of Destination Marketing & Management, 5*(1), 1–4.

Croes, R., & Kubickova, M. (2013). From potential to ability to compete: Towards a performance-based tourism competitiveness index. *Journal of Destination Marketing and Management, 2*(3), 146–154.

Croes, R., & Semrad, K., (2018). Destination competitiveness, in C. Cooper, S. Volo, W. Gartner and N. Scott (eds), *The Sage handbook of tourism management: Application of theories and concepts to tourism* (pp. 77–90), London: Sage.

Croes, R., Ridderstaat, J., & Shapoval, V. (2020). Extending tourism competitiveness to human development, *Annals of Tourism Research, 80*, p.102825.

Crouch, G., & Ritchie, B. J. R. (2012). Destination competitiveness and its implications for host-community QOL. In M. Uysal, R. Perdue & M. J. Sirgy (eds), *Handbook of Tourism and Quality-of-Life Research: Enhancing the lives of tourists and residents of host communities* (pp. 491–514). Dordrecht, Netherlands: Springer.

Dalziel, P., Saunders, C., & Saunders, J. (2018). *Wellbeing economics: The capabilities approach to prosperity*. Dordrecht: Springer Nature.

De Smedt, M., Giovannini, E., & Radermachier, V. (2018). Measuring sustainability. In J. E. Stiglitz, J.-P. Fitoussi, & M. Durand (eds) *For good measure: Advancing research on wellbeing metrics beyond GDP* (pp. 243–284). Paris: OECD Publishing.

Diener, E., & Biswas-Diener, R. (2019). Wellbeing interventions to improve societies. In J. Sachs, R. Layard, & J. F. Helliwell (eds), *Global Happiness Policy Report 2019* (pp. 95-112). Dubai: Global Happiness Council.

Diener, E., Oishi, S., & Tay, L. (2018). Advances in subjective wellbeing research. *Nature Human Behaviour, 2*(4), 253–260.

Durand, M. (2015). The OECD better life initiative: How's life? and the measurement of wellbeing. *Review of Income and Wealth, 61*(1), 4–17.

Durand, M., (2020). What should be the goal of public policies? *Behavioural Public Policy, 4*(2), 226–235.

Durand, M., & Exton, C. (2019). Adopting a wellbeing approach in central government: Policy mechanisms and practical tools. In J. Sachs, R. Layard, & J. F. Helliwell (eds), *Global Happiness Policy Report 2019* (pp. 141–159). Dubai: Global Happiness Council.

Dwyer, L. (2018). Saluting while the ship sinks: The necessity for tourism paradigm change. *Journal of Sustainable Tourism, 26*(1), 29–48.

Dwyer L. (2020). Tourism development and sustainable wellbeing: A Beyond GDP perspective. *Journal of Sustainable Tourism, 28*, 1–18.

Dwyer, L. (2021). Resident wellbeing and sustainable tourism development: The capitals approach. *Journal of Sustainable Tourism.* https:// doi .org/ 10 .1080/ 09669582 .2021.1990304.

Dwyer, L. (2022a). Tourism contribution to the SDGs: Applying a wellbeing lens. *European Journal of Tourism Research, 32*, 3212. https://doi.org/10.54055/ejtr.v32i .2500.

Dwyer, L. (2022b). Destination competitiveness and resident wellbeing. *Tourism Management Perspectives, 43*, 100996. https://doi.org/10.1016/j.tmp.2022.100996.

Dwyer, L. (2022c). Productivity, destination performance, and stakeholder wellbeing. *Tourism and Hospitality, 3*(3), 618–633.

Dwyer L. (2022d). Why tourism economists should treat resident wellbeing more seriously. *Tourism Economics, 0*(0)1–20. https://doi.org/10.1177/13548166221128081.

Dwyer, L. (2023a). Tourism development to enhance resident wellbeing: A strong sustainability perspective. *Sustainability 15*(4), 3321. https:// doi .org/ 10 .3390/ su15043321.

Dwyer, L. (2023b). Sustainable development of tourism; research and policy challenges. *Highlights of Sustainability.*

Dwyer L., and Forsyth, P. (2019). Evaluating special events: Merging two essential approaches. *Event Management, 23*(6), 897–911.

Easterlin, R. A., & O'Connor K. J. (2020). The Easterlin Paradox IZA DP No. 13923 Institute of Labor Economics (IZA). Discussion Paper Series, December.

Ekins, P., Dresner, S., & Dahlström, K. (2008). The four-capital method of sustainable development evaluation. *Environmental Policy and Governance, 18*, 63–80.

Exton, C., & Shinwell, M. (2018). Policy use of wellbeing metrics: Describing countries' experiences. *OECD Statistics Working Papers*, No. 2018/07, OECD Publishing, Paris. https://doi.org/10.1787/d98eb8ed-en.

Fioramonti, L., Coscieme, L., & Mortensen, L. F. (2019). From gross domestic product to wellbeing: How alternative indicators can help connect the new economy with the Sustainable Development Goals. *The Anthropocene Review, 6*(3), 207–222.

Fleurbaey, M., & D. Blanchet (2013). *Beyond GDP: Measuring welfare and assessing sustainability.* Oxford: Oxford University Press.

Frijters, P., Clark, A. E., Krekel, C., & Layard, R. (2020). A happy choice: Wellbeing as the goal of government. *Behavioural Public Policy, 4*(2), 126–165.

Fuchs, D., Schlipphak, B., Treib, O., Long, L., & Lederer, M. (2020). Which way forward in measuring the quality of life? A critical analysis of sustainability and wellbeing indicator sets. *Global Environmental Politics*, *20*(2), 12–36.

Hartwell, H., Fyall, A., Willis, C., Page, S. Ladkin, A., & Hemingway, A. (2018). Progress in tourism and destination wellbeing research. *Current Issues in Tourism*, *21*(16), 1830–1892.

Helliwell, J, Layard, R., Sachs, J., & De Neve, J. (eds) (2020). *World Happiness Report 2020*. New York: Sustainable Development Solutions Network.

Iriarte, L., & Musikanski, L. (2019). Bridging the gap between the Sustainable Development Goals and happiness metrics. *International Journal of Community Wellbeing*, *1*(2), 115–135.

Kubickova, M., Croes, R., & Rivera, M. (2017). Human agency shaping tourism competitiveness and quality of life in developing economies. *Tourism Management Perspectives*, *22*, 120–131.

Lee, C. C., Chen, M. P., & Peng, Y. T. (2021). Tourism development and happiness: International evidence. *Tourism Economics*, *27*(5), 1101–1136.

Llena-Nozal, A., Martin, N., & Murtin, F. (2019). The economy of wellbeing. Creating opportunities for people's wellbeing and economic growth. *OECD Statistics Working Papers* 2019/02.

Musikanski, L., Cloutier, S., Bejarano, E., Briggs, D., Colbert, J. Strasser, G., & Russell, S. (2017). Happiness index methodology. *Journal of Social Change,* *9*(1), 4–31. https://doi.og/10.5590/JOSC.2017.09.1.01.

Nikolova, M., & Graham, C. (2020). *The Economics of Happiness*, GLO Discussion Paper, No. 640, Global Labor Organization (GLO), Essen.

OECD. (2020). *How's life?: Measuring wellbeing*. Paris: OECD Publishing. https://doi.org/10.1787/9870c393-en.

Qasim, M., & Grimes, A. (2018). Sustainable economic policy and wellbeing: The relationship between adjusted net savings and subjective wellbeing (No. 18_06). Motu Economic and Public Policy.

Ridderstaat, J. R., Croes, R., & Nijkamp, P. (2016). The tourism development–quality of life nexus in a small island destination. *Journal of Travel Research*, *55*, 79–94.

Rivera, M., Croes, R., & Lee, S. H. (2016). Tourism development and happiness: A residents' perspective. *Journal of Destination Marketing & Management*, *5*(1), 5–15.

Smith, M. K., & Diekmann, A. (2017). Tourism and wellbeing. *Annals of Tourism Research,* *66*, 1–13.

Stiglitz, J., Fitoussi, J., & Durand, M. (2018a). *Beyond GDP: Measuring what counts for economic and social performance*. Paris: OECD Publishing. https://doi.org/10.1787/9789264307292-en.

Stiglitz, J. E., Fitoussi, J.-P., & Durand, M. (eds) (2018b). *For good measure: Advancing research on wellbeing metrics beyond GDP*. Paris: OECD Publishing. https://dx.doi.org/10.1787/9789264307278-en.

Stone, A., & Krueger, A. B. (2018). Understanding subjective wellbeing. In J. E. Stiglitz, J.-P. Fitoussi & M. Durand (eds), *For good measure: Advancing research on well-being metrics beyond GDP* (pp 163–202), Paris: OECD Publishing. https://dx.doi.org/10.1787/9789264307278-en.

Tov, W. (2018). Wellbeing concepts and components. In E. Diener, S. Oishi, & L. Tay (eds), *Handbook of wellbeing*. Salt Lake City, UT: DEF Publishers.

United Nations General Assembly Resolution 65/309. (2012) Happiness: Towards a holistic approach to development. Draft Note, 6 November.

UNWTO. (2018). Tourism and the Sustainable Development Goals: Journey to 2030. https://www.e-unwto.org/doi/pdf/10.18111/9789284419401.

Uysal, M., Perdue, R., & Sirgy, M. J. (eds). (2012). *Handbook of tourism and quality-of-life research: Enhancing the lives of tourists and residents of host communities*. Dordrecht: Springer Science & Business Media.

Uysal, M., & Sirgy, M. J. (2019). Quality-of-life indicators as performance measures. *Annals of Tourism Research, 76*, 291–300.

Uysal, M., Berbekova, A., & Kim, H. (2020). Designing for quality of life. *Annals of Tourism Research, 83*, 102944.

Woo, E., Uysal, M., & Sirgy, M. (2018). Tourism impact and stakeholders' quality of life. *Journal of Hospitality & Tourism Research, 42*(2), 260–286.

Yu, N. N., Mair, J., Lee, A., & Ong, F. (2022). Subjective wellbeing and events. *Event Management, 26*(1), 7–24.

3   Indicators of quality of life in tourism: the perspective of demand and supply interaction

Adiyukh Berbekova and Muzaffer Uysal

3.1   Introduction

The rapid development of quality of life (QOL) and wellbeing research in the tourism context has contributed to an extensive research area that focuses on nonconventional outcome measures of tourism. Many empirical studies were conducted to investigate the potential impacts of tourism experiences on tourists' QOL, as well as the effects of tourism development on the wellbeing of residents and communities in a travel destination, as well as the industry employees. With the evolvement of this research stream, numerous constructs, indicators, and measures were employed to operationalize wellbeing and quality of life as it pertains to tourism research setting. A proper conceptualization reflective of the unit of research analysis and consequent measurement of these constructs are essential in establishing the true effects of tourism on QOL (Uysal et al., 2016). Thus, reliable and valid measurements of wellbeing and QOL are critical and pose challenges in tourism research. It should be noted that primarily, the concepts of wellbeing and QOL are used in tourism research interchangeably. However, there are slight differences in their definitions. Wellbeing is based solely on subjective evaluations of one's life, and the QOL concept is used as a more encompassing, umbrella term (Land & Michalos, 2018). Following the practice established in the tourism literature, in this chapter, we use the terms interchangeably.

One of the approaches to categorizing the existing measures in the tourism context is to classify them based on the measurement focus (i.e., objective and subjective [Sirgy, 2012]). The current studies mostly utilize the so-called subjective approach to measuring QOL and focus on assessing the effects of tourism activities and experiences on stakeholders' subjective, individual assessment of the satisfaction in their lives in general or certain life domains (e.g., Cummins, 2005; Kim et al., 2015; Rapley 2003; Wang et al., 2021). In this regard, the assessment of subjective wellbeing includes both negative and positive emotions associated with the evaluation as outcome measures. Examples of such measures are happiness, perceived QOL, satisfaction with life domains, and overall life satisfaction. On the contrary, the objective indicators reflect the external conditions, including economic (e.g., gross income per capita), environmental QOL (e.g., air and water pollution), state of health (e.g., infant mortality rate), education (e.g., adult literacy rate) sectors, and so on (Berbekova & Uysal, 2021). It is important to note that it is challenging to capture a holistic and comprehensive state of QOL by employing just objective or subjective indicators (Land & Michalos, 2018). They both independently and collectively serve different purposes and functions based on targets, goals, and locations. Ideally, the impacts of tourism on stakeholders' QOL and wellbeing would be analyzed by combining both indicator types. It is observed that quality of life is almost always measured by subjective indicators using surveys of individuals' perceptions, evaluations and satisfaction with their living conditions or objective indicators using secondary data reflective of the place where the study takes place (McCrea et al., 2006). It is also argued and agreed upon that objective and subjective indicators constitute independently useful estimates of the QOL construct (Cummins, 2000). It has also been demonstrated that the relationship between variables measured within each dimension is complex. Cummins (2000) concluded that while objective and subjective indicators are generally fairly independent, their degree of dependency increases when the objective conditions of living are poor. This contention is supported by a study (McCrea et al., 2006) that examined the link between objective and subjective indicators of urban QOL and found that the relationships between the two are weak, suggesting that care must be taken while making inferences about improvements based the interaction of the two. While it is essential to understand the distinction between objective and subjective approaches to measuring QOL and wellbeing, in this chapter, we take a different angle on the measurement tools in the tourism context.

This chapter discusses the constructs and measures utilized in wellbeing and quality of life research in the tourism context and assesses the most commonly applied measures and indicators. First, the demand and supply perspectives on measurement indicators for wellbeing and quality of life are reviewed. Specifically, the measures of individual and community wellbeing are presented. Second, drawing on a service-dominant (S-D) logic, the chapter further details the importance of accounting for operand and operant resources in measuring quality of life and wellbeing in tourism. It concludes with recommendations and future research directions relating to measurement tools for wellbeing and quality of life in tourism.

3.2   Demand and Supply Perspectives on Measurement Indicators for Wellbeing and QOL

Any tourism experience occurs as a function of the demand and supply inter-action (Uysal et al., 2012). The challenge is then to manage the flow of visitors in relation to attractions in a given destination, whether it be manmade or natural settings. This can be possible if the nature of the interaction between demand and supply is fully understood in a given experience context. Mansfeld (1990) discussed two basic streams that conceptualize tourist flows in the liter-ature: (1) travel flows as a function of demand-supply interaction (functional approach) and (2) travel flows as a result of political-economic prosperity/superiority. The latter approach argues that travel flows occur "from the desire of affluent classes in metropolitan countries to travel to dependent and deprived countries". The implicit assumption of this approach is that the flow between an origin and destination(s) is unidirectional as a function of the "political and economic superiority" of the generating place. This approach is considered radical in its research orientation and does not consider the behavioural and functional or evolutionary aspects of tourists. However, there is enough evidence to suggest that a significant volume of international visitation and tourism may still be attributable to this theoretical framework. Regardless of the emphasis and approach in each flow model, the essence of the interaction between demand and supply helps managing the consequences (socioeconomic, environmental, and cultural impacts) of tourism activities on the wellbeing of both participants and residents, including providers of goods and services.

The physical setting of the destination, available attractions, facilities and amenities, residents and industry employees form the supply side of the tourism ecosystem, while the demand is represented by travellers and encom-passes their personal characteristics, needs and expectations (Uysal et al., 2020). Inevitably, the nature and the quality of this interaction will affect the perceived benefits of tourism experiences and tourism development for all parties involved. Consequently, the quality of life and wellbeing of the main stakeholders is affected (Berbekova & Uysal, 2021). The measures and indica-tors that are utilized in tourism research to evaluate the wellbeing and quality of life also characterize both supply and the demand side of tourism activities.

3.2.1   Indicators and Measurement Tools for Wellbeing and QOL From a Demand Perspective

From the demand perspective, the wellbeing and QOL in the tourism context are examined by analysing the effects of tourism experiences on tourists' perceived quality of life and life satisfaction (Puczkó & Smith, 2012). Puczkó and Smith (2012) note that from the demand side, the analysis of tourists' QOL should encompass several domains of one's wellbeing and wellness (i.e., material, physical, spiritual, emotional, social, and safety), as well as the overall life satisfaction and happiness. These measures are commonly collected on an individual level and through either qualitative techniques (e.g., participant observation, in-depth interviews) or cross-sectional surveys.

There is extensive research that investigates the effects of tourism experience on individuals' QOL (e.g., Backer, 2019; Farkić et al., 2020; McCabe et al., 2010). Thus, some studies confirm that participation in tourism activities can have a positive effect on tourists' wellbeing (Kruger, 2012; Puczko & Smith, 2011). For instance, the study by Kim et al. (2015) focused on a sample of elderly tourists and found that satisfaction with one's trip experience leads to satisfaction with the leisure life domain and consequently positively affects one's overall wellbeing (both physical and mental). Moreover, the authors confirmed that the higher tourists' involvement in the experience is, the higher their overall trip satisfaction will be – in other words, their wellbeing. The concept of involvement in tourism experience has been discussed as an important predecessor of satisfaction with travel/destination and furthermore, as a potential factor that can moderate the link between tourism experience to quality of life (Neal et al., 1999, 2007; Uysal et al., 2020). Thus, Gilbert and Abdullah (2004) found that involvement in planning the trip and the associated anticipation of travel lead to similar levels of happiness as if measured after the trip. Similar results were obtained by Nawijn et al. (2010) that analysed the pre- and posttrip levels of happiness among vacationers and nonvacationers and found differences in the degree of happiness only before the trip. Nonetheless, there is research that does not confirm an unequivocal positive effect of traveling on wellbeing and QOL. Thus, Michalkó et al.'s (2009) results showed that traveling had no effect on respondents' satisfaction with life and thus, did not support the positive link between tourism and tourists' QOL. Such findings suggest that other confounding factors (from both supply and demand side of tourism) moderate this relationship and should be accounted for in future research.

The studies investigating the impact of tourism activities on tourists' wellbeing employ a subjective approach to QOL assessment and utilize constructs and measures at the individual level. Some research may concentrate on pre-, on- and post-trip experiences, others measure tourists' satisfaction with certain life domains (e.g., leisure, emotional, spiritual). Finally, the majority of studies employ the overarching concept of overall life satisfaction or perceived happiness. As noted by Genç (2012a, b), when applying any QOL measure, it is critical to consider both cognitive and affective components. Thus, the cognitive factors are formed through thoughts and evaluations, while the affective components include emotions such as joy and anger, sadness and happiness, and shame and pride (Genç, 2012a).

Some focused research may employ additional constructs depending on the context of the study (i.e., if a specific tourism experience is explored) (e.g., Lee et al., 2014; Lin et al., 2022). Recently, considering the ongoing effect of COVID-19 new factors surrounding the experience that may affect QOL and wellbeing are being examined. Thus, Kim and Han (2022) explored how certain in-room amenities shape hotel guests' sense of wellbeing. In their study, the authors refer to the sense of wellbeing as reflecting both emotional and cognitive satisfaction with life. The study results suggested that protective (e.g., cleanliness, contactless service) and sensory (e.g., room furniture, interior) in-room facilities as well as the amenities related to food and beverage play a significant role in predicting guests' wellbeing. Such findings reinforce the notion that tourism experiences can be designed to impact and enhance QOL actively (Uysal et al., 2020; Vogt et al., 2020). Designing the experience that can positively contribute to quality of life is defined by the successful integration of both demand and supply factors and thus, measures that assess both are important (Uysal et al., 2020).

3.2.2   Indicators and Measurement Tools for Wellbeing and QOL From a Supply Perspective

From the supply perspective, the QOL and wellbeing are evaluated for destination residents and industry employees. The industry employees include a wider group of stakeholders, including owners and suppliers of tourism and industry-related businesses, employees, and their families. Similar to tourists, residents' and employees' wellbeing and QOL can be assessed on an individual level. Thus, industry employees' wellbeing is generally measured through the construct of quality of work life (QWL) (Sirgy et al., 2001), which accounts for employees' satisfaction with seven work and nonwork-related domains. The QWL is grounded in need hierarchy and spill over theories (Sirgy et al., 2001) and posits that QWL is a function organization's capability to satisfy workers' basic and growth needs.

The topic of residents' QOL, as they are important stakeholders in the tourism industry, has received extensive attention in the literature. One of the main reasons for the heightened interest is the practical implication of improving residents' wellbeing through tourism development (Ramkissoon, 2020). Several studies found that residents' satisfaction with certain life domains, as an outcome of tourism, has a direct positive effect on their attitude toward tourism and the further development of the industry in the destination (e.g., Wang et al., 2022; Woo et al., 2015). On an individual level, locals' wellbeing is examined through constructs similar to those utilized for tourists and include satisfaction with life domains and overall life satisfaction. For instance, Kim et al. (2013) investigated the connection between perceived impacts of tourism and residents' sense of material, health and safety, community, and emotional wellbeing, and overall life satisfaction. The indicators of each domain represented locals' satisfaction with each wellbeing dimension. Their results suggested that satisfaction with certain life domains is a function of locals' perceptions of specific tourism impacts (i.e., economic, social, cultural, environmental). Depending on the research focus, only certain life domains may be of interest. Thus, the study by Wang et al. (2021) was set to analyze the effects of emotional connections between tourists and residents (i.e., the level of emotional solidarity) on residents' emotional wellbeing, measured through leisure and spiritual life, and consequently on their support for tourism development. The authors established the explanatory power of emotional antecedents in explaining locals' satisfaction with emotional wellbeing and confirmed the positive connection between residents' QOL and their attitudes toward tourism.

Nonetheless, the analysis of the effects of tourism development on residents' QOL is not complete without accounting for community wellbeing (Hu et al., 2022). Community wellbeing measures include several dimensions, such as economic or material, health and safety, environmental, social and educational attainment, and leisure wellbeing. These external conditions are generally assessed through objective indicators such as per capita income, adult literacy rate, life expectancy, air and water pollution, and more. These indicators are collected by statistical agencies, along with local and national organizations, and can reflect the wellbeing at city, county, and country levels.

Table 3.1 summarizes some examples of individual and community wellbeing measures employed in tourism research from both the demand and supply perspectives.

Table 3.1   Examples of individual and community wellbeing measures

Individual wellbeing measures	Community wellbeing measures
Tourists	*Economic or material wellbeing*
Satisfaction with all stages of tourism	Income per capita
experience (i.e., pre-, on-, post-trip)	Consumer expenditure
Satisfaction with travel/tourism services and	Prices of goods and services
the experience overall	Housing costs and costs of land
Satisfaction with leisure life domain	Unemployment rate
Satisfaction with emotional and spiritual life	*Health and safety wellbeing*
Satisfaction with life in general/Overall life	Life expectancy
satisfaction	Number of hospitals and hospital beds
Perceived happiness	Number of doctors
Positive affect	Crime rate
Negative affect	*Social wellbeing and educational attainment*
	Adult literacy rate
	Mean years of schooling
	Expected years of schooling
	Quality of the public transportation system in
	the area
	Leisure wellbeing
	Number of recreational areas and programs
	Environmental wellbeing
	Land pollution in the area
	Air pollution in the area
	Water pollution in the area
	Crowdedness of the area
	Living conditions in general
	Accessibility to amenities
Residents	
Satisfaction with material wellbeing	
Satisfaction with community wellbeing	
Satisfaction with health and safety wellbeing	
Satisfaction with emotional wellbeing	
Industry employees (i.e., owners and suppliers	
of tourism and industry-related businesses,	
employees, and their families)	
Quality of work life, including:	
Satisfaction of health and safety needs	
Satisfaction of economic and family needs	
Satisfaction of social needs	
Satisfaction of esteem needs	
Satisfaction of actualization needs	
Satisfaction of knowledge needs	
Satisfaction of aesthetics needs	

Note: This table is not intended to be exhaustive, but rather it provides examples of possible indicators under each category.
Source: Adapted from Uysal & Sirgy (2019), Sirgy et al. (2001).

As this discussion demonstrates, several measures are commonly employed to assess the wellbeing and QOL in tourism. We have reviewed these constructs and measures drawing on a supply-demand interaction in a functioning tourism system that points to two groups of measures, those that pertain to an individual and community wellbeing. It should be further emphasized that the nature of the community wellbeing measures discussed in Table 3.1 could differ depending on the destination and commonly reflect specific issues and challenges (Uysal & Sirgy, 2019). Furthermore, the stage of tourism development in the destination should be considered in estimating the effects of tourism on residents' and community wellbeing (Uysal et al., 2012). The strength and the direction of the relationship between perceived impacts of tourism and locals' satisfaction with certain life domains may differ contingent on the level of tourism development (Kim et al., 2013).

Overall, as a general rule of thumb, the choice of the variable and the focus on a specific life domain should be theoretically driven and correspond with the theoretical framework chosen and the study focus (Uysal & Sirgy, 2019). In the next section, we consider the S-D logic perspective on QOL measurement in tourism.

3.3   The Importance of Resource Configuration: Operant and Operand Resources as 'Indicators' of Wellbeing

A functioning tourism system is dependent on the availability of certain resources and, thus, monitoring and managing these resources in a sustainable manner is of critical significance. It is important to note that resources required for a tourism experience to occur can be both tangible and intangible. S-D logic emphasizes that the interaction of both tangible (operand) and intangible (operant) resources is crucial in creating value (Vargo, 2008). Operand resources are defined as physical, tangible assets and goods, while operant resources are characterized as intangible, skill-based, and present resources that either create an effect or can act on other resources to create the effect (Akaka & Vargo, 2014; Constantin & Lusch, 1994). The operant resources are further classified as human, organizational, relational, and informational (Madhavaram & Hunt, 2008). It should be noted that S-D logic recognizes the dominant role of operant resources in value cocreation (Vargo & Lusch, 2004).

As noted in the previous section, the tourism experience takes place as an outcome of supply-demand interaction in the tourism system (Gunn & Var, 2020). Thus, the operand and operant resources represent both supply and demand sides. For instance, tourism destinations can be conceptualized as an ecosystem that is formed by both operand and operant resources (Prebensen et al., 2018). The destination's tangible resources generally encompass the facilities, amenities, natural and manmade attractions, cultural and heritage sites, as well as service providers (i.e., physical equipment, servicescape elements) and destination management and marketing organizations (Prebensen et al., 2013). The operant resources in a travel destination are presented through community residents and industry employees and include their knowledge, skills, personal travel experiences and relationships formed with tourists, and perceptions of the industry in general (Prebensen et al., 2018).

S-D logic views the customer as a central actor in value co-creation and posits that value is created only in use, thus shifting from the value-in-exchange concept to value-in-use (Grönroos, 2008; Grönroos & Ravald, 2011). Inevitably, the interaction between operand and operant resources shapes the tourism experience and thus, consequently, impacts satisfaction with the experience and the stakeholders' wellbeing. Previous research demonstrates that cocreated value has a positive impact on tourists' overall travel satisfaction and QOL (e.g., Mathis et al., 2016; Prebensen & Xie, 2017). Thus, the tourist is an active participator in creating value through the tourism experience. Tourists' operant resources include knowledge, skills, energy, and emotions that, together with the destination ecosystem, contribute to value cocreation (Prebensen et al., 2018). Uysal et al. (2020) proposed that destinations and tourists act as resource integrators and their active engagement in value cocreation is essential in improving stakeholders' QOL.

Both operand and operant resources have the potential to independently or in combination to influence how both objective and subjective assessments of indicators may be perceived to contribute to one's wellbeing or QOL. In a way, resources are also reflective of tourism development and living conditions. Perceived living conditions in a given place may consist of host attributes, including the health of the local economy, perceived liveability of the place, types of amenities, safety, level of attachment to that community, economic and political stability, ease of access to amenities, availability of open space, employment level, cost of living, perceived crowding and congestion, support for education and public services, level of public spending, and the like (Uysal, 2010). The assumption is that there is a reciprocal interaction between perceived living conditions and wellbeing. In other words, the types of resources emanating from either supply or demand side can play a moderating role in understanding QOL outcome measures. Limited research in tourism exists that makes such a connection. One of the earliest studies in this area was conducted by Perdue et al. (1991). The study used a list of objectives indicators of resident QOL as a function of tourism development and explored the effects of tourism development on the selected objective QOL indices within the domains of economics, education, medical services, welfare services, and crime. The unit of analysis for the study was the counties of North Carolina, categorized into five levels based on tourism expenditures. A similar study by Meng et al. (2010) found a correlation between different levels of living conditions and QOL indicators. The results revealed that the residents of provinces with the highest level of development lead a significantly 'better life' than those who are in the regions with a medium or low level of tourism development, as measured with a select number of objective indicators of QOL. Thus, the study indirectly demonstrated the connection between levels of economic living conditions and its impact on tourism QOL. An earlier study by Crotts and Holland (1993) using objective indicators of the impacts of rural tourism found that income, health, recreation, and personal services had a positive relationship with the QOL of rural populations but was negatively connected with poverty. As we move more toward general societal goals and improvement of QOL of individuals as tourists and residents as providers, there is room for further research that could explore the interaction between living conditions in relation to tourism impact and overall community wellbeing (Uysal et al., 2012).

It could be argued that the level of tourism development that is characterized by changes in the infrastructure and the general setting of the destination should be considered as an overarching operand resource. Moreover, the community wellbeing indicators (see Table 3.1) can be viewed as reflecting the state of the operand resources in the area. The challenge here is how to best integrate both operand and operant resources over time as the destination experiences structural changes and behavioural responses to the nature of structural changes. This reality implies that both objective and subjective indicators in relation to a given destination are dynamic and can also change in their meanings and connotation attributed to them. Although the constructs or indicators of quality of life may be the same, the way they are operationalized may be a function of how indicators are evaluated with respect to their perceived utility and contribution or centrality to the quality of life of a given destination. Figure 3.1 summarizes the configuration of operand and operant resources from the perspective of supply-demand interaction within the tourism ecosystem. As the figure demonstrates, there is a mutual connection between community and individual wellbeing and the resources that constitute the tourism experience. Moreover, some of these resources, either objectively or subjectively evaluated, may be utilized as proxies of wellbeing and QOL measures.

3.4   Conclusion and Future Research Directions

This chapter focused on measures and constructs of wellbeing and QOL in tourism. Drawing on the framework of supply-demand interaction and S-D logic, we discussed the commonly employed measures on both individual and community levels and related relevant issues. Undoubtedly, indicators of QOL should represent both demand and supply elements. At the same time, types of resources, either operand or operant, along with levels of development (living conditions) should be part of the process of identifying and developing appropriate indicators, and their operationalization needs to be done within the scope and parameters of the place in question. It is important to acknowledge that the functional operationalization of these indicators is subject to change over time; thus, they need to be monitored by either collecting regular data for objective indicators or conducting interval surveys for subjective indicators.

The challenge is establishing the link between objective and subjective indicators or operand and operant resources as QOL indicators using theoretical underpinnings. The extant literature reveals that, based on homeostasis theories, an individual's QOL can vary over time with objective life events (e.g., buying a car, getting married or divorced, taking a trip) but tend to return to an equilibrium level of satisfaction (McCrea et al., 2006). This implies an adaptive state as events induce negative or positive emotions. Thus, homeostasis theories in general help explain (low) correlations between subjective QOL indicators and objective life occurrences or events (Cummins, 2000).

The literature on QOL using both top-down and bottom-up models also sheds some light on the relationships between objective and subjective indicators (within the realm of operand and operant resource configuration). For example, personality traits and characteristics of individuals may have a stabilizing influence on life satisfaction. So, there is evidence that personality traits influence overall QOL and flow down to affect satisfaction judgment in specific life domains (Hayes & Joseph, 2002; McCrea, et al., 2006). In this sense, the influence of personality traits weakens the relationship between subjective and objective indicators. In contrast, bottom-up models propose direct relationships between objective and subjective indicators. However, the degree to which the relationship is assessed is a context matter. Despite the argument presented, we have limited empirical studies within tourism settings that directly link objective indicators to subjective wellbeing. We believe that there is ample opportunity to conduct research in this area. It should also be noted that with a few exceptions (e.g., Lee et al., 2014) tourism and hospitality researchers adopt measures and indicators, developed in social indicators

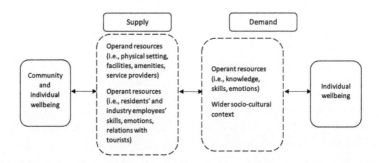

Figure 3.1   Resource configuration within the tourism ecosystem

and QOL research. There are no specific scales and measures developed for tourism experiences exclusively. Thus, more mixed-methods inquiries are needed to explore the possibility of creating and validating a tourism wellbeing index.

The other practical challenge is that each destination is unique with its level of development and living conditions including cultural dispositions and the nature of social capital of the place – thus, how locals and tourists as stakeholders perceive the influence of tourism on their wellbeing can be and are different according to the stage of tourism development. The list of both objective and subjective QOL indicators should also reflect the level of development, as well as the sociocultural fabric of the place. Although the quantification or measure of objective indicators are straightforward and may be easily obtainable, their perceived importance in contributing to wellbeing of individuals and residents may show variation. Recalibrating or weighing the relative importance of objective indicators of QOL by subjective evaluation based on standardized scores is crucial in linking objective and subjective indicators of QOL for a given destination.

Furthermore, it is important to investigate the impact of successful resource configuration (operand and operant) in cocreating value and designing for quality of life. Thus, more integrated models that account for these resources in explaining wellbeing and QOL are needed. Moreover, contingent on the setting, the importance of a certain resource in creating value for the actors could vary (Madhavaram & Hunt, 2008). Thus, for instance, depending on the stage of tourism development, the reconfiguration of available resources for quality experience could be different.

References

Akaka, M. A., & Vargo, S. L. (2014). Technology as an operant resource in service (eco) systems. *Information Systems and E-Business Management, 12*(3), 367–384. https://doi.org/10.1007/s10257-013-0220-5.

Backer, E. (2019). VFR travel: Do visits improve or reduce our quality of life? *Journal of Hospitality and Tourism Management, 38*, 161–167. https://doi.org/10.1016/j.jhtm.2018.04.004.

Berbekova, A., & Uysal, M. (2021). Wellbeing and quality of life in tourism. In J. Wilks, D. Pendergast, P. A. Leggat, & D. Morgan (eds), *Tourist health, safety and wellbeing in the new normal* (pp. 243–268). Springer. https://doi.org/10.1007/978-981-16-5415-2_10.

Constantin, J. A., & Lusch, R. F. (1994). *Understanding resource management: How to deploy your people, products, and processes for maximum productivity.* Irwin Professional Publishing.

Crotts, J. C., & Holland, S. M. (1993). Objective indicators of the impact of rural tourism development in the State of Florida. *Journal of Sustainable Tourism, 1*(2), 112–120, DOI: 10.1080/09669589309450709.

Cummins, R. A. (2000). Objective and subjective quality of life: An interactive model. *Social indicators research, 52*(1), 55–72.

Cummins, R. A. (2005). The domains of life satisfaction: An attempt to order chaos. In A. C. Michalos (ed) *Citation classics from social indicators research* (pp. 559–584). Dordrecht: Springer. https://doi.org/10.1007/1-4020-3742-2_19.

Farkić, J., Filep, S., & Taylor, S. (2020). Shaping tourists' wellbeing through guided slow adventures. *Journal of Sustainable Tourism, 28*(12), 2064–2080. https://doi.org/10.1080/09669582.2020.1789156.

Genç, R. (2012a). Subjective aspects of tourists' quality-of-life (QOL). In M. Uysal, R. Perdue, & M. J. Sirgy (eds), *Handbook of Tourism and Quality-of-Life Research* (pp. 149–167). Springer Netherlands. https://doi.org/10.1007/978-94-007-2288-0_9.

Genç, R. (2012b). Tourist consumption behavior and quality-of-life. In M. Uysal, R. Perdue, & M. J. Sirgy (eds.), *Handbook of Tourism and Quality-of-Life Research* (pp. 135–148). Springer Netherlands. https://doi.org/10.1007/978-94-007-2288-0_8.

Gilbert, D., & Abdullah, J. (2004). Holidaytaking and the sense of well-being. *Annals of Tourism Research, 31*(1), 103–121. https://doi.org/10.1016/j.annals.2003.06.001.

Grönroos, C. (2008). Service logic revisited: Who creates value? And who co-creates? *European Business Review, 20*, 298–314. https://doi.org/10.1108/09555340810886585.

Grönroos, C., & Ravald, A. (2011). Service as business logic: Implications for value creation and marketing. *Journal of Service Management, 22*(1), 5–22. https://doi.org/10.1108/09564231111106893.

Gunn, C. A., & Var, T. (2020). *Tourism planning: Basics, concepts, cases* (4th edn.). Routledge. https://doi.org/10.4324/9781003061656.

Hayes, N., & Joseph, S. (2003). Big 5 correlates of three measures of subjective well-being. *Personality and Individual Differences, 34*(4), 723–727.

Hu, R., Li, G., Liu, A., & Chen, J. L. (2022). Emerging research trends on residents' quality of life in the context of tourism development. *Journal of Hospitality & Tourism Research.* https://doi.org/10.1177/10963480221081382.

Kim, H., Woo, E., & Uysal, M. (2015). Tourism experience and quality of life among elderly tourists. *Tourism Management, 46*, 465–476. https://doi.org/10.1016/j.tourman.2014.08.002.

Kim, J. J., & Han, H. (2022). Redefining in-room amenities for hotel staycationers in the new era of tourism: A deep dive into guest well-being and intentions. *International Journal of Hospitality Management, 102*, 103168. https://doi.org/10.1016/j.ijhm.2022.103168.

Kim, K., Uysal, M., & Sirgy, M. J. (2013). How does tourism in a community impact the quality of life of community residents? *Tourism Management, 36*, 527–540. https:// doi .org/ 10 .1016/j.tourman.2012.09.005.

Kruger, P. S. (2012). Perceptions of tourism impacts and satisfaction with particular life domains. In M. Uysal, R. Perdue, & M. J. Sirgy (eds), *Handbook of tourism and quality-of-life research* (pp. 279–292). Springer Netherlands. https:// doi .org/ 10 .1007/ 978–94–007–2288–0_16.

Land, K. C., & Michalos, A. C. (2018). Fifty years after the social indicators movement: Has the promise been fulfilled?: An assessment an agenda for the future. *Social Indicators Research, 135*(3), 835–868. https://doi.org/10.1007/s11205–017–1571-y.

Lee, D.-J., Kruger, S., Whang, M.-J., Uysal, M., & Sirgy, M. J. (2014). Validating a customer well-being index related to natural wildlife tourism. *Tourism Management, 45*, 171–180. https://doi.org/10.1016/j.tourman.2014.04.002.

Lin, M.-P., Marine-Roig, E., & Llonch-Molina, N. (2022). Gastronomy tourism and well-being: Evidence from Taiwan and Catalonia Michelin-starred restaurants. *International Journal of Environmental Research and Public Health, 19*(5), 2778. https:// doi .org/ 10 .3390/ ijerph19052778.

Madhavaram, S., & Hunt, S. D. (2008). The service-dominant logic and a hierarchy of operant resources: Developing masterful operant resources and implications for marketing strategy. *Journal of the Academy of Marketing Science, 36*(1), 67–82. https:// doi.org/ 10.1007/ s11747–007–0063-z.

Mansfeld, Y. (1990). Spatial patterns of international tourist flows: Towards a theoretical framework. *Progress in Human Geography, 14*(3), 372–390.

Mathis, E. F., Kim, H., Uysal, M., Sirgy, J. M., & Prebensen, N. K. (2016). The effect of co-creation experience on outcome variable. *Annals of Tourism Research, 57*, 62–75. https://doi.org/10.1016/j.annals.2015.11.023.

McCabe, S., Joldersma, T., & Li, C. (2010). Understanding the benefits of social tourism: Linking participation to subjective well-being and quality of life. *International Journal of Tourism Research, 12*(6), 761–773. https://doi.org/10.1002/jtr.791.

McCrea, R., Shyy, T. K., & Stimson, R. (2006). What is the strength of the link between objective and subjective indicators of urban quality of life? *Applied Research in Quality of Life, 1*(1), 79–96.

Meng, F, Li, X. and Uysal, M. (2010). Tourism development and regional quality of life: The case of China. *Journal of China Tourism Research, 6*, 164–182. https:// doi.org/ 10.1080/ 19388160.2010.481602.

Michalkó, G., T. Rátz, & A. Irimiás (2009). Health tourism and quality of life in Hungary: Some aspects of a complex relationship. In G. De Santis (ed) *Salute e lavoro. Atti del nono seminario internazionale di geografia medica* (pp. 79–90). Edizioni RUX.

Nawijn, J., Marchand, M. A., Veenhoven, R., & Vingerhoets, A. J. (2010). Vacationers happier, but most not happier after a holiday. *Applied Research in Quality of Life, 5*(1), 35–47. https:// doi.org/10.1007/s11482–009–9091–9.

Neal, J. D., Sirgy, M. J., & Uysal, M. (1999). The role of satisfaction with leisure travel/tourism services and experience in satisfaction with leisure life and overall life. *Journal of Business Research, 44*(3), 153–163. https://doi.org/10.1016/S0148–2963(97)00197–5.

Prebensen, N. K., & Xie, J. (2017). Efficacy of co-creation and mastering on perceived value and satisfaction in tourists' consumption. *Tourism Management, 60*, 166–176. https://doi .org/10.1016/j.tourman.2016.12.001.

Prebensen, N. K., Vittersø, J., & Dahl, T. I. (2013). Value co-creation significance of tourist resources. *Annals of Tourism Research, 42*, 240–261. https://doi.org/10.1016/j.annals.2013 .01.012.

Prebensen, N. K., Uysal, M. S., & Chen, J. S. (2018). Perspectives on value creation–resource configuration. In N. K, Prebensen, J. S. Chen, & M.S. Uysal (eds), *Creating experience value in tourism*, (pp. 228–237), 2nd edn. CAB International 2018.

Puczkó, L., & Smith, M. (2011). Tourism-specific quality-of-life index: The Budapest model. In M. Budruk & R. Phillips (eds), *Quality-of-life community indicators for parks, recreation and tourism management* (pp. 163–183). Springer.

Puczkó, L., & Smith, M. (2012). An analysis of tourism QOL domains from the demand side. In M. Uysal, R. Perdue, & M. J. Sirgy (eds), *Handbook of tourism and quality-of-life research* (pp. 263–277). Springer Netherlands. https://doi.org/10.1007/978–94–007–2288–0_15.

Ramkissoon, H. (2020). Perceived social impacts of tourism and quality-of-life: A new conceptual model. *Journal of Sustainable Tourism, 31*(2), 442–459. https://doi.org/10.1080/ 09669582.2020.1858091.

Rapley, M. (2003). *Quality of life research: A critical introduction.* Sage.

Sirgy, M. J. (2012). *The psychology of quality of life* (Vol. 50). Springer Netherlands. https://doi .org/10.1007/978–94–007–4405–9.

Sirgy, M. J., Efraty, D., Siegel, P., & Lee, D.-J. (2001). A new measure of quality of work life (QWL) based on need satisfaction and spillover theories. *Social Indicators Research, 55*(3), 241–302. https://doi.org/10.1023/A:1010986923468.

Uysal, M. (2010). The effects of tourism impacts upon QOL of residents and sustainability in the community. Invited presentation at International Conference on Tourism Sustainability, Mbombela – Nelspruit, South Africa, November 15–19, 2010.

Uysal, M., Berbekova, A., & Kim, H. (2020). Designing for quality of life. *Annals of Tourism Research, 83*, 102944. https://doi.org/10.1016/j.annals.2020.102944.

Uysal, M., & Sirgy, M. J. (2019). Quality-of-life indicators as performance measures. *Annals of Tourism Research, 76*, 291–300. https://doi.org/10.1016/j.annals.2018.12.016.

Uysal, M., Sirgy, M. J., Woo, E., & Kim, H. (2016). Quality of life (QOL) and well-being research in tourism. *Tourism Management, 53*, 244–261. https://doi.org/10.1016/j.tourman .2015.07.013.

Uysal, M., Woo, E., & Singal, M. (2012). The tourist area life cycle (TALC) and its effect on the quality-of-life (QOL) of destination community. In M. Uysal, R. Perdue, & M. J. Sirgy (eds), *Handbook of tourism and quality-of-life research* (pp. 423–443). Springer Netherlands. https://doi.org/10.1007/978–94–007–2288–0_25.

Vargo, S. L. (2008). Customer integration and value creation: Paradigmatic traps and perspectives. *Journal of Service Research, 11*(2), 211–215. https:// doi .org/ 10 .1177/ 1094670508324260.

Vargo, S. L., & Lusch, R. F. (2004). Evolving to a new dominant logic for marketing. *Journal of Marketing, 68*(1), 1–17. https://doi.org/10.1509/jmkg.68.1.1.24036.

Vogt, C. A., Andereck, K. L., & Pham, K. (2020). Designing for quality of life and sustainability. *Annals of Tourism Research, 83*, 102963. https://doi.org/10.1016/j.annals.2020.102963.

Wang, S., Berbekova, A., & Uysal, M. (2021). Is this about feeling? The interplay of emotional well-being, solidarity, and residents' attitude. *Journal of Travel Research, 60*(6), 1180–1195. https://doi.org/10.1177/0047287520938862.

Wang, S., Berbekova, A., & Uysal, M. (2022). Pursuing justice and quality of life: Supporting tourism. *Tourism Management, 89*, 104446. https:// doi .org/ 10 .1016/ j .tourman .2021 .104446.

Woo, E., Kim, H., & Uysal, M. (2015). Life satisfaction and support for tourism development. *Annals of Tourism Research, 50*, 84–97. https://doi.org/10.1016/j.annals.2014.11.001.

PART II

INDIVIDUAL WELLBEING IN TOURISM

4   Healthy hotels: contribution of employee wellness programs

Susan E. Gordon and Xinran Lehto

4.1   Introduction

Researchers have been proposing various lenses to shed insights as to how best to deliver wellbeing values through designing, communicating, delivering, and managing products, services, and experiences (e.g., Lehto, 2013; Lehto & Lehto, 2019; Lehto et al., 2021). However, much of the literature on wellbeing in the hospitality and tourism area centres more on the consumer side of the phenomenon. Efforts in examining the employee side of the picture is not as pronounced. In the employee wellbeing literature, researchers mostly focus on topics pertaining to the antecedents (e.g., coworker, supervisor, and organizational support, career development, work/life balance, emotional labour, stress, and work/life conflict) and consequences (e.g., increased productivity, satisfaction, and retention, burnout, turnover, and healthcare costs) of employee wellbeing. Much less attention is given to the actual wellbeing programs themselves, especially in terms of how they are being structured, delivered, and perceived by employees. Among the existing studies that do attempt to shed light on these programs, they oftentimes assess these programs in the settings of businesses that largely follow the standard Monday through Friday 9:00 am to 5:00 pm work schedule. These studies miss aspects that pertain to hospitality, given the industry's characteristics, including long hours, nonstandard schedules, temporary employment due to seasonality, constant guest interactions, emotional labour, and physical work, among others. Therefore, there is a need for researchers to shine a spotlight on the hospitality employees in this regard.

Further, as we transition out of the COVID-19 pandemic era, wellbeing research focusing on hospitality businesses bears an even greater importance than the prepandemic era. The toll it took on the hospitality employees is severe as they directly interface with guests and are concerned with not only guest health safety but also that of their own and their families. Such stressors for hotel employees have led to negative wellbeing consequences, reaching far beyond employees' physical health domain into the mental and family domains (Kim et al., 2023). From a business perspective, employee wellbeing is a key component of the service profit chain as customer satisfaction starts with a business's treatment of its own employees. In this sense, the chain of service profit can only be set in motion when employees are well cared for, and they can then convey their satisfaction to best care for the customers. As such, research examining the various aspects of programs for hospitality employee wellbeing is particularly imperative. This study attempts to examine hotel employee wellbeing programs utilizing a case study of a hotel management company headquartered in the United States.

4.2   Literature Review and Study Objectives

4.2.1   Wellbeing and Wellness

It is worth noting that in the United States, employee wellbeing-oriented programs are usually termed as "wellness programs", instead of "wellbeing programs". While there is no consensus on a definition of wellbeing nor consensus as to the difference between the concepts wellbeing and wellness, Gallup says that wellness typically focuses on physical health, whereas wellbeing focuses on the whole person, and because work and life cannot be separated, organizations should care for the whole person by focusing on the wellbeing of employees (Gallup, n.d.). As such, this study takes a holistic lens to understand employee wellbeing, which often comprises aspects of quality of life, happiness, physical health, and mental health.

Wellness programs aimed at intentional and individual efforts have been found to increase employee wellbeing. Furthermore, offering a variety of activities to achieve goals and facilitating peer-to-peer discussions in small groups was found to be impactful (Page & Vella-Brodrick, 2013). A study by Gubler et al. (2018) revealed that a short-term focus by companies on employee wellbeing will not be sustained over the long-run and thus, short-term interventions are not enough. Recently, research has shown that online delivery of wellness programs can be effective in improving employee wellbeing (Neumeier et al., 2017).

4.2.2   Employee Wellbeing

Employees are key to organizational success and because of this, employee wellbeing is critical to organizations. Employees who have higher levels of wellbeing are more satisfied in their jobs (Satuf et al., 2018), more productive (Taris & Schreurs, 2009), experience a higher quality of life (Dodge et al., 2012) and are less likely to be absent (Carter et al., 2011), have workplace accidents (Danna & Griffin, 1999), feel burned out, and quit (Gordon et al., 2019). Given this, employee wellbeing is important both as a result in itself and as a precursor to organizational results (Agarwal, 2021). Van De Voorde et al.'s (2012) systematic review of the impact of human resources management (HRM) practices on employee wellbeing revealed that studies have found that psychological and social wellbeing were positively associated with organizational performance, but health wellbeing, including both physical and mental wellbeing, was negatively associated performance, possibly due to high workloads and stress. However, managers have been found to impact employee physical health through the mediating effect of intrinsic motivation (Huo et al., 2020). In addition, emotional support from managers can increase employee wellbeing (Vakkayil et al., 2017). Given that these aspects are intertwined, this case study takes a holistic view of these three dimensions when considering employee wellbeing using the singular term wellbeing.

Company wellness programs gained attention in the 1970s in the United States as organizations began to focus on healthcare costs due to the increasingly sedentary lives of employees (Gebhardt & Crump, 1990). Employee assistance programs (EAPs) were put in place to help employees deal with substance abuse while continuing to work (Jacobson & Sacco, 2012). These programs have grown to include aspects such as financial planning, mental health, weight loss, and smoking cessation, among others (Gebhardt & Crump, 1990). Employee wellness programs can be delivered in person or digitally through wellbeing websites and apps, virtual workout classes, virtual doctor visits, mindfulness programs, and more. The effectiveness of this mode of delivery is supported by Neumeier et al. (2017) who found that self-administered programs delivered online were effective at increasing employee wellbeing. The COVID-19 pandemic gave rise to the many virtual options to deliver wellness to employees. Benefits of employee wellness programs include increased productivity and employee retention, improved health behaviours by employees, reduction of diseases and stress, lower healthcare costs, higher profitability, and a favourable company image (Chaturvedi & Rathore, 2021; Gubler et al., 2018). Despite these benefits, many organizations see low employee participation (Zhang, 2018), especially among those most in need of the programs (Merrill et al., 2011). This can lead to organizations perceiving a low return on investment (ROI) in these programs despite their aforementioned benefits. Gubler et al. (2018) found that employers can earn an ROI for investing in wellness programs if employee participate and stay with the program and company. Thus, undertaking a strategy of supporting employee wellbeing is critical to an organization's success.

4.2.3   Employee Wellbeing in Hotels

The hospitality industry is known for nonstandard working conditions such as seasonality leading to temporary employment, irregular schedules, long hours, lower pay, physical labour, and emotional labour when serving guests. As such, the wellbeing of employees is a critical issue facing hospitality organizations especially as wellbeing impacts business success (Agarwal, 2021) in terms of providing service to guests and by extension profits and guest loyalty. Within the hotel context, subjective wellbeing was shown to negatively impact turn-over and mediate the relationship between supervisor support and turnover among line-level employees in select-service hotels (Gordon et al., 2019). A study of employees in full-service hotels confirmed the daily fluctuation of wellbeing and turnover intention meaning that employees' feelings and intentions can changed based on the job demands encountered and resources received (Shi et al., 2021). This is of particular interest in the hotel context as employees never have the same day twice, so support of employee wellbeing by hotel leaders is a key to success. Coworkers have also been found to positively impact employee wellbeing in the hotel context (Nilgün, 2017).

A study focused on hotel employees found that because of the pandemic, HRM practices moved from the typical business-focus practices to those that focused on employees' personal lives to ensure organizational outcomes such as job performance (Agarwal, 2021). As such, Agarwal (2021) suggested hotels continue to employ wellbeing-centred HRM practices that benefit both the employees and organization. Another note of interest from this study are that flexibility in HRM practices is key in terms of managing employee wellbeing (Agarwal, 2021). As the pandemic continues to shine a very bright light on the need to ensure hospitality employee wellbeing no matter what the environ-ment, understanding how employee wellbeing is considered at all levels of an organization is critical. Thus, this case study focuses on how employee wellness programs are infused within a hotel management company from the perspec-tives of a corporate benefits decision-maker, hotel human resources directors, hotel operations managers, and hotel employees. The focus of this study is to understand what values wellbeing practices deliver to employees that allow them to better serve their guests.

4.2.4   Theoretical Background

Our theoretical underpinning draws on three concepts: the Job Demands-Resources (JD-R) model (Baaker & Demerouti, 2014), the Conservation of Resources (COR) theory (Hobfoll, 1989), and the Health Resources typology (Lehto & Lehto, 2019). Demands are aspects of work that require employees to expend energy and may be challenging or hindering, whereas resources help employees reach goals and mitigate demands (Baaker, 2015). Baaker (2015) proposed that exhaustion, a form of unwellbeing, and engagement, which can increase wellbeing (Gordon et al., 2021), will fluctuate on momentary, daily, and weekly basis as employees' job demands and resources change. In this vein, Shi et al. (2021) confirmed that hotel employees' subjective wellbeing fluctuates daily. Furthermore, managerial support, which is a type of resource, has been shown to increase employee wellbeing (Gordon et al., 2019). These conceptual arguments seem to suggest that wellness programs offered to hotel employees may be perceived and received in a varied fashion by the employees because of the nature of work, the fluctuation of work demand at different times, situational scenarios, and management support.

The COR theory also lends support to the importance of employee wellbeing (Hobfoll, 1989), as it posits that employees who are experiencing the kind of stress that can decrease wellbeing (Yu et al., 2021), may look for ways to cope with this by preserving their resources, which could come from other individuals such as managers, coworkers, and family members or by the employee withdrawing from work either temporarily or permanently. Thus, COR has been used to underpin wellbeing studies as employees may look to preserve their wellbeing as one resource to combat job demands. As such, organizations that support employee wellbeing will be providing a resource for employees to better handle job demands.

Lehto and Lehto (2019) proposed a "Vacation as a Health Resource" four-dimensional structure of wellness. The prevention function helps people conserve wellbeing resources. Under the restorative function, people regain their optimal mental and physical conditions. The instorative function is the potential to cultivate new personal resources such as creative resources. The transformative function instigates transformational changes for an individual. This health resource typology sheds light on wellbeing values that could be created and delivered to hospitality employees. While this typology is proposed in the context of tourism consumers, the four functions may provide a framework to understand the nature of hotel wellness programs and practices and how they benefit employees especially considering the JD-R and COR theories.

4.2.5   Study Objective

Using the typology proposed by Lehto and Lehto (2019) for vacation as a health resource, we propose that the four dimensions of this framework (protective, restorative, instorative, and transformative) can be extended to workplace wellbeing practices to employees. In the vein of the service profit chain, where taking care of employees leads to taking care of guests, we also propose that employees who receive and engage in wellbeing practices will then enhance the wellbeing of guests. Specifically, this study aims to understand how one hospitality organization engages in wellness programs from a holistic view of employee wellbeing. The following research questions provide a broad guide as we investigate our case. However, given the open-ended nature of this qualitative study, we intend to address our case study as patterns evolve to allow for possible new unexpected themes and patterns to emerge.

(1) the nature of wellness-oriented practices and programs in hotels;
(2) how wellness programs are perceived and practiced by hotel employees;
(3) how the practices were selected and designed to meet various wellbeing needs;
(4) the program structure and flexibility for localizing the programs at the hotel level; and
(5) how operations managers support the programs.

4.3   Methodology

This research took a case study approach situated in a hotel management company headquartered in the Midwest of the United States. The organization owns and operates full-service hotels across the country. A qualitative approach to the research was deemed most appropriate because it allowed us to depict a nuanced view of reality of our case company as it pertains to employee wellbeing. Situating the phenomenon of employee wellbeing in context enabled us to effectively reveal the multifaceted nature of employee wellbeing with the idea that it would extend to guest wellbeing.

Semi-structured interviews were employed to better understand what wellness programs are offered, which programs are most valuable, how programs meet different wellbeing needs, how managers encourage participation, and the rationale for which programs are offered. This method employs "open-ended questions [that] are developed in advance, along with prepared probes. Unplanned, unanticipated probes may also be used" (Richards & Morse, 2007,

p. 111). Interviews were conducted with one corporate benefits manager, three hotel human resources directors and managers, five hotel managers, and three hotel hourly associates. When new information was no longer being revealed, it was deemed that saturation had been reached. Interviews lasted approximately 30 minutes each and were recorded for transcription purposes.

The interview data was analyzed using a thematic content analysis approach to identify themes (Braun & Clarke, 2006). We coded the data by creating units of meaning (Gordon & Parikh, 2021), which necessitated the use of multiple codes due to the complexity of the interview data (Campbell et al., 2013; Gordon & Parikh, 2021). Eighteen patterns were revealed that subsequently contributed to the five overarching themes. These themes are "nature of the wellness programs", "wellness program structure", "champions and advocates", "wellness as a brand strategy", "meeting people where they are", and "wellness as a business philosophy". Table 4.1 presents the five overarching themes with the 18 patterns located under each one. It should be noted that some of the patterns appeared in more than one theme.

4.4   Results and Discussion

Based on our interviews with the corporate office benefits manager, hotel managers, and frontline associates, we unpacked the following themes that pertain to the state of wellness programs and perceptions about them as to how they influence hotel employees' sense of wellbeing. Rather than presenting our results by strictly corresponding to our set of study questions, we discussed themes and topics emerged from the data that were gained using the study questions in our interviews. Table 4.1 provides an overview of the 18 topics we noted, which were later grouped into five broad themes. Some topics can be relevant to more than one theme. Our discussions are organized and presented accordingly.

4.4.1   Nature of Wellness Programs

Our interviews revealed that the understanding of wellbeing is different given the perspectives that each person expressed. In other words, each person has their own perceptions of what constitutes wellbeing and wellbeing needs and support. For example, when asked what wellness programs the company offers, some associates mentioned leadership programs they are in, regular meetings with managers regarding their personal development, and tuition reimbursement, which pertain to the instorative domain of the health resource

Table 4.1   Five themes and 18 topics revealed in the interviews

Theme	Topic
Nature of Wellness Programs	Wellbeing programs offered can be viewed as core and augmented
	Personal growth-oriented programs are popular
	"Change the work narrative": it is okay not to work long hours*
	Managers walk-the-talk leads to the trigger down effect of associates adopting healthy wellness-oriented behaviours*
	Various aspects of wellbeing and the interconnectedness of these aspects
Wellness Program Structure	Flexible, organic, grass roots wellness initiatives as versus structured and standardized
	"Change the work narrative": it is ok not to work long hours*
	"Meet people in their space" *
	Hourly associates need unique care programs
	Financial security is important
	Partnerships with local wellness providers are welcomed
	Social wellbeing needs are acute
Champions and Advocates for Self-Care	Employee's readiness to serve helps with the transfer of wellbeing to the delivery of "care" and "wellbeing mindset" for guests
	Balanced scorecard: need to incorporate wellbeing as a measurement pillar for success (in addition to market share, financial wellbeing/revenue, associate satisfaction, and guest satisfaction)
	Service profit chain updated: feeling well, serving well
	COVID effect: The pandemic heightened imperative
Meeting People Where They Are	"Meet people in their space"

Theme	Topic
	Time effect: programs helping with better scheduling and few hours really help. The benefits go beyond personal physical wellbeing, but also social wellbeing and family wellbeing
	Meals included can directly help with multiple aspects of one's sense of wellbeing

Note: * Indicates a topic that fit more than one theme

typology (Lehto & Lehto, 2019). These actions are viewed as "care" from the company and help with mental wellbeing. This finding echoes Vakkayil et al. (2017), who found that senior human resources managers viewed professional development as an element of employee wellbeing.

Wellness program components seem to fall into core and augmented categories much like Grönroos's (2000) grouping of services for customers. Benefits such as health insurance and employee assistance programs (EAPs) are expected by employees as standard benefit offerings like core services whereas offerings such as a telemedicine program are considered unique benefits so would be considered augmented. Managers mentioned that some associates do not have primary care doctors or cannot get an appointment with their doctor in a timely manner or take time off for the appointment but can make use of the telemedicine offering that allows them to be "seen" by a doctor and obtain a prescription, if needed. The telemedicine program was revealed to be extremely popular among managers and associates alike. Thus, these augmented wellbeing products such as telemedicine adds value to employees not just in the immediate benefits they perceive, but they also positively influence how employees view the wellbeing image of the corporation. This impact on wellbeing aligns with Neumeier et al.'s (2017) finding that online wellness programs delivered through smartphones and tablets can increase employee wellbeing. They further speculated that this may be particularly effective for organizations that have high mobility jobs or jobs that do not utilize computers, two characteristics prevalent in the hospitality and tourism industry.

We noted that wellness program components do fit within the four health resources typology proposed by Lehto and Lehto (2019), albeit in a different way than for consumers. The standard benefits that address physical and mental wellbeing needs fits within the preventative resource. Some of these benefits are provided by partnerships with local organizations such as gym membership discounts but could also be extended to paying employees to volunteer within their community as proposed by a human resources director. Adding to this resource are programs that meet social wellbeing such as associate rallies that bring feelings of connectedness and associate recognition, which echoes previous studies that have found coworker support increases wellbeing (Nilgün, 2017). As previously mentioned, personal growth programs add to the instorative resource. Interestingly, these programs were viewed as wellness program components not only by associates, but by managers and the corporate benefits director, too. Thus, the company seems to recognize the contribution of personal development to employee wellbeing, hence the emphasis on its importance.

Restorative resources come in the form of some core benefit offerings such as EAPs, but also in the augmented offerings such as telemedicine and mental health counselling sessions available to associates regardless of whether they are enrolled in the company's health insurance. The transformative resource came in the form of managers actively working to change the work narrative in terms of encouraging associates not to work long hours. The pandemic seems to have helped those in the organization realize that it is not okay to work long hours and that reducing the stigma of hospitality as an industry plagued by long hours for little pay is key moving forward to provide work–life balance. Thus, managers are walking the talk by not working long hours themselves and encouraging those who can to work from home one day per week to engage in self-care by modelling this behaviour. Managers are also actively encouraging participation in wellness programs and function as champions for the programs when associates come to them with personal situations. This is in line with Gubler et al.'s (2018) finding that employees are more apt to participate over the long term when supported by the organization and not by one short-term intervention. Associates reported that the managers who have been with the company longer know more about the wellness programs and are able to provide them with information in addition to those who work in human resources. Associates may view this as supervisor support, which has been shown to increase wellbeing (Gordon et al., 2019). This suggests that incorporating wellbeing initiatives into a manager's annual review or into a company's metrics and balanced scorecard would elevate wellbeing as a focus in the same way as guest satisfaction, employee satisfaction, financials, and market share.

4.4.2   Wellness Program Structure

Many wellness programs come from the hotel management company's corporate office as part of the overall benefits offerings for associates. They are standardized across the organization and address long-term needs such as health insurance. The corporate benefits administrator is highly selective in terms of which vendors are chosen to provide programs and considerable time is spent curating the programs. However, the local hotels are also given the flexibility to create offerings for their own associates or in partnership with other hotels nearby under the same management, so grassroots initiatives are also incorporated into the program structure. For example, some hotels offered weight-loss programs locally or brought in local fitness instructors to hold classes at the hotel for associates. In addition to these programs that can help address momentary wellbeing, hotels are also free to address breakroom design and meal offerings and departments are free to develop wellness practices such as allowing associates to take a ten-minute walk after handling a stressful guest situation or providing bottled water to associates. Hotels also hold associate rallies multiple times throughout the year that are customized to the needs of the hotel's associates and help provide recognition to them. Interviewees mentioned that these rallies impact their social wellbeing by helping them feel connected to others at the hotel and especially those in other departments who they may not see often.

The nature of work and changing the mindset of long hours are addressed by individual departments, as they determine when associates can work from home or where and when those who lead operations and are constantly on their feet can take time away from the operation to complete administrative tasks. Other initiatives include how operations can ensure the leader is not "on call" 24 hours per day and that they truly can step away from the operation to restore during their days off. These types of initiatives are also aimed at addressing associate stress in the workplace. All these practices help the organization to "meet people in their space" through offering a variety of programs, allowing choice, and designing local programs and so on. The offering of multiple ways to address needs and providing employees the freedom to choose is in line with Page and Vella-Brodrick's (2013) finding to successfully increase employee wellbeing. These actions show that the organization understands that associates are all in different life stages, which means they have different needs to address. For example, one associate spoke about the financial security she enjoys from her organization through the financial counselling that is available and the retirement packages, as those are important to her as someone who is getting closer to retirement and no longer has children at home.

4.4.3   Champions and Advocates for Self-care

A theme that stood out across multiple interviews involved advocating for and championing the wellness programs. Interviewees shared that managers who have been with the organization for several years were instrumental in helping them understand what wellness programs are available especially in times of need. Thus, the communication from managers in the form of pre-shift meetings, one-on-one sessions, and informal conversations is key to ensuring associates take advantage of the programs offered. In addition, communications from the corporate office in the form of weekly emails is also beneficial to associates and serve as reminders in times such as open enrolment and as an encouragement signal for self-care.

Perhaps even more important than communication are actions. Managers who walk the talk and demonstrate a focus on wellbeing are seen as championing wellbeing and wellness programs. This behaviour and sharing their own personal use of programs trickles down to the associates and signals to them that it is ok to focus on your wellbeing or work from home or make use of programs like mental health counselling. Managers also shared that they are actively trying to show associates the importance of self-care by working from home one day per week or telling the associates about their own experiences with the virtual mental health counsellor or telemedicine doctor. According to Kim et al. (2023), employees' work environments are most impacted by their direct manager, which can impact their wellbeing. As such, managers walking the talk of self-care create a positive environment where employees can feel comfortable addressing their own wellbeing needs, especially around mental health.

4.4.4   Wellness as a Brand Strategy

Interviewees strongly felt that if their wellbeing needs are met, they have a readiness to serve guests and impact the guests' wellbeing by delivering care to them. This resonates with the idea of the service profit chain where employees feeling well means they can serve well. It was mentioned that guests can detect the level of an associate's efforts because of that associate's wellbeing even if the associate is working to mask it. One way the organization has impacted employee wellbeing is by increasing the pay of hourly associates, which has allowed many to drop a second job they once held, and this is a positive outcome from the pandemic. This in turn has helped to reduce turnover and increase satisfaction, which, of course, are fundamental performance metrics for organizations. Another initiative the company has taken is to create a new associate pledge and branding that incorporates wellbeing. Job advertisements emphasize the benefits available and how the brand thinks about employee wellbeing. These strategies signal to associates that the organization cares about their wellbeing, also characterized as organizational support (Eisenberger et al., 1986).

4.4.5   Meeting People Where They Are

As mentioned previously, meeting people in their space or meeting them where they are resonated throughout many interviews to the point that it seemed to be a key to success in ensuring employee wellbeing. The ways associates feel they are seen as individuals with varying needs comes across in the flexibility of plan choices, variety of offerings, localized programs created to address needs, and the understanding that everyone is in a different stage in life and, thus, a one-size-fits-all approach will not work. For example, a hotel in one area is heavily staffed by local college students and, as such, needs such as tuition reimbursement, flexible scheduling, and time off are important for them. Another example is the nature of the work being done in the job. For example, hourly employees and operations managers may need more mental health programs, as the nature of their work provides physical activity, but they are constantly serving guests. Meanwhile, those managers in support roles may need more physical health programs due to their sedentary work. A time effect was apparent in that programs and actions by managers that addressed associate scheduling needs were seen as going beyond the associate's own wellbeing and contributing to family wellbeing and social wellbeing as time spent with family and friends became more accessible. Previous research has shown that working with hourly operations employees to accommodate their scheduling needs is seen as a form of supervisor support (Gordon & Parikh, 2021), which has led to increased wellbeing (Gordon et al., 2019). These actions and the ability for some to work from home can help to stimulate creativity which can benefit the workplace and guests. Finally, associates see meals to impact their wellbeing both in terms of healthy options as well as financially. If a hotel can offer meals to associates, this is viewed as caring by the organization. Even extending this beyond the hotel is viewed as care. For example, one interviewee mentioned a time when the hotel gave away food boxes for associates in need to take home.

4.5   Further Reflections and Directions

This research set out to examine a case study of wellness programs employed by one hotel management company in the United States. Through our interviews, we developed a case-based understanding of the nature of wellbeing-oriented practices and programs offered to hotel employees, how these programs are being implemented and participated, what the rationales behind them are, and whether and how these programs are factored into the larger context of the strategic aspects of hotel management such as service profit chain and brand considerations. The results have revealed a nuanced picture of wellness programs and practices of hospitality businesses in the United States. Our analysis allows us to further reflect on the ramifications for practice and for theory development. We developed a wellness flow chart and a model to depict an ecological cycle of the wellness system. Although as previously noted, wellness tends to imply physical health in the United States (Gallup, n.d.), we use the term wellness in our reflections to invite organizations to rethink wellness programs in the spirit of caring for the whole person. We invite future researchers to use the flow chart in a company or cultural setting to determine if the practices hold true and to discover the prevalence of the practices.

4.5.1   Wellness as a Business Philosophy

The interviews and themes above brought about the theme of wellness as a business philosophy. By infusing wellness throughout the organization and the strategies and decision made, the organization can impact employees and guests alike. Changing the culture to one oriented towards wellness can help achieve this. For example, starting with changing the narrative about working long hours to one of working smarter no longer can set the tone and expectations for all employees that it is not ok to work tirelessly and that it is ok to take time away from work. Many interviewees mentioned a renewed focus on work–life balance because of the pandemic where self-care is encouraged by the organization and managers. COVID certainly heightened the imperative for work–life balance and this organization is one that heeded the call. The actions taken by the organization revealed frequently throughout the conversations with the interviewees brought about a sense of wellness driving decision-making, instilling a spirit of hospitality and care for others, a permeation of wellness throughout the organization, and the need to sustain employee wellbeing. All of this culminates in a sense that wellness as a business philosophy is the way for organizations to move from a technology-driven orientation to a wellness-driven orientation.

4.5.2   A Wellness Flow Chart

As Figure 4.1 suggests, we can identify a wellness flow pattern where the hotel management company's wellness programs and policies are designed and offered at the headquarter level. However, these programs and policies are carried out at the individual hotel level but with situational adaptations at the departmental level and freedom of choice or participation at the associate level. Further, there are specific characteristics associated with each level. At the corporate level, wellness-oriented programs tend to be structured and longer-term oriented. These programs include employee health benefits (e.g., insurance), and they are concerned with the cultivation of a wellbeing culture, tying wellness offerings to brand identity, brand value, employee retention strategy, talent development, and company performance indicator. It is interesting to note that wellness programs and benefits were not explicitly considered as a strategy for branding and other bigger picture aspects of the company until 2022. Prior to the COVID-19 pandemic, they were just simply treated as employee benefits. As wellbeing is being increasingly prioritized for today's society, and considering the challenges that hotels are facing in recruiting hospitality workers, there is growing strategic thinking about projecting a corporate image of a company that places wellbeing of people as a central focus and a brand differentiation point. This strategy has worked well as our interviews with employees at various levels – from managers to supervisors to hourly associates – suggest that employees recognize and appreciate not just the wellness programs but also the hospitality care that the hotel management company exhibits towards its employees. At the department level, the wellness-oriented practices appear to be more spontaneous and more situational in nature. For example, the nature of work and individual life circumstances were factored into consideration. The hotels recognize that wellness needs can vary because of an employee's work responsibilities (i.e., office work versus work that entails physical exertion versus work that entails direct guest contact). Needs can also vary because of employees' life stage variabilities (e.g., families, age, financial situation, etc.). "Meet people where they are" becomes not just an internal marketing slogan but an orientation that has guided the design and delivery of wellness programs geared towards employees.

4.5.3   An Ecological Cycle of Wellness System

An interesting observation is that employees' understanding of "wellness" programs seem to be broader and more holistic than the company. For example, associates view higher-than-industry-standard pay as a way for the company to not only take care of their financial wellbeing but also mental wellbeing (stress reduction) and social wellbeing (reducing need for second jobs and more time for family and socialization). The fact that financial assistance (such as investment portfolio assistance or free meals/discounted hotel stays) are being seen as "wellness" programs is notable. Another aspect of wellness practices that are somewhat out of the conventional definition of "wellness" program is for professional development programs and opportunities to be seen as wellness initiatives and representation of company care. These observations are meaningful. It suggests that "wellness" and "wellbeing" should not been treated as something of a "plus", or "extra", they should be essential to a business. In fact, it needs to become an overarching guiding principle for business processes,

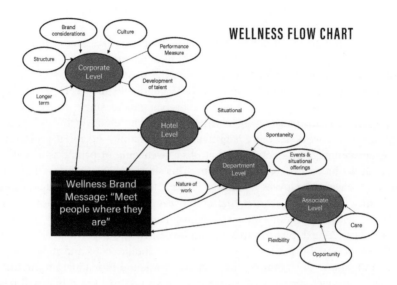

Figure 4.1   A wellness flow chart

operations, and other management strategies. Wellness should permeate into the fine grain of a hospitality company.

We propose a conceptual model of an ecological cycle of wellness system for a hospitality business (Figure 4.2). In this model, we advocate for a wellness-centred business model for the hospitality businesses. Changing the narrative of work culture is imperative. As shown in this research, employees in our case study are encouraged that the company views taking days off for vacation or self-care as positive and that it is actively supported. This is exemplified by the fact that mid-level managers and front-line employees take positive cues from the corporate managers – it is okay to work smart, not long. This wellness orientation governs "goals", "people", "products", and "activities" of a hospitality business. When wellness is valued as "employee care" and as a "performance measure", it inspires and encourages people in the company to actively act on it by championing for wellness practices and initiating more or better tailored practices for employees. When the entire company embraces and celebrates a wellness/care culture, it will nudge employees to participate in the various wellness initiatives for self enhancement, be it physical, mental, social, or developmental (professional growth).

It is interesting to note that this research suggests that the various domains of wellbeing work together to allow employees to create the best possible product – wellness principle guided experiences and services for the consumers, which lead to a hospitality company's financial wellbeing and wellness brand enhancement. Our case company is building a wellness culture within the company, realizing a wellness-instigated service profit chain effect. This "feeling well– serving well" approach can be a performance advantage for an organization that prioritizes employee wellbeing, as it will then transfer to guests in much the same way that satisfaction is posited to transfer from employees to guests in the service profit chain. By including a wellness metric on an organization's balanced scorecard, wellness could become a pillar of success, in addition to market share, profits, and employee and guest satisfaction.

AN ECOLOGICAL CYCLE OF WELLNESS SYSTEM

Figure 4.2   A conceptual model of an ecological cycle of wellness system for a hospitality business

4.6   Conclusion

As society moves from a technology-driven orientation to one driven by wellbeing of individuals, communities, and the environment, there is a need for hospitality and tourism industries to increasingly embrace their caretaking role: safeguarding consumer health resources and enhancing the wellbeing of their various stakeholders (Lehto & Lehto, 2019). In fact, researchers have suggested that the spirit of hospitality and wellbeing should be the overarching governing principles upon which hospitality and tourism business operations, processes, and management rest. This orientation is being seen as a departure from a traditional business model (Lehto et. al., 2022). It represents not just a philosophical principle but also opportunities for brands, and strategic advantages for businesses. As showcased in this case study, the business philosophy of being wellness-centric can work well for all facets of a business. The hospitality and tourism industries are collectively encouraged to play a bigger role and stake a bigger share of today's wellbeing-oriented society by adopting the ecological cycle of wellness system proposed by this research. As such, wellness programs should be orchestrated considering larger company goals related to branding and other strategic considerations in addition to caring for employees as whole people.

Given the scarcity of the wellness program literature focused on hospitality employees, our case study allows a greater understanding of the specificities of a wellness program offered to hospitality employees: its structure, the nature of the offerings, the value perceptions of the program, and how the program is situated in a company as it relates to branding and other strategic considerations of hospitality. We acknowledge that our insights are derived from one company. However, the case in point, being a typical case for hotel management companies in the United States, allows for reasonable transferability of our results and insights. While more research is needed, our analysis and proposed model contribute to the literature of hospitality employee wellbeing. It is a timely study that enriches the ongoing discussion about the increasing role of wellbeing in hospitality and tourism management. In a broader sense, this research contributes to the larger conversation about the need for a wellbeing driven society.

References

Agarwal, P. (2021). Shattered but smiling: Human resource management and the wellbeing of hotel employees during COVID-19. *International Journal of Hospitality Management, 93*, 102765.

Braun, V., & Clarke, V. (2006). Using thematic analysis in psychology. *Qualitative Research in Psychology, 3*(2), 77–101.

Campbell, J. L., Quincy, C., Osserman, J., & Pederson, O. K. (2013). Coding in-depth semistructured interviews: Problems of unitization and intercoder reliability and agreement. *Sociological Methods & Research, 42*(3), 294–320.

Carter, M. R., Kelly, R. C., Alexander, C. K., & Holmes, L.M. (2011). A collaborative university model for employee wellness. *Journal of American College Health, 59*(8), 761–763.

Chaturvedi, S., & Rathore, A. S. (2021). Virtual wellness program for employees during pandemic Covid-19. *International Journal of Recent Advances in Multidisciplinary Topics, 2*(6), 218–221.

Danna, K., & Griffin, R. W. (1999). Health and well-being in the workplace: A review and synthesis of the literature. *Journal of Management, 25*(3), 357–384.

Dodge, R., Daly, A. P., Huyton, J. and Sanders, L. D. (2012). The challenge of defining wellbeing. *International Journal of Wellbeing, 2*(3), 222–235.

Eisenberger, R., Huntington, R., Hutchison, S., & Sowa, D. (1986). Perceived organizational support. *Journal of Applied Psychology, 71*(3), 500–507.

Gallup. (n.d.) What is employee wellbeing and why does it matter? Retrieved December 17, 2022, from https://www.gallup.com/workplace/404105/importance -of-employee-wellbeing.aspx.aspx?utm_source=workplace&utm_medium=email& utm_campaign=wellbeing_pillar_page_email_1_december_12152022&utm_term= alert&utm_content=focus_on_employee_wellbeing_textlink_1.

Gebhardt, D. L., & Crump, C. E. (1990). Employee fitness and wellness programs in the workplace. *American Psychologist, 45*(2), 262–272.

Gordon, S., Jolly, P., Self, T., & Shi, X. (2021). Is subtle toxicity worse for racial-ethnic minority employees? The impact of coworker incivility on employee well-being. *Journal of Foodservice Business Research, 26*(4), 587–608.

Gordon, S., & Parikh, A. (2021). Supporting employee well-being: The case of independent restaurants. *Journal of Foodservice Business Research, 24*(2), 215–234.

Gordon, S., Tang, C. H. H., Day, J., & Adler, H. (2019). Supervisor support and turnover in hotels: does subjective well-being mediate the relationship? *International Journal of Contemporary Hospitality Management, 31*(1), 496–512.

Grönroos, C. (2000). *Service management and marketing: A customer relationship management approach.* Chichester: John Wiley & Sons.

Gubler, T., Larkin, I., & Pierce, L. (2018). Doing well by making well: The impact of corporate wellness programs on employee productivity. *Management Science, 64*(11), 4967–4987.

Hobfoll, S. E. (1989). Conservation of resources: a new attempt at conceptualizing stress. *American Psychologist, 44*(3), 513.

Huo, M. L., Boxall, P., & Cheung, G. W. (2020). How does line-manager support enhance worker wellbeing? A study in China. *The International Journal of Human Resource Management, 31*(14), 1825–1843.

Jacobson, J. M., & Sacco, P. (2012). Employee assistance program services for alcohol and other drug problems: Implications for increased identification and engagement in treatment. *The American Journal on Addictions, 21*(5), 468–475.

Kim, M., Ma, E., & Wang, L. (2023). Work-family supportive benefits, programs, and policies and employee well-being: Implications for the hospitality industry. *International Journal of Hospitality Management, 108*(2023). https://doi.org/10 .1016/j.ijhm.2022.103356.

Lehto, X. Y. (2013). Assessing the perceived restorative qualities of vacation destinations. *Journal of Travel Research, 52*, 325–339.

Lehto, X., & Lehto, M. (2019). Vacation as a public health resource: Toward a wellness-centered tourism design approach. *Journal of Hospitality and Tourism Research, 43*(7), 935–960.

Lehto, X. Y., Park, S., Mohamed, M. E., & Lehto, M. R. (2021). Traveler attitudes toward biometric data-enabled hotel services: Can risk education play a role? *Cornell Hospitality Quarterly, 64*(1), 74–94. https://doi.org/10.1177/19389655211063204.

Merrill, R. M., Hyatt, B., Aldana, S. G., & Kinnersley, D. (2011). Lowering employee health care costs through the Healthy Lifestyle Incentive Program. *Journal of Public Health Management and Practice, 17*(3), 225–232.

Neumeier, L. M., Brook, L., Ditchburn, G., & Sckopke, P. (2017). Delivering your daily dose of well-being to the workplace: A randomized controlled trial of an online well-being programme for employees. *European Journal of Work and Organizational Psychology, 26*(4), 555–573.

Nilgün, A. V. C. I. (2017). The relationship between coworker supports, quality of work life and wellbeing: An empirical study of hotel employees. *Uluslararası Yönetim İktisat ve İşletme Dergisi, 13*(3), 577–590.

Page, K. M., & Vella-Brodrick, D. A. (2013). The working for wellness program: RCT of an employee well-being intervention. *Journal of Happiness Studies, 14*(3), 1007–1031

Richards, L. and Morse, J. (2007). *Readme First for a user's guide to qualitative methods,* 2nd edn. London: Sage Publications.

Satuf, C., Monteiro, S., Pereira, H., Esgalhado, G., Marina Afonso, R., & Loureiro, M. (2018). The protective effect of job satisfaction in health, happiness, well-being and self-esteem. *International Journal of Occupational Safety and Ergonomics, 24*(2), 181–189.

Shi, X., Gordon, S., & Tang, C. H. (2021). Momentary well-being matters: Daily fluctuations in hotel employees' turnover intention. *Tourism Management, 83,* 104212.

Taris, T. W., & Schreurs, P. J. G. (2009). Well-being and organizational performance: An organizational-level test of the happy-productive worker hypothesis. *Work & Stress, 23*(2), 120–136.

Vakkayil, J., Della Torre, E., & Giangreco, A. (2017). "It's not how it looks!" Exploring managerial perspectives on employee wellbeing. *European Management Journal, 35*(4), 548–562.

Van De Voorde, K., Paauwe, J., & Van Veldhoven, M. (2012). Employee well-being and the HRM–organizational performance relationship: a review of quantitative studies. *International Journal of Management Reviews, 14*(4), 391–407.

Yu, J., Park, J., & Hyun, S. S. (2021). Impacts of the COVID-19 pandemic on employees' work stress, well-being, mental health, organizational citizenship behavior, and employee-customer identification. *Journal of Hospitality Marketing & Management, 30*(5), 529–548.

Zhang, T. (2018). Employee wellness innovations in hospitality workplaces: Learning from high-tech corporations. *Journal of Global Business Insights, 3*(2), 52–66.

5   Tourist idleness and eudaimonic wellbeing: an exploratory study

Jelena Farkić, Gorana Isailović and Dušan Perić

5.1   Introduction

Idleness has long been a contested notion. Thinkers, such as Aristotle, Paul Lafargue, or Bertrand Russell, have argued that doing nothing is paramount in having a full life and is central to human wholeness. In the past, people of higher standing would often relocate to the countryside for leisure, which allowed for boredom and idleness. Doing nothing was considered beneficial for mental and physical health, as well as for bolstering creativity and imagination. Yet, in our speed-bound world, characterised by tech acceleration and workaholism, being lazy, bored or idle are not considered virtues. Rather, they are claimed to lead us to exclusion from certain social circles in which 'time wasters' are not particularly welcome (Foley, 2017).

Moreover, in our capitalist society, labour to make money seems to be entirely devoid of eudaimonistic perspectives and is considered solely as an aim in itself, which, in comparison to the individual's happiness appears transcendent and irrational. Recognising the destructive power of industrialisation, Lafargue (2021 [1883]) argued that people, instead of claiming the right to work, should claim the right to be lazy. In addressing the capitalist condition, he offered laziness as a solution, that is, the reappropriation of time off work for the development of people's nonproductive potential. He did not suggest laziness to discredit the purposefulness of work, but rather as a way to promote the right to leisure and rest.

Similarly, Russell (2004 [1935]) addressed the cult of workaholism by considering how our manipulated mentality has hypnotised us into worshiping work as a virtue and scorning laziness as weakness or folly, rather than recognising it as the raw material of social justice and the locus of our power. Russell claimed that the true, authentic self can be achieved when we situate ourselves outside the demands of work and everyday busyness. His conceptualisation of idleness is similar to the classical Greek notion of leisure or *scholé*, implying the opportunity for contemplation dedicated to improving one's life and community. Unlearning busyness and learning how to more frequently pause and do nothing should become the crucial priority in achieving purpose, meaning and good, well-lived life.

Spending time away from busyness and doing what we enjoy may therefore alleviate stress, which can take its toll on people's mental and physical wellbeing. While it is important to take short breaks during the day, longer periods of rest are key to our wellbeing. Yet, many workers do not take enough time off. A study has shown that 75% of surveyed Americans never use their holiday leave. More than 700 million leave days remain unused each year, which equates to 5.6 billion hours that could be spent relaxing, rather than working (Giurge et al., 2020). However, things have somewhat changed postpandemic. For example, a nascent movement of quiet quitting, which prioritises people's wellbeing in that it encourages 'clocking out' to enjoy leisure activities after work hours, has reshaped the cultural attitudes toward paid labour. By reducing their performance to the 'bare minimum' within work hours, people are making a small effort to avoid burnout and secure emotional and mental stability, resilience and coping. There has also been an exponential growth in interventions that address stress, anxiety or burnout, which in their own right help achieve people's physical, mental and emotional regeneration (Morrison-Beedy, 2022). To this end, positive, preventative interventions that focus on people's wellbeing have been increasingly developed, not only in the realm of public health but also in tourism.

In this exploratory study, we move away from the capitalocentric worldview and adopt more regenerative way of thinking which suggests that 'the economy can serve systemic health within its own unique context' (Mathisen et al., 2022, p. 331). To this end, we explore the ways in which tourism can support wellbeing of humans and other living beings by encouraging idleness. We situate the discussion within the broader regenerative tourism discourse and approach the notion of idleness from the positive psychology perspective as a productive way of achieving eudaimonic wellbeing. In doing so, we build on the scholarship that prioritises the modalities of holidays that encourage simplified experiences, and which celebrate post-capitalist economic alternatives. We move the focus away from profit-driven tourism economies towards more meaningful and regenerative pursuits to discuss how this paradigm shift may contribute to a more sustainable and prosperous future for all. We aim to pave new avenues for understanding and thinking about idleness as a meaningful holiday pursuit, which not only enhances people's wellbeing but also holistically contributes to and cocreates wellbeing of our planet.

5.2   Intersecting Regenerative Tourism, Wellbeing and Idleness

The COVID-19 pandemic has been an impetus for developing various approaches to tourism recovery – the ones that rebuild, strengthen or regenerate communities by way of creating jobs, promoting culture, or protecting heritage (Duxbury et al., 2020). In aiming to add to the new avenues of research and practice towards achieving sustainability in tourism, the relatively new concept of regenerative tourism has emerged. Emanating from the ecological worldview and regenerative development paradigm, it builds on the idea of regeneration as a process of constant coming into being (Cave & Dredge, 2020; Pollock, 2019). Broadly, regenerative tourism focuses on the ways in which it can contribute to local communities' wellbeing, revitalisation and sustainability. It supports activities that continually harmonise places, local communities and their guests with the environments within which tourism is taking place (Bellato et al., 2022). The underlying quality of interconnectedness of such ecosystems is claimed to work towards the enhancement of human and non-human wellbeing whilst enabling the processes of flourishing and prospering (Bellato & Cheer, 2021). Sheldon (2020) referred to this idea of 'caring for us' as an engaged contribution. It is reflected in shifting the focus away from one's own welfare ('ego consciousness') to a more noble and generous concern about the wellbeing of the whole ('eco consciousness'). While this mutual care, compassion and generosity are difficult to quantify, not least monetise, they may nonetheless enable the processes of regeneration at all levels and scales, and ultimately lead to people living healthier and more meaningful lives.

While sustainability discourse has been critiqued for failing to consider ethical aspects to create wellbeing for humans and nature, regenerative tourism goes a step further by placing far greater emphasis on the moral act of 'giving back' (Mathisen et al., 2022). To this end, it proactively contributes to the regeneration of communities, cultures, heritage, places or landscapes by advocating primarily for those interventions that make a positive societal impact by embracing the 'alternative non-capitalist forms of ownership, non-monetary exchange and beneficial community-based development' (Sheller, 2021, p.2). It prioritises the local rather than the global, and gives way to microscale regeneration initiatives which think beyond capitalism (Mura & Wijesinghe, 2021). Scholars have argued that within the regenerative tourism paradigm, all stakeholders should be equally and actively involved in the creation of long-term social, cultural, environmental and economic wellbeing (Fusté-Forné & Hussain, 2022). Mathisen et al. (2022) further explained that tourism planners and researchers alike should adopt an ecocentric and just way of thinking and acting to create wellbeing for all. Therefore, the cocreation of value through tourism practices should reflect broader moral and ethical responsibility towards the social and natural environment and their reciprocal relationships. Following these priorities, we consider the notion of tourist idleness and its capacity to bring about positive change, wellbeing and meaningful transformation of 21st-century societies.

The improvement of wellbeing and prevention of ill health have become key priorities in the public health realm (McDaid et al., 2019), as well as in tourism (Ohe et al., 2017; Lee et al., 2014; Smith & Reisinger, 2013). Even in the prepandemic era, the World Health Organization (WHO) addressed the issue of mental health and advocated for the improvement of wellbeing of the global population as a sustainable way forward. The WHO considers mental health to be more than the absence of mental health conditions, describing it as a mental state that 'enables people to cope with the stresses of life, to realize their abilities, to learn well and work well, and to contribute to their communities' (WHO, 2022). Wellness tourism plays an important role in preventative healthcare, as it offers tourists opportunities to maintain or improve their health and wellbeing through the concept of social and green prescribing, or consumption of wellness services, such as detox programmes, Eastern practices, healthy menus, cooking classes, fitness concierge services and others (Huang et al., 2022; Farkic et al., 2021; He et al., 2021; Hjalager & Konu, 2011). Particularly after the pandemic, there has been a significant increase in the bookings of wellness retreats or holidays in outdoor spaces – all aimed at the regeneration of human health by (re)connecting with the self, the natural environment, and local communities.

To better understand the regenerative aspects of tourism, positive psychology is helpful in explaining the underlying conditions that enable people to live meaningful, fulfilled lives. Wellbeing is broadly viewed both as a pleasure, happiness or positive feelings (*hedonia*) and the achievement of deeper states such as meaning or greater purpose in life (*eudaimonia*) (Mackenzie & Raymond, 2020). In the context of tourism, scholars have particularly discussed eudaimonic wellbeing, which focuses on the construction of meaning, processes of self-actualisation, or achieving vitality in life (Filep et al., 2022; Smith & Diekmann, 2017). This notion is closely related to happiness and encapsulates the virtues of living a fulfilled life with contemplation (Ryan & Deci, 2001; Deci & Ryan, 2008). Aristotle is often cited as the pioneer of the concept of eudaimonia. He claimed that true happiness can be found in living a good life and accomplishing what is worthwhile. He contended that living in accordance with one's *daimon*, or the true, authentic self, and realising one's full potential is the ultimate human goal. To this end, living a meaningful life, while striving for change and gaining a deeper knowledge of oneself and the environment, has a regenerative capacity, as it enables personal development and flourishing.

Hedonic and eudaimonic dimensions are undeniably crucial in understanding tourist wellbeing. However, there appears to be considerable heterogeneity amongst the components that contribute to wellbeing. According to Butler and Kern (2016), interpersonal relationships, in addition to emotions and meanings, are important components of psychological wellbeing. Furthermore, the experience of togetherness and sharing meaningful moments, promote eudaimonic experiences (Shahvali et al., 2021; Farkic et al., 2020). There is also evidence that spending extended time in nature, combined with the relaxation of the mind, boosts positive feelings and emotions. Recreational activities, in particular, foster a sense of purpose and meaning, long-term happiness, and life satisfaction, all considered the inherent eudaemonic qualities (Sharma-Brymer & Brymer, 2020; Houge Mackenzie et al., 2021; Houge Mackenzie & Hodge, 2020; Buckley, 2020). Filep et al. (2013) found that joy, interest and contentment were most commonly linked to experiences that involved observations of natural scenery, strengthening the importance of spending time in nature, preferably at an idle, slow pace. Through slow immersion in the natural environment and sharing experiences with others, people feel the restoration of their physical and mental health, generate positive emotions, develop a sense of belonging and unity with nature, and construct meaning through such moments of restoration and regeneration (Farkic et al., 2020).

Honoré (2005), in challenging the cult of speed, chronicled what we, both individually and as a society, have lost in our race against time. We should slow down the pace of life and savour the moments which have been replaced by constant, often technology-driven, activities. In doing so, he claimed, slowness should not be about doing everything at a snail's pace, or about a rebellion against technology; it should bring about balance and control over our own lives. The emergence of the slow movement as an antidote to the fast-paced way of life that counter productivity, exhaustive work and conspicuous consumption has also been long discussed within leisure and tourism (Foley, 2017). Scholars have argued that personal happiness and wellbeing can be achieved when the pace of life is slowed down (Parkins & Craig, 2006). Crucial here is taking time to enjoy the slow process of discovering the place, the people, the foods or the stories of that place (Fullagar et al., 2012). By facilitating such connections, tourism provides a number of regenerative benefits for the tourist experience, the local environment, the host community and the region's economy (Heitmann et al., 2011). Importantly, slowness encourages both personal and communal wellbeing, allowing for the generation of qualities such as conviviality, trust, friendship, a sense of belonging or the purposeful utilisation of leisure time (Foley, 2017). It is therefore important to highlight that enabling activities that do not hold economic value account for crucial aspects of holidaying, which may greatly contribute to achieving eudaimonic wellbeing.

In extending works on slow travel some researchers have argued that when on holidays, tourists should 'do nothing' (Farkic et al., 2022). The underlying idea of tourist idleness is the relinquishment of busyness and the constant striving for the achievement of goals. Engaging in slow-paced activities, such as sitting and pondering, gazing at landscapes or taking part in creative workshops, can make us happier, more creative and eventually, more productive. Mecking (2021) defined idleness as doing nothing on purpose, without a purpose. She observed the act of doing nothing as different from other wellness trends and self-care techniques in that it pushes people to find alternatives to conventional treatments and improvement of their health and wellbeing. Alongside a multitude of wellbeing trends and philosophies, such as mindfulness, Zen, hygge or *ikigai*, which have been proposed as quick-fix solutions to our blues, anxieties, burnout or ill-being, Mecking (2021) proposed that the more we practice doing nothing, the more we will reject the idea of ubiquitous busyness.

The essence of idleness is rooted in the Aristotelean proposition of *daimon*, that is, embracing what makes us human: creativity, social connections, the ability for reflective thought and our capacity for joy (Headlee, 2020). However, despite the initiatives to slow down, waste time and do nothing, individuals in our capitalist, speed-bound society find it challenging to disengage from work and engage more frequently in activities that have no economic value, and which would allow for regeneration, inner growth, self-fulfilment and meaningful development. To this end, this chapter seeks to make the first steps towards an analytical understanding of tourist idleness as a wellbeing-focused practice and in its small way make a contribution to the wellbeing and regenerative tourism research agenda.

5.3   Method

Following a tradition of exploratory studies into novel or underresearched phenomena, our study takes a web-based approach and is of descriptive transversal design. Utilising the survey as an efficient data collection tool, we aimed to generate insights into people's lifestyles whilst focusing on the role, meaning, and position that idleness takes in their everyday life, and on holidays. The survey contained 35 questions, formulated in understandable terms without difficult constructs and vague concepts. The first part of the survey consisted of six predetermined questions that were aimed at eliciting demographic data. They also involved 18 close-ended, topic-based questions on, for example, people's lifestyle and everyday habits, the meaning of idleness, and their imaginations of an 'idle holiday'. While qualitative surveys remain a relatively underused method, we followed Braun et al. (2021) in their claim that they have great potential in harnessing qualitative data which offer nuanced, in-depth and potentially novel understandings of social issues. Therefore, the survey also contained 11 open-ended questions which invited participants to describe, in their own words, their ideal holiday, the activities they do when they are idle, how they rest and their own understanding of the concept of idleness. This produced rich and complex accounts of their experiences, narratives, practices and positionings (Braun & Clarke, 2013); the data we found useful in the construction of a broad understanding of idleness and the ways in which the newly generated knowledge can be used in developing tourism practices and services aimed at regeneration and enhancing wellbeing.

5.3.1   Data Collection

Empirical data were collected in the period from March to August 2022. The survey was created as a Google form and was bilingual, in English and Serbian – Serbian being the native language of all three authors. The link was distributed via direct mailout and on social media networks such as LinkedIn and Facebook. The increase in response rate was achieved through snowballing, whereby the authors' contacts shared the link on their own online platforms, which generated a larger sample across 14 countries. Participation in the study was entirely voluntary, meaning that the respondents were self-selected, which resulted in all surveys being completed and subjected to analysis.

The convenience sampling technique was not intended to infer from the sample to the general population in statistical terms (Vaske, 2011). This is the main limitation of this exploratory study, and we thus propose that the results should be interpreted with caution. There has been a lot of criticism of this data collection method which raised legitimate concerns around the coverage error, nonresponse error, and sampling error (Gigliotti, 2011). Furthermore, the common assumption is that surveys are rigid and inflexible tools due to the lack of opportunities for probing deeper into participants' experiences and must therefore be supplemented with interviews to provide rich and trustwor-

Table 5.1   Distribution of participants according to age and gender

Age	Male	Female	Total
18–26	0	9	9
27–41	10	25	35
42–54	3	18	21
55–64	2	7	9
65+	1	4	5
Total	16	63	79

thy data. However, we achieved depth and richness by offering open-ended questions which allowed the participants to create their own narratives around the topic in question.

While an online survey is typically used in large-scale research, it can also be a useful tool for small-scale study. We generated a sample of 79 respondents (Table 5.1) distributed across 14 countries (Table 5.2). Despite the sample not being representative and unequally distributed across the countries, the attitudinal differences were minimal, which enabled us to observe the sample as a coherent whole based on the lifestyle criterium. The rich dataset that the study generated was therefore of an appropriate scope to address the research questions and present the credible findings.

5.3.2   Data Analysis

Empirical data collected through close-ended questions were statistically analysed and expressed as empirical frequencies. To this end, the Chi-Square test was used as the appropriate statistical procedure, which showed that there were no significant differences between the subgroups in any variable. Essentially, none of the demographic characteristics (e.g., gender, age, education, occupation, nationality) influenced the differences between the responses. Because of this, the analysis was performed on the whole sample using IBM SPSS v.21 statistical software package (License Stats Prem: 761b17dcfd1bf20da576 by Hearne software), with the statistical significance set at $p < 0.05$. The results obtained are presented and interpreted in relation to the findings from the analysis of the open-ended questions.

To analyse responses, we took a realist stance, as it allowed us to better understand 'reality' from the participants' perspectives. We followed Braun and Clarke's (2006) method in thematically analysing the data obtained through 11

Table 5.2   The respondents' countries of residence

Country	Frequency	Country	Frequency
Serbia	49	China	1
Slovenia	5	Croatia	4
Netherlands	1	Austria	1
Germany	6	Montenegro	1
USA	2	Lithuania	1
Thailand	1	Brazil	1
United Kingdom	5	Sweden	1

open-ended questions. This was done across the entire dataset to give a broad account of the data, which can be helpful when the topic is underresearched (Ivanski & Kohut, 2017). Coding was done by the first author with additional input from the third author. The analysis involved an initial reading of the responses to generate a general understanding of the data. This was followed by making detailed notes of the main ideas found in the responses, which created an initial coding structure. Next, the previously identified ideas were translated into themes by identifying related constructs such as 'time', 'solitude' or 'quietude', each of which contributed to our multidimensional understanding of the benefits of idleness, and which were eventually subsumed into a broader theme, 'eudaimonic wellbeing and regeneration'.

We found Braun et al.'s (2020, p. 2) study particularly encouraging regarding the trustworthiness of the data generated through open-ended survey questions in their suggestion that 'qualitative survey datasets can provide richness and depth when viewed in their entirety, even if individual responses might themselves be brief'. The responses were analysed at the semantic level in order to generate surface level meanings, while some responses lent themselves well to richer and more interpretative theorisations around, for example, eudaimonic experiences and regeneration through idleness.

In the following sections, we first provide the presentation of the results emanating from the close-ended questions, which show qualitative indicators of participants' perception of laziness/idleness, and their habitual relationship with free time and digital devices, all of which paint a somewhat concerning picture. Next, we turn to the presentation of findings through several sub-themes that we distilled through the thematic analysis, which helped us to

Table 5.3   The meaning of laziness

	Frequency	Percent
Unproductivity	22	27.9%
Bad habits	13	16.5%
Procrastination	19	24.1%
Opportunity to enjoy activities	8	10.1%
Opportunity to rest	17	21.5%

more closely understand the relationality between idleness and eudaimonic wellbeing, and their regenerative potentials.

5.4   Results and Discussion

5.4.1   The Ambiguousness of Laziness, Ubiquitous Business, and Understanding Idleness

In our aim to understand the lifestyle and everyday habits of participants, we initially asked them about the meaning of laziness, the term often used interchangeably with idleness. The results suggest that 67.1% of participants were unable to decide whether it is a good or bad thing, while 15.2% suggested it was good and 17.7% thought it was bad. In further unpacking what laziness meant for them, or what they associated it with, we can see how the terms with negative connotations, such as lack of productivity, bad habits or procrastination, dominated their responses (Table 5.3). However, laziness was also viewed as a chance to rest and recuperate from work or do the activities they enjoy.

The fact that the majority of participants associated laziness with a negative quality rather than the free time that belongs to them, we can relate to the condition of the capitalist world in which we live and work, and in which we do not have much 'right to be lazy' (Lafargue, 2021 [1883]). We always strive to do something rather than nothing, particularly the activities that bring monetary gain. This resonates with Hodgkinson's (2005, cited in Foley, 2017, p.11) suggestion that 'idleness is good goes against everything we have ever been taught. Industry, hard work, duty, self-sacrifice, toil: surely these are the virtues that lead to success in life'. Slothfulness and lack of productivity are not welcome in our society, and periods of doing nothing are regarded as empty labour (Paulsen, 2014). The present results illustrate this, and as such should

Table 5.4   Rest hours

	Frequency	Percent
Hardly ever	3	3.8%
Less than one hour	31	39.2%
1–3 hours	36	45.6%
More than 3 hours	9	11.4%

represent a serious concern, and be an impetus for modern-day humans to reconsider their perception of free time and the ways of its consumption.

Another disappointing result is related to the amount of time the respondents spend resting during the day. The fact that only 11.4% suggested that they allow themselves more than three hours for rest in their wake state is yet another serious concern (Table 5.4). The others, sadly, reported very little to no time spent in a way that is associated with rest and relaxation. Here, we can see how the demands of life, family commitments or work are consuming the majority of people's time, and they have very little free time to engage in their favourite pastimes; instead, they feel the constant necessity to 'do something' (Foley, 2017). Further, 27.2% of participants reported that they spend seven to nine hours per day in front of screens, while 16% spend more than ten hours doing that. This makes nearly half of the total number of our participants over-dependent on digital devices, which in 30.9% of surveyed participants leads to technostress.

Scholars have argued that routinised everyday practices in many ways restrict idleness and greatly diminish people's innate potential for creativity and lead to inner impoverishment and illbeing (Rosa, 2013; Perrons, 2003). The near-constant expenditure of mental energy constraints people's creativity and leads to physical and mental exhaustion. Moreover, flexible work arrangements have created tensions between the need to work and the desire to spend more time with family, engage in leisure activities, or relax (Bourne & Forman, 2014; Walsh, 2012). The need to do something rather than nothing has found its way to transcend time and space boundaries. This leaves very few opportunities for people to truly disentangle from work commitments and allow themselves to be idle and rest. As a result, people's free time has been devalued, their quality of life has been diminished and physical and psychological health has become one of the major concerns. Being overdependent on digital technologies, overwhelmed with work and not having enough time for the things that fulfil us is making an increasing number of individuals chronically

Table 5.5   Meaning of idleness

	Frequency	Percent
Enjoying free time	20	25.3%
Being lazy	5	6.3%
Relax / Rest	10	12.7%
Doing nothing	22	27.8%
Boredom	4	5.1%
Meditation	8	10.1%
Wasted free time	2	2.5%
Engaging in hobbies	3	3.8%
Rarely available luxury	1	10.1%
Undecided	4	5.1%

stressed, fatigued, burnt out or mentally depleted (Moreno-González et al., 2020; Kim et al., 2019). Therefore, more frequent practicing of idleness in an 'offline environment', and going back to basics by immersing oneself in nature may be a way forward for those 42% of participants who expressed nostalgic feelings about the analogue world.

We further wanted to know what idleness means and what connotations it has in the minds of our participants. More than half of them related it to enjoying their free time and doing nothing (53.1%), while other commonly cited activities were rest, relaxation and meditation (Table 5.5).

However, these moments of doing nothing and engaging in creative and restful activities, which are claimed to be crucial for wellbeing, are rare for the majority of participants. As Foley (2017) suggested, despite knowing that we need to slow down the tempo of living, people continue to devote very little time to idleness, laziness or wasting time. This inability to relax, and having the feeling of 'uselessness' when we do nothing we can relate to the inability of Western society to experience idleness as a calm and contemplative state of being. The illustration of this we can find in statements such as 'I rest and after a bit of time I try to do something that needs to be done' or 'I very quickly end up being distracted by to-do lists, news, Instagram, errands'.

According to Lafargue (2021 [1883]), the fallacy that we have is *Homo Faber's* culturally constructed love of labour. He viewed laziness as the essence of satisfying people's intrinsic needs and space for achieving their creative capacity. Falling into the productivity trap can lead to physical and mental health issues. Increased efficiency or better time management will not alleviate stress, increase wellbeing or free up time for the things that are truly important and fulfil us. Instead, this will only create more space for busyness.

5.4.2   Achieving Eudaimonic Wellbeing and Regeneration Through Idle Holidays

Having provided evidence of people's connectivity and busyness and thus the inability to use their free time to rest, we argue that tourism can greatly help in promoting idleness as a way of achieving wellbeing. Following regenerative tourism scholarship that emphasise the necessity for transformation of relationships with and between the self, other humans and nonhumans (Bellato et al., 2022), we suggest that incorporating idle tourism practices within local communities and relational ecological processes may ultimately work towards enhancing human and nonhuman wellbeing. We argue that, when they are idle and do nothing of economic value, people fulfil their creative potential by doing things and engaging in processes that *mean* to them. Through such meaningful moments, they activate eudaimonic processes of happiness, self-actualisation, sense of purpose or life satisfaction. We further argue that achieving eudaimonic wellbeing is therefore vital in the processes of regeneration. If people are fulfilled and content with themselves, the environment and the life they live, they will be more prone to radiate compassion, generosity or care, not only for other human beings but also for nonhuman species.

For the majority of our participants, being idle is not that easy, however. In trying to maintain their productivity, they have difficulty breaking away from routines, such as checking emails, and reading news or social media feeds. For this reason, encouraging idleness on holiday is crucial in achieving the pleasure of being completely unproductive, or productively bored and lazy. In what follows, we listen to the voices of our participants and critically discuss how they interpret the act of being idle, which may enable our awareness of the relational processes across time-space-species horizon. We distilled three subthemes through which we discuss how encouraging idleness on holiday can contribute to achieving wellbeing and regeneration.

5.4.3   Slowness, Quietude and Nature

We aimed to understand what participants normally do when they are idle and what makes them feel well. The responses related to slowing down the pace of movement and stilling the body, even engaging in meditative states, were most frequently associated with the idea of being idle. This adds to the argument that decompression of time has the capacity to create eudaimonic experiences and positively influence happiness (Parkins & Craig, 2006). Here, we turn to Foley's (2017) study, which is encouraging in suggesting that there still are those who readily let go of time thrifting and utilise holidays for time wasting. The value is created through spending time *unpurposively* and *meaningfully*: through slow, idle holiday experiences underpinned by socialities, moments of relaxation and convivial atmospheres within natural environs.

In idle tourism scenarios, time then becomes qualitative, rather than a chronological category. It is lived, rather than clocked and measured. The duration of activities, their order or hierarchy is irrelevant; the unstructuredness is the key aspect of an idle holiday; tourists can do activities in whichever order they want and for however long they want (Farkic et al., 2022), as suggested by one participant:

> a holiday without much planning ahead. Doing things I want to do when I feel like it… I'm also imagining there's no electricity, so we can go to bed early. I'd like to eat healthy, organic food and to be able to slow down.

The ability to let go of chronological time is imperative for a productive idle holiday, which alludes to the importance of attending to natural rhythms. Following circadian rhythms, that is, the patterns of day and night, initiates various biological processes within our bodies to keep us functioning at our best and to rest and recover when we need to. The slow pace of living and being, extended immersion in the landscapes and attentiveness to the dynamics different from busy, structured everydayness may allow for creative absent-mindedness, learning about and deep appreciation of the traditions, foods, the land and local communities. This is precisely what regenerative tourism aims to do; it uses place-based processes which reflect, honour and enhance their unique social-ecological systems (Sanford, 2019). Tourists are more deeply and meaningfully connected with the hyperlocal, traditional character of the place and may thus more meaningfully contribute to the local economy and communal wellbeing.

Not rare were the responses that combined physical and mental relaxation with natural settings, such as gazing at the sea or river, watching the sky or greenery, gazing at the moon or sun or through the window or just having the view of the outside. The natural environment is cited as the space in which idleness can be best savoured. The participants explained how they imagine a place in which an idle holiday happens:

> In a small cottage with a fireplace, in the unspoiled nature so I could take long walks and swim in the nearby lake.
> I would go to the mountain, to a woodland house far from civilization. To meditate with the birds chirping and bathe in the sun rays…. To enjoy the crackling fire and the warmth of a mountain hut.

As Farkic et al. (2022) suggested, such environments have their distinct spatiality that draws clear boundaries between noise and silence, easy access and seclusion. These places offer an atmosphere different from that found in urban environs and foster a different kind of attention, to the natural environment, to the senses or to the way in which idle time is lived. Time spent in the natural environment also has a transformative capacity as it generates positive, harmonious emotions, encourage feelings of connection to self and nature, develop intuition, and creates a sense of belonging, wellbeing and being-well with nature (Sheldon, 2020). Moreover, the interplay between tourists and the natural environments may promote self-esteem, contentment and happiness; the universal values associated with eudaimonia and flourishing (Sharma-Brymer & Brymer, 2020).

5.4.4   Relinquishment of Digital Devices

The participants' responses implied the tendency to temporarily leave behind their phones, laptops, social media, news, crowds or car keys, and take control over their lives by engaging in more idle states and practices. We surely live in an era in which smartphones have replaced objects like alarm clocks, cameras or money and, while we can justify their utilitarian value, they nonetheless demand constant connectivity when travelling, as explained by one of the participants:

> I would leave my phone behind but it serves as my map, and I need the vaccination pass for COVID so I need to have it. But I turned off all app notifications so that I don't see them on my home screen

Being even temporarily disconnected or unavailable may produce a sense of disorientation and inconvenience, even guilt and anxiety, particularly in our workaholic and networked society in which digital has become the norm. For this reason, people find different 'excuses' for having their phones at hand at all times (albeit they have their notifications switched off). However, our participants also voiced the need for respite from smartphones, explicitly emphasising that the internet or any technologies are not welcome on their holiday. They imagined their idle holiday takes place:

> in the forest, in a house without the internet… Being on the phone is not being idle, I think, it's being distracted

and

> in a place with a dense forest and a small swimming spot, no Wi-Fi, phones, emails, or cars.

Breaking away from technology-induced realities, and spending holidays in natural environments, as mentioned in the above examples, may allow for that much-needed psychological relief. Therefore, facilitating disconnection from digital devices and reducing the temptation to reengage in, for example, checking emails or social media, can be achieved by the mere presence of an 'obstacle' to deter people from getting online, or at least encourage a moment of pause (Aranda & Baig, 2018). A number of slow or 'sedentary' activities can be offered, such as sit spots, knitting yoga, creative workshops, drawing mandalas, storytelling, forest bathing, stargazing or fly fishing. Engaging in such activities has numerous wellbeing benefits, such as more frequent and immediate connection among travel companions, which allows for bonding and developing a sense of communal belonging. Sharing experiences with others may contribute to emotional stability and engender a certain sense of ontological security and therefore contribute to people's eudaimonic wellbeing.

Following Lafargue (2021 [1883]), taking time for the development of people's nonproductive potential through tourism is essential for the achievement of eudaimonic wellbeing. Utilising holidays for satisfying our intrinsic needs and creating space, specifically outside of the virtual world, for achieving our creative capacity may pave the productive path toward thinking about life differently, and ultimately lead to the achievement of a better quality of life and wellbeing. Following Duxbury et al. (2021), creativity can be perceived as a regenerative element that contributes to local wellbeing, preserving local cultural heritage or revitalising disappearing arts, crafts and traditions. To this end, local communities should be actively engaged and take the central place of local tourism development, natural and cultural heritage preservation and regeneration.

5.4.5   Simplicity, Solitude and Authentic 'Me'

Sheldon (2020) explained that a desire for the authenticity of experience often accompanies the desire for simplicity. There is more interest in minimalism and simplification of the experience, and creating an environment in which less is more. Some of the participants voiced the urge to 'be me', the authentic self which flourishes through engaging in meaningful moments (Farkic et al., 2020). For some, solitude and simplicity are seen as crucial aspects of the idle holiday, coupled with small hedonic pleasures. They explained that their expectation from an idle holiday is:

> Nothing special. A good book and nap in the shade under the pine tree... In the evening a glass of wine or cocktail would be nice.

Having privacy and the time to relax on one's own as opposed to working or getting things done is seen as an opportunity to reduce stress or restore energy and do what one truly enjoys. The way in which such eudaimonic experiences are constructed is seen in the following responses:

> I went to a monastery in the mountains. Stillness and quiet. No questions about my whereabouts... No questions about my job or my personal background. Just be, sing, pray, eat, hike. Alternatively, I'd go to the seaside, but same here – be by myself and stay outside as much as possible, and walk.
> I like to be alone with myself in peace, silence, and tranquillity, that no one asks for anything and expects nothing from me; I enjoy being "me", away from the chaos of modern life, I stay away from social media.

This urge to break away from chaotic realities we can associate with the phenomenon of 'joy of missing out' (JOMO), referring to feelings of enjoyment prompted by being able to choose not to participate, to opt out of busy or digital worlds and having the freedom to choose where to direct one's attention (Brinkmann, 2019). Idleness is an openminded and unbounded construct that enables the formulation of alternative views of life that encompass the universal human values in order to achieve a balanced, happy life, colived with the self, others, nature and the more-than-human world. By being idle and engaging in processes of self-reflection, tourists may become more aware and sensitive to their environment, and can contribute to the broader regeneration processes by regenerating themselves.

5.5   Conclusion

In this chapter we argued that in our agenda-driven lives, people should take more time for slowing down and doing nothing. We suggest that idleness may in many ways contribute to our wellbeing, as we help our body and mind to regenerate. Recognising that time is finite, we should give priority to the things that make us happy or give us meaning and purpose, make a step towards self-fulfilment, and realisation of our authentic being. Work–life balance is crucial to maintaining general wellbeing and long-term productivity. We are much more efficient, creative, and productive at work if we maximise our free time. Tourism may therefore make its own small contribution to regeneration by encouraging idleness. Even on short holidays, or weekend getaways, we should practice doing nothing by resisting the urge to check work email and instead entirely unplug and make a conscious decision to appreciate the moments of quietude, solitude or collective, creative 'sedentary' activities.

While restoring the dignity of idleness is a crucial prerequisite for recalibrating our satisfaction with life and happiness to better reflect modern realities, it is not sufficient. Russell (2004) explained that the mingling of needs and wants at the heart of capitalist materialism and conspicuous consumption exacerbates our already distorted relationship with the digitalised, accelerated and interconnected world. The profound change that would occur if we stopped viewing the value of labour as a goal in itself, we should instead see as a means to a condition of being in which work (in its current form) is no longer a priority. By restoring the right to be idle, we may return to the authentic self and achieve a better balance and comfort in life. Russell (2004) saw idleness as a multifaceted phenomenon that takes us outside of rules or customs. Resisting all of the disturbing expectations that are imposed on us, and instead participating in noncompulsion and drift, where the lack of purpose delivers peaceful and joyful qualities, could be a modest step towards an alternative, yet regenerative, way of life.

In a similar vein, tourism destinations need to make conscious decisions and make fundamental changes if they are to ensure wellbeing of all involved agents. Creating spaces of idleness can help the tourism industry in its efforts to contribute to the wellbeing of all living beings and their conscious development. As Hussain (2021) claims, a truly regenerative tourism model requires a shift in our conscious travel paradigm, and creative, adaptive, and resilient communities and destinations. This can be achieved through conscious policymaking, responsible product development, and creative promotion of idle holidays as a way of wellbeing, flourishing and thriving, and as a way of regenerating the tourism industry as a whole. After all, we need to give ourselves, and our planet, back.

References

Aranda, J. H., & Baig, S. (2018). Toward JOMO the joy of missing out and the freedom of disconnecting. In *Proceedings of the 20th international conference on human-computer interaction with mobile devices and services* MobileHCI'18, September 3-6, Barcelona, Spain (pp. 1–8).

Bellato, L., & Cheer, J. M. (2021). Inclusive and regenerative urban tourism: Capacity development perspectives. *International Journal of Tourism Cities, 7*(4), 943–961.

Bellato, L., Frantzeskaki, N., & Nygaard, C. A. (2022). Regenerative tourism: a conceptual framework leveraging theory and practice. *Tourism Geographies, 25*(1), 1–21.

Bourne, K. A., & Forman, P. J. (2014). Living in a culture of overwork: An ethnographic study of flexibility. *Journal of Management Inquiry, 23*(1), 68–79.

Braun, V., Clarke, V., Boulton, E., Davey, L., & McEvoy, C. (2021). The online survey as a qualitative research tool. *International Journal of Social Research Methodology, 24*(6), 641–654.

Braun, V., & Clarke, V. (2013). *Successful qualitative research: A practical guide for beginners.* Sage.

Braun, V., & Clarke, V. (2006). Using thematic analysis in psychology. *Qualitative Research in Psychology, 3*(2), 77–101. https://doi.org/10.1191/1478088706qp063oa.

Brinkmann, S. (2019). *The joy of missing out: The art of self-restraint in an age of excess.* John Wiley & Sons.

Buckley, R. (2020). Nature tourism and mental health: Parks, happiness, and causation. *Journal of Sustainable Tourism, 28*(9), 1409–1424.

Butler, J., & Kern, M. L. (2016). The PERMA-Profiler: A brief multidimensional measure of flourishing. *International Journal of Wellbeing, 6*(3), 1–48. https://doi.org/10.5502/ijw.v6i3.526.

Cave, J., & Dredge, D. (2020). Regenerative tourism needs diverse economic practices. *Tourism Geographies, 22*(3), 503–513.

Deci, E. L., & Ryan, R. M. (2008). Facilitating optimal motivation and psychological well-being across life's domains. *Canadian Psychology/Psychologie canadienne, 49*(1), 14.

Duxbury, N., Bakas, F. E., Vinagre de Castro, T., & Silva, S. (2020). Creative tourism development models towards sustainable and regenerative tourism. *Sustainability, 13*(1), 2.

Farkic, J., Isailovic, G., & Lesjak, M. (2022). Doing nothing on holiday – conceptualising tourist idleness and creating places of otium in nature-based tourism. *Academica Turistica-Tourism and Innovation Journal, 15*(1), 11–23, https://doi.org/10.26493/2335-4194.15.11-23.

Farkic, J., Isailovic, G., & Taylor, S. (2021). Forest bathing as a mindful tourism practice. *Annals of Tourism Research Empirical Insights, 2*(2), 100028.

Farkic, J., Filep, S., & Taylor, S. (2020). Shaping tourists' wellbeing through guided slow adventures. *Journal of Sustainable Tourism, 28*(12), 2064–2080.

Filep, S., Cao, D., Jiang, M., & DeLacy, T. (2013). Savouring tourist experiences after a holiday. *Leisure/Loisir, 37*(3), 191–203.

Filep, S., Moyle, B. D., & Skavronskaya, L. (2022). Tourist wellbeing: Re-thinking hedonic and eudaimonic dimensions. *Journal of Hospitality & Tourism Research*, https://doi.org/10.1177/1096348022108796.

Foley, C. (2017). The art of wasting time: Sociability, friendship, community and holidays. *Leisure Studies, 36*(1), 1–20.

Fullagar, S., Markwell, K., & Wilson, E. (eds). (2012). *Slow tourism: Experiences and mobilities* (Vol. 54). Channel View Publications.

Fusté-Forné, F., & Hussain, A. (2022). Regenerative tourism futures: a case study of Aotearoa New Zealand. *Journal of Tourism Futures, 8*(3), 346–351. https://doi.org/10.1108/JTF-01-2022-0027.

Gigliotti, L. M. (2011). Comparison of an internet versus mail survey: A case study. *Human Dimensions of Wildlife*, 16, 55–62.

Giurge, L. M., Whillans, A. V., & West, C. (2020). Why time poverty matters for individuals, organisations and nations. *Nature Human Behaviour, 4*(10), 993–1003.

He, M., Liu, B., & Li, Y. (2021). Tourist inspiration: How the wellness tourism experience inspires tourist engagement. *Journal of Hospitality & Tourism Research*, https://doi.org/10.1177/10963480211026376.

Headlee, C. (2020). *Do Nothing: How to Break Away from Overworking, Overdoing, and Underliving*. New York: Harmony.

Heitmann, S., Robinson, P., & Povey, G. (2011). Slow food, slow cities and slow tourism, in S. Heitmann, P., Robinson, & P. Diecke (eds) *Research themes for tourism*, (pp. 114–127). Wallingford: CABI.

Hjalager, A. M., & Konu, H. (2011). Co-branding and co-creation in wellness tourism: The role of cosmeceuticals. *Journal of Hospitality Marketing & Management, 20*(8), 879–901.

Honoré, C. (2005). *In praise of slowness: Challenging the cult of speed*. HarperOne.

Houge Mackenzie, S., & Hodge, K. (2020). Adventure recreation and subjective well-being: A conceptual framework. *Leisure Studies, 39*(1), 26–40.

Houge Mackenzie, S., Hodge, K., & Filep, S. (2021). How does adventure sports tourism enhance well-being? A conceptual model. *Tourism Recreation Research, 48*(1), 3–16, https://doi.org/10.1080/02508281.2021.1894043.

Huang, Y. T., Tzong-Ru, L., Goh, A. P., Kuo, J. H., Lin, W. Y., & Qiu, S. T. (2022). Post-COVID wellness tourism: providing personalized health check packages through online-to-Offline services. *Current Issues in Tourism, 25*(24), 3905–3912, https://doi.org/10.1080/13683500.2022.2042497.

Hussain, A. (2021). A future of tourism industry: Conscious travel, destination recovery and regenerative tourism. *Journal of Sustainability and Resilience, 1*(1), 5.

Ivanski, C., and Kohut, T. (2017). Exploring definitions of sex positivity through thematic analysis. *The Canadian Journal of Human Sexuality*, 26, 216–225.

Kim, I., Koo, M. J., Lee, H. E., Won, Y. L., & Song, J. (2019). Overwork-related disorders and recent improvement of national policy in South Korea. *Journal of Occupational Health, 61*(4), 288–296.

Lafargue, P. (2021 [1883]). *The right to be lazy: And other studies*. CH Kerr.

Lee, D. J., Kruger, S., Whang, M. J., Uysal, M., & Sirgy, M. J. (2014). Validating a customer well-being index related to natural wildlife tourism. *Tourism Management*, 45, 171–180.

Mackenzie, S. H., & Raymond, E. (2020). A conceptual model of adventure tour guide well-being. *Annals of Tourism Research*, 84, 102977.

Mathisen, L., Søreng, S. U., & Lyrek, T. (2022). The reciprocity of soil, soul and society: the heart of developing regenerative tourism activities. *Journal of Tourism Futures*, 8(3) 330–341. https://doi.org/10.1108/JTF-11-2021-0249.

McDaid, D., Park, A. L., & Wahlbeck, K. (2019). The economic case for the prevention of mental illness. *Annual Review of Public Health*, 40, 373–389.

Mecking, O. (2021). *Niksen: Embracing the Dutch art of doing nothing*. Houghton Mifflin.

Moreno-González, A. A., León, C. J., & Fernández-Hernández, C. (2020). Health destination image: The influence of public health management and well-being conditions. *Journal of Destination Marketing & Management*, 16, 100430.

Morrison-Beedy, D. (2022). Are we addressing "quiet quitting" in faculty, staff, and students in academic settings? *Building Healthy Academic Communities Journal*, 6(2), 7–8.

Mura, P., & Wijesinghe, S. N. (2021). Critical theories in tourism – a systematic literature review. *Tourism Geographies*, 25(2-3), 487-507. https://doi.org/10.1080/14616688.2021.1925733.

Ohe, Y., Ikei, H., Song, C., & Miyazaki, Y. (2017). Evaluating the relaxation effects of emerging forest-therapy tourism: A multidisciplinary approach. *Tourism Management*, 62, 322–334.

Parkins, W., & Craig, G. (2006). *Slow living*. University of New South Wales Press.

Paulsen, R. (2014). *Empty labor: Idleness and workplace resistance*. Cambridge University Press.

Perrons, D. (2003). The new economy and the work–life balance: Conceptual explorations and a case study of new media. *Gender, Work & Organization*, 10(1), 65–93.

Pollock, A. (2019, October 1). Regenerative tourism: The natural maturation of sustainability. *Regenerate the Future*. https://medium.com/activate-the-future/regenerative-tourism-the-natural-maturation-of-sustainability-26e6507d0fcb.

Rosa, H. (2013). *Social acceleration: A new theory of modernity*. Columbia University Press.

Sanford, C. (2019). he regenerative paradigm: Discerning how we make sense of the world. In B. Caniglia, B. Frank, J. L. Knott, Jr, K. S. Sagendorf, & E. A. Wilkerson (eds.), *Regenerative urban development, climate change and the common good* (pp. 13-33). Routledge.

Shahvali, M., Kerstetter, D. L., & Townsend, J. N. (2021). The contribution of vacationing together to couple functioning. *Journal of Travel Research*, 60(1), 133–148.

Russell, B. (2004). *In praise of idleness and other essays*. Psychology Press.

Ryan, R. M., & Deci, E. L. (2001). On happiness and human potentials: A review of research on hedonic and eudaimonic well-being. *Annual Review of Psychology*, 52, 141.

Sharma-Brymer, V., Brymer, E. (2020). Flourishing and eudaimonic well-being. In W. Leal Filho, T. Wall, A. M. Azul, L. Brandli, & P. G. Özuyar (eds), *Good health and well-being. Encyclopedia of the UN Sustainable Development Goals*. Springer.

Sheldon, P. J. (2020). Designing tourism experiences for inner transformation. *Annals of Tourism Research*, 83, 102935.

Sheller, M. (2021). Reconstructing tourism in the Caribbean: Connecting pandemic recovery, climate resilience and sustainable tourism through mobility justice. *Journal of Sustainable Tourism*, 29(9), 1436–1449.

Smith, M. K., & Diekmann, A. (2017). Tourism and wellbeing. *Annals of Tourism Research*, 66, 1–13.

Smith, M., & Reisinger, Y. (2013). Transforming quality of life through wellness tourism. *Transformational Tourism: Tourist Perspectives, 55*, 67.

Vaske, J. J. (2011). Advantages and disadvantages of internet surveys: Introduction to the special issue. *Human Dimensions of Wildlife, 16*(3), 149–153.

Walsh, J. (2012). Work–life balance: The end of the "overwork" culture? In S. Bach & M. R. Edwards (eds) *Managing human resources: Human resource management in transition* (pp. 150–177). London: Wiley.

World Health Organization. (2022). WHO guidelines on mental health at work. Accessed 20 September 2022 from https:// www .who .int/ publications/ i/ item/ 9789240053052.

6 Nature as a contributor to wellbeing and future tourism: Finnish Gen Zers seeking happiness and meaning in life

Miia Grénman, Juulia Räikkönen and Fanny Aapio

6.1 Introduction

We have entered the Anthropocene Epoch, in which human activity is so massive that it leaves a lasting imprint on the entire planet and its systems. We are also living in a time of transition, where the ecological crisis – the combination of accelerating climate change and biodiversity loss – challenges our future on Earth. Profound questions regarding the nature of the "good life" are critical since human activities, particularly consumption and global business structures, are amongst the root causes of the ongoing ecological crisis (Dasgupta, 2021; Díaz et al., 2019; Jayasinghe & Darner, 2020). Simultaneously, the COVID-19 pandemic is undoubtedly one of the most disruptive events faced by humankind in recent times, critically changing our everyday lives, practices, consumption, and tourism behaviour (Gössling et al., 2020).

These crises have also heavily impacted the global tourism industry, revealing the need for tourism transformation. This shift can only occur if the values and consciousness of the whole industry and all involved in tourism are transformed (Sheldon, 2020). Accordingly, the future of tourism must embrace the awakening of consciousness towards more sustainable practices that enhance the wellbeing of tourists and the planet. This chapter discusses how nature can contribute to wellbeing and future tourism by drawing on philosophical and psychological understandings of wellbeing and the biophilia hypothesis of human–nature connection.

Wellbeing has become one of the decade's most essential concepts and is omnipresent in almost all discourse relating to human life (Smith & Diekmann, 2017). Wellbeing has a myriad of conceptualisations, and it can be measured either through objective (e.g., gross domestic product [GDP] and income) or subjective indicators (e.g., life satisfaction and happiness), all relating to quality of life that indicates human development (Pancer & Handelman, 2012). With the advent of quality of life and subjective wellbeing research (Diener et al., 1999), as well as positive psychology (Seligman, 2012), more emphasis has been placed on subjective conceptualisations and measures as indicated, for example, in the World Happiness Report, which measures people's own life evaluations and subjective wellbeing (Helliwell et al., 2022). Wellbeing has also been widely acknowledged in recent tourism studies through a broad range of concepts inspired by philosophy and psychology, such as "quality of life" and "life satisfaction" (Dolnicar et al., 2012; Pearce et al., 2010), "happiness" (Nawijn, 2011; Nawijn et al., 2010), "wellness" (Smith & Puczkó, 2008; Voigt et al., 2011), and "hedonic" and "eudaimonic" paradigms of wellbeing (Ateljevic, 2020; Konu, 2016; Pritchard et al., 2011; Sheldon, 2020; Voigt et al., 2011).

However, wellbeing has been a philosophical and psychological concern since the beginning of intellectual history; conceptions of happiness and the "good life" have been central concerns for philosophers and great thinkers from Aristotle's time to the present (Ryan & Deci, 2001). The current psychological understanding of wellbeing is based on two significant perspectives: hedonia and eudaimonia. The hedonic approach focuses on happiness and defines wellbeing in terms of pleasure, enjoyment, and pain avoidance (Diener et al., 1999; Kahneman et al., 1999). Conversely, the eudaimonic approach focuses on meaningfulness and self-realisation, capturing aspects of optimal living and psychological functioning (Ryff, 1989; Ryff & Singer, 2008).

The natural environment is an integral part of hedonic and eudaimonic wellbeing. Within research on sustainability attitudes and environmentally sustainable behaviour, scholars have suggested an examination of nature relatedness – a psychological construct that reflects an individual's relationship with the natural world (Nisbet & Zelenski, 2013; Nisbet et al., 2011). Previous research has acknowledged that a disconnection from nature damages human and environmental wellbeing, while a strong connection with nature is associated with greater happiness, wellbeing, and environmental concern (Dutcher et al., 2007; Mayer & Frantz, 2004; Nisbet & Zelenski, 2013; Nisbet et al., 2011; Zelenski & Nisbet, 2014). Instead of focusing on nature's well-documented health or recuperative benefits (Nisbet et al., 2011; Puhakka et al., 2017), this chapter discusses nature as a source of wellbeing by addressing nature relatedness (NR), which refers to a sense of subjective connectedness with nature (Nisbet et al., 2009).

To this end, this chapter examines hedonic and eudaimonic wellbeing, nature relatedness, and tourism transformation among Gen Zers in Finland, the "happiest country in the world" (Helliwell et al., 2022). The chapter sheds light on future tourism, which will be increasingly shaped by Gen Z, born between the late 1990s and the late 2000s (White, 2017). Gen Z forms a significant future consumer and tourist cohort, as they come equipped with notably different values, attitudes, beliefs, expectations, and behaviours than previous generations; having been born into the digital era and growing up with increasing environmental consciousness, Gen Z takes sustainability seriously due to having a global mindset with ethical sensitivities (Corey & Grace, 2018).

This chapter contributes to tourism literature by drawing a future research and development agenda for tourism and wellbeing, highlighting key aspects of happiness, meaningfulness, and nature relatedness for Finnish Gen Zers. Examining the philosophical and psychological understandings underpinning wellbeing and nature relatedness can also contribute to a deeper understanding of future tourism and the required tourism transformation and the need for more meaningful, transformational, and eudaimonic tourist experiences (Ateljevic, 2020; Sheldon, 2020; Smith & Diekmann, 2017).

6.2   Theoretical Background

6.2.1   Hedonia and Eudaimonia: Two Perspectives on Wellbeing

Conceptions of happiness and the "good life" have been central concerns for philosophers and great thinkers – from Aristotle's time to the present (Ryan & Deci, 2001). Originally, the concept of wellbeing evolved around two philosophical perspectives: hedonism and eudaimonism. *Hedonism* posits that the pursuit of pleasure is the greatest good and that happiness is the totality of one's hedonic moments (Ryan & Deci, 2001). Conversely, *eudaimonism* holds that one should pursue a life of virtue and excellence by focusing on psychological wellbeing connected to meaningful and valuable actions in opposition to "vulgar" pleasure seeking (Waterman, 2008). According to Aristotle's definition of eudaimonia, true happiness is found by leading a virtuous life and doing what is worth doing, meaning realising human potential is the ultimate human goal (Ryan et al., 2008; Waterman, 2008).

The search for an understanding of human wellbeing has extended to various fields. Interest in the hedonia–eudaimonia distinction has proliferated in recent years, especially in positive psychology (Huta & Ryan, 2010; Huta & Waterman, 2014). Towards the hedonic end, researchers (Diener et al., 1999; Kahneman et al., 1999) argue that wellbeing consists of the pleasantness of one's moments. Hedonia defines wellbeing as *happiness* (or subjective well-being [SWB]), focusing on satisfaction with one's life, the quantity of positive affect, and the absence of negative affect (Diener, 2009; Diener et al., 1999). Accordingly, hedonic wellbeing is most often defined by life satisfaction, happiness, pleasure, enjoyment, and comfort, thus emphasising positive emotions (Diener, 2009; Huta & Ryan, 2010).

Although wellbeing is mostly conceptualised as SWB following the hedonic approach, researchers have advocated examining dimensions of wellbeing beyond subjective wellbeing: eudaimonic wellbeing stressing psychological functioning (Ryff, 1989; Ryff & Singer, 2008; Waterman, 2008). Eudaimonia, originating from humanistic psychology, captures aspects of optimal living and argues that wellbeing involves applying and developing oneself to the fullest (Huta & Ryan, 2010; Waterman, 2008). Eudaimonia is connected to *meaningfulness* and *self-realisation* – commonly defined as a sense of meaning and purpose, authenticity, personal growth, self-development, psychological functioning, full engagement, autonomy, and vitality (Huta & Ryan, 2010; Ryff & Singer, 2008).

While hedonia requires engaging in joyful and relaxing activities, eudaimonia also necessitates engagement in effortful and challenging pursuits that often result in greater wellbeing in the long term: more life satisfaction, increased positive affect, greater meaning in life, and a higher potential to reach one's best self (Huta & Ryan, 2010). However, researchers have argued that hedonic and eudaimonic wellbeing indicators tend to be positively correlated and influence one another, implying they are not mutually exclusive but overlapping and distinct (Huta & Ryan, 2010; Huta & Waterman, 2014).

The positive psychology movement has also influenced tourism studies addressing wellbeing within these paradigms (Smith & Diekmann, 2017). In wellness tourism, beauty spas rely on more hedonic experiences, while spiritual retreats provide more eudaimonic ones (Voigt et al., 2011). However, tourism experiences usually consist of both hedonic and eudaimonic elements, forming combinations of hedonism and pleasure, rest and relaxation, meaningful experiences, philanthropic activities, and sustainability (Smith & Diekmann, 2017). Experiential tourism services appeal to tourists' hedonic and/or eudaimonic motivations and lead, through involvement, to internal and emotionally engaging experiences (Konu, 2016) or even to inner transformations through deep human connectivity, deep environmental connectivity in natural settings, self-inquiry, and/or tourists' engaged contribution to the destination (Sheldon, 2020).

6.2.2   Nature Relatedness and Wellbeing

The theoretical background of nature relatedness draws on Wilson's (1984) biophilia hypothesis, according to which humans possess an innate need to connect with all living things. Kellert and Wilson (1993) have argued that, due to biological evolution, humans have an inherent appreciation for nature that is embedded in their biology and has not been negated by modern lifestyles. Evidence of the biophilia hypothesis is found, for example, in the popularity of outdoor wilderness activities, gardening, our relationships with animals, and the fondness for natural scenery (Nisbet et al., 2009, 2011). The biophilia hypothesis helps explain the human–nature connection and the consequences of disconnection from the natural world (Nisbet & Zelenski, 2013). However, individual differences exist in how people connect with nature; objective contact with nature is not entirely equivalent to the subjective sense of connection that likely fosters wellbeing and environmentally sustainable behaviour (Mayer & Frantz, 2004; Nisbet et al., 2009; Nisbet & Zelenski, 2013).

Schultz (2000) has argued that environmental concerns directly relate to how people see themselves as part of nature. The more connected people are to nature, the more they are aware of their actions and concern for all living things (Nisbet et al., 2009; Schultz, 2000). This so-called "biospheric" attitude reflects a strong human-nature connection. Conversely, concerns for oneself (i.e., "egoistic" attitude) indicate a damaged relationship that may contribute to unhappiness and environmentally destructive behaviour (Nisbet & Zelenski, 2013). Research has shown that human–nature connection and biospheric concern are associated with less self-interest and more environmental concern (Dutcher et al., 2007; Mayer & Frantz, 2004; Schultz, 2000), increased happiness and wellbeing (Capaldi et al., 2014; Nisbet et al., 2011; Zelenski & Nisbet, 2014), and self-reported environmentally sustainable behaviour (Clayton, 2003; Nisbet et al., 2009, 2011; Schultz, 2001).

Various concepts and measures have been developed to assess the human–nature connection, including the inclusion of nature in self (Schultz, 2001), environmental identity (Clayton, 2003), connectedness to nature (Mayer & Frantz, 2004), and connectivity with nature (Dutcher et al., 2007). Nisbet et al. (2009) proposed the construct of nature relatedness (NR) to capture the subjective sense of connectedness with nature that refers to the affective, experiential, and cognitive relationship individuals have with the natural world. NR differs from other environmental attitude measures, especially in predicting and assessing happiness and wellbeing, going beyond merely measuring environmental attitudes or concerns, also encompassing one's appreciation for and understanding of human interconnectedness with all other living things

(Nisbet et al., 2009, 2011). A strong sense of nature relatedness should predict happiness and wellbeing more broadly (Nisbet & Zelenski, 2013).

NR is relatively stable over time and across situations and is considered to be like a trait. From a biophilia perspective, NR indicates how much a person's innate need to connect with nature has been supported, while individual differences reflect the strength of connectedness with the natural environment (Nisbet et al., 2011). As research interest in NR has grown, Nisbet and Zelenski (2013) developed and validated a short-form version of the original 21-item Nature Relatedness Scale (NR-6), comprising six items from two subscales of a sense of identification ("self") and contact with nature ("experience") to offer an alternate when time and space are limited and the research context requires an assessment of connected elements rather than environmental attitudes.

NR has been frequently investigated with happiness and wellbeing, and studies have drawn on hedonic and eudaimonic approaches (Capaldi et al., 2014; Howell et al., 2013; Mayer & Frantz, 2004; Nisbet et al., 2011; Nisbet & Zelenski, 2013). Studies have revealed that an individual with a high nature relatedness is also likely to experience more subjective and psychological wellbeing. Nisbet et al. (2011) found that NR correlated positively with positive affect, autonomy, personal growth, a sense of purpose in life, and self-acceptance. Capaldi et al.'s study (2014) suggested that those more connected to nature tended to experience more vitality, positive affect, and life satisfaction than those less connected to nature. Furthermore, Howell et al. (2013) found that nature connectedness correlated positively with meaning in life.

6.3   Research Methods

Survey data were collected at one Finnish university in 2021 as part of a basic-level course on business ethics to better understand Gen Zers' sources of wellbeing and nature relatedness. The survey included open- and closed-ended questions on the following themes: 1) happiness and meaning in life, 2) nature in everyday life, 3) nature relatedness, and 4) COVID-19's impact on nature relatedness (Table 6.1).

The survey was administered via Qualtrics and completed by 68 students aged 19 to 24. Concerning gender, the answers were equally distributed (women, 53%; men, 47%). The open-ended responses were analysed with content analysis facilitated by NVivo20 and closed-ended responses through descriptive statistical methods with SPSS28. Notably, all participants were guaranteed

Table 6.1   Research design, operationalisation and analysis

Themes	Questions	Operationalisation and analysis
Happiness and meaning in life	What makes you happy? What brings meaning into your life?	Open-ended question; content analysis Open-ended question; content analysis
Nature in everyday life	What do you do in nature? How would you evaluate the following statements concerning the meaning of nature? What does nature mean to you?	Open-ended question; content analysis Closed-ended question with a five-point Likert scale: 1 = strongly disagree to 5 = strongly agree (adapted from Haanpää & Laasonen, 2020); descriptive statistical methods Open-ended question; content analysis
Nature relatedness (NR-6 scale)	How would you evaluate the following statements related your connection with nature?	Closed-ended question with a five-point Likert scale: 1 = strongly disagree to 5 = strongly agree (adapted from Nisbet & Zelenski, 2013); descriptive statistical methods
Covid-19's impact on nature relatedness	Has your relationship with nature changed due to COVID-19? If the change has been positive, how would you describe it?	Closed-ended question with a three-point scale: 1 = yes, the change has been positive; 2 = no, there has been no change; 3 = I don't know; descriptive statistical methods Closed-ended question with a five-point Likert scale: 1 = strongly disagree to 5 = strongly agree; descriptive statistical methods

anonymity and were asked to provide written consent granting permission to utilise their responses for research. Research participation was voluntary yet encouraged for class credit.

6.4   Results and Discussion

6.4.1   Sources of Happiness and Meaning in Life

The research data included two open-ended questions related to hedonic and eudaimonic wellbeing: "What makes you happy?" and "What brings meaning into your life?" As previous literature suggests (Huta & Ryan, 2010; Huta & Waterman, 2014), happiness and meaning in life are not mutually exclusive but interconnected and overlapping. The analysis also indicated that respondents interpreted these broad notions rather similarly.

As presented in Table 6.2, we identified 181 references addressing happiness and 119 addressing meaning in life, classifying them into the following categories based on previous literature (Diener, 2009; Huta & Ryan, 2010; Ryff & Singer, 2008; Seligman, 2012): positive affect, relationships, sense of meaning and purpose, sense of accomplishment, vitality, and autonomy. Positive affect represents hedonic wellbeing, while the rest of the categories emphasise eudaimonic wellbeing.

As the findings revealed, relationships are a significant source of happiness and meaning. Happiness was strongly associated with positive affect and enjoyable activities, such as playing sports, engaging in hobbies, laughing, relaxing, enjoying little moments, seeking adventure, and travelling. Conversely, meaning in life was largely addressed concerning a sense of accomplishment; achieving goals, succeeding, practising self-development, getting an education, and working seemed to strongly resonate with meaningfulness. A sense of meaning and purpose, such as doing meaningful things and enjoying meaningful moments, being a good person, acting for the common good, enjoying nature, and practising sustainability, seemed to be valued by Gen Zers and were equally important sources of happiness and meaning. Interestingly, vitality regarding health and wellbeing, and autonomy – including freedom, hope for a better future, economic independence, and safety – were not considered to be primary sources of happiness and meaning in life.

6.4.2　Nature in Everyday Life

Nature's role in Gen Zers' everyday life was analysed through open- and closed-ended questions. Respondents were first asked to briefly describe "What do you do in nature?" Based on short written answers, we identified 191 references to different nature activities, classified into three categories: outdoor activities, observing and admiring nature, and recuperative activities. The largest category, with 119 references, was named *outdoor activities*, including a wide range of nature-based activities such as walking, jogging, hiking, biking, horse riding, swimming, skiing, picking mushrooms and berries, fishing, hunting, camping, boating, and spending time at the summer cottage.

> I run and let my thoughts run by themselves. It has solved many challenges in my life.

Table 6.2 Gen Zers' interpretations of happiness and meaning in life

Main categories	Happiness (181 references)	Meaning in life (119 references)
Hedonic wellbeing		
Positive affect	Sports and hobbies; laughter; lazy mornings; relaxation; sleeping; summer and sunshine; enjoying little moments; adventure; travelling; vacation; food and drinks; active living (50 references; 28%)	Doing enjoyable things; hobbies; enjoying little moments (12 references; 10%)
Eudaimonic wellbeing		
Relationships	Family and friends; home; pets (63 references; 35%)	Family and friends; pets (36 references; 30%)
Sense of meaning and purpose	Doing meaningful things; doing important things; the common good; nature; living environment (25 references; 14%)	Enjoying meaningful moments; the common good; being a good person; being useful; sustainability; life's uniqueness and finiteness (19 references; 16%)
Sense of accomplishment	Goals; success; self-development; routines; self-efficacy; education and work (25 references; 14%)	Goals; success; self-development; education and work (43 references; 36%)
Vitality	Health and wellbeing (10 references; 5%)	Health and wellbeing (3 references; 3%)
Autonomy	Freedom; future; economic independence; safety (8 references; 4%)	Freedom; future (6 references; 5%)

The second category, *observing and admiring nature*, included 44 references related to spending time and enjoying nature, being in the moment, living in the lap of nature, admiring beautiful sceneries, listening to nature's sounds, learning new things, and observing or photographing different species.

> I try to be silent while listening to birds singing, looking into the sky, and exploring new places. In nature, you notice how little you actually need to enjoy life.

The third category, *recuperative activities*, consisted of 28 references to resting, relaxing, enjoying the silence, slowing down, breathing, escaping everyday life, and getting refuelled with fresh air and freedom.

I sojourn, admire, breathe, calm, reflect, move, and grow in nature.

Respondents were also asked to evaluate six statements concerning the meaning of nature with a five-point Likert scale from 1 = strongly disagree to 5 = strongly agree (Haanpää & Laasonen, 2020). The statements included the following themes: nature as a part of Finnish identity, nature's appreciation at the municipality and national levels, nature's conservation, nature and biodiversity, and humans' relationship with nature.

Nearly all respondents (97%) stated that pure nature is an integral part of Finnish identity (M = 4.76, SD = 0.63) and over 82% expressed their interest in nature and biodiversity (M = 4.00, SD = 0.79). Almost 70% opined that appreciating nature is evident in their municipality (M = 3.78, SD = 0.88). However, only 28% stated that nature is adequately conserved at the national level (M = 2.75, SD = 1.07). Fewer than half (44%) of the respondents received enough information about the state of the ecological environment and nature conservation (M = 3.26; SD = 0.82), while hardly anyone (2%) agreed that nature is primarily for human use (M = 1.94, SD = 0.77).

Gen Zers were asked to also describe what nature means to them. Altogether, we identified 123 references, classifying them into four categories: healing and recreation, life and vitality, diversity, and valuable and worth conserving. The most common category was *healing and recreation* (47 references), which primarily described nature as a source of calmness, silence, and recovery – only secondary as a source of physical activity, recreation, and adventure.

Nature is my place of calm and grounding, where I ultimately feel like being myself

The second category, *life and vitality*, consisted of 31 references accentuating the necessity of nature in Gen Zers' lives and how nature epitomizes life in the broader sense.

If there were no nature, there would be no humans either. Nature is a lifeline.

The third category was named *diversity* (26 references) as it described nature as pure, beautiful, versatile, diverse, unknown, and pristine. Moreover, the meaning of nature was illustrated by comparing it to freedom, home, and nostalgia.

> Authenticity, peace, and freedom. Unfortunately, modern humans have somewhat forgotten our original habitat and its role in empowering us.

Finally, 19 references described how nature is *valuable and worth conserving*. Moreover, this category highlights nature's essential role in providing resources while shaming humankind for not treating nature with respect.

> Nature is the beginning and end of all things, which must also be protected and cherished.

6.4.3   Nature Relatedness

In order to gain insights on Gen Zers' sense of identification ("self") and contact with nature ("experience"), we utilised a short-form version of the Nature Relatedness Scale (NR-6; Nisbet & Zelenski, 2013). Respondents answered to statements using a 5-point Likert scale from 1 = strongly disagree to 5 = strongly agree, after which items were averaged with higher scores indicating stronger nature relatedness.

As illustrated in Figure 6.1, three out of four respondents (74%) stated that they take notice of wildlife wherever they are (M = 3.79, SD = 0.87), while three out of five (62%) indicated that they reflect on how their actions affect the environment (M = 3.53, SD = 0.78). Interestingly, a clear majority (57%) saw their connection to nature as part of their spirituality (M = 3.49, SD = 1.09), and over one-third (43%) stated that their relationship with nature is linked to the fundamental question of who they are (M = 3.21, SD = 1.07). Nevertheless, only about a third of the respondents (32%) stated that their ideal vacation destination would be a remote wilderness (M = 2.94, SD = 1.06). In comparison, every fourth respondent (25%) felt very connected to all living things and the Earth (M = 2.85, SD = 1.07).

As the findings indicate, Gen Zers have a strong sense of connectedness to nature that is especially reflected in awareness and subjective knowledge about the environment, spirituality, and feelings of oneself with nature. Conversely, experiencing nature was particularly echoed in the awareness of local wildlife and nearby nature.

Respondents were further asked whether and how the COVID-19 pandemic impacted their connection with nature: over 40% of Gen Zers stated that the pandemic's impact has been positive and increased their sense of connected-

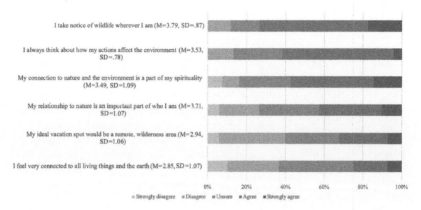

I take notice of wildlife wherever I am (M=3.79, SD=.87)

I always think about how my actions affect the environment (M=3.53, SD=.78)

My connection to nature and the environment is a part of my spirituality (M=3.49, SD=1.09)

My relationship to nature is an important part of who I am (M=3.21, SD=1.07)

My ideal vacation spot would be a remote, wilderness area (M=2.94, SD=1.06)

I feel very connected to all living things and the earth (M=2.85, SD=1.07)

0%   20%   40%   60%   80%   100%

■ Strongly disagree   ■ Disagree   ■ Unsure   ■ Agree   ■ Strongly agree

Figure 6.1   Gen Zers' nature relatedness

ness, especially their increased appreciation of nature, as 40% stated. One-third also mentioned that due to COVID-19, they now spend more time in nature. One-fourth indicated they had discovered new ways of relaxing in nature, while another 25% said nature had enhanced their wellbeing. Furthermore, 13% of Gen Zers also mentioned they are now more interested in conserving nature's diversity.

6.5   Conclusion

This chapter discussed how nature could contribute to wellbeing and future tourism by drawing on philosophical and psychological understandings of wellbeing and the biophilia hypothesis of the human–nature connection. More precisely, the chapter examined hedonic and eudaimonic wellbeing and NR among Gen Zers in Finland. The chapter sheds light on future tourism, which will be increasingly shaped by Gen Z – the future generation whose values, attitudes, beliefs, expectations, and behaviours differ greatly from previous cohorts (Corey & Grace, 2018).

Tourism can enable inner transformations by directing the focus from individual needs towards a more comprehensive notion of wellbeing or turning the attention inwards and examining one's true nature (Ateljevic, 2020; Sheldon, 2020; Smith & Diekmann, 2017). Transformation calls for living with compassion; being concerned for others; acting on the greater good; having a sense of unity with others and nature; contributing to the wellbeing of other living beings; valuing generosity over greed; simplifying lifestyles with less interest in possessions and outward demonstrations of success; living in the present; and achieving inner peace, even amid chaos (Sheldon, 2020).

Based on our findings, Finnish Gen Zers interpreted the notions of happiness and meaning in life somewhat similarly. Relationships were an essential source of happiness and meaningfulness, indicating deep human connectivity (Sheldon, 2020). A sense of meaning and purpose, such as doing meaningful things and enjoying meaningful moments, being a good person, and acting on behalf of the common good, were equally important sources of happiness and meaningfulness, reflecting engaged contribution to the greater good (Ryan et al., 2008; Waterman, 2008). Similarly, the valuation and appreciation of nature and sustainability – another reflection of a sense of meaning and purpose – echo deep environmental connectivity and a biospheric attitude (Nisbet et al., 2009; Schultz, 2000). However, differences were found between these notions. Gen Zers associated happiness with positive affect and enjoyable activities, such as hobbies, relaxation, adventure, and travelling, while meaning in life seemed to resonate with self-realisation, especially regarding achieving goals, self-development, education, and work. Happiness and meaning in life represented self-inquiry but from two different perspectives (Diener, 2009; Huta & Ryan, 2010).

Our findings also showed evidence of the biophilia hypothesis (Nisbet et al., 2011; Wilson, 1984). Gen Zers had a strong sense of connectedness to nature, reflecting a high awareness and environmental knowledge, which increased due to the COVID-19 pandemic. Moreover, nature was considered an essential part of self-identification – a part of Gen Zers' spirituality and the self in a broader sense. While various physical outdoor activities were common to them, nature's esthetic aspects and healing powers were also largely recognised. For Gen Zers, nature was primarily a source of healing and recreation and equalled life and vitality. Nature was considered a valuable and multifaceted entity – pure, beautiful, versatile beyond biodiversity, and well worth conserving. This also represented their quest for meaning and purpose (Howell et al., 2013; Nisbet et al., 2011).

As previous tourism literature suggests, nature is an essential stimulus for transformative experiences (Ateljevic, 2020; Pritchard et al., 2011; Sheldon, 2020; Voigt et al., 2011). It generates positive emotions, enhances connections to self and nature, creates a sense of belonging and wellbeing, calms the mind, and brings inner peace. Wilderness experiences, in particular, seem to profoundly influence tourists' consciousness by minimising one's sense of control, while vast spaces, pure air, and silence can connect the soul to nature in transformative ways (Sheldon, 2020).

Gen Zers considered pure nature an integral part of the Finnish identity, valuing nature and biodiversity highly and agreeing that appreciating nature was evident in their living environment. According to the latest World Happiness Report, Finland is the happiest country in the world for the fifth year in a row (Helliwell et al., 2022). Along with the other Nordic countries, Finland has built a society that possesses an infrastructure of happiness: universal social, healthcare, and educational systems, which increase people's feelings of trust and safety. These social systems offer a basis for maintaining happiness and wellbeing. However, as our findings revealed, Finnish Gen Zers' happiness seems to be strongly related to positive nature relatedness and the search for eudaimonic wellbeing.

6.6   Recommendations

Smith and Diekmann (2017) asked tourism professionals to prepare for future tourism in which long-term self-development or transformation outcomes outweigh the current desire for episodic happiness and hedonic pleasures. Their integrative wellbeing tourism experience model combined elements of hedonism and pleasure, rest and relaxation, meaningful experiences, philanthropic activities, and sustainability. According to our study, Gen Zers long for experiences that, along with mere pleasure, are meaningful and enable personal growth, and compassion for others. As nature offers various possibilities for rest and relaxation and tourism activities that advance ecological sustainability and the wellbeing of other species, future research and development must further address Gen Zers' preferences and interests.

Regarding inner transformations in tourism based on deep environmental connectivity, Sheldon (2020) highlighted the role of guided experiences in sacred and natural landscapes in facilitating tourist transformation and the importance of incorporating the natural world, even in urban tourism destinations. In our study, Gen Zers connected nature to healing and recreation and life and vitality. Future research must examine how Gen Zers wish to consume and cocreate nature-based tourism experiences and how service providers could best respond to their needs in facilitating the possibility for inner transformations. For instance, developing nature-based science tourism (Räikkönen et al., 2021) or modern-day nature pilgrimage tourism (cf. Sheldon, 2020) to Gen Zers offers interesting avenues for researchers and service providers.

Young generations, in particular, often prefer urban tourism destinations, which was indicated also in our study. Therefore, urban nature experiences and their transformative power must be examined with Gen Zers. One topical aspect is digitalisation, often discussed with Gen Z or digital natives. The key to engaging with Gen Zers in leisure activities is to target their desire for social interaction, involvement, and the cocreation of experiences that may occur in the virtual world (Skinner et al., 2018).

The COVID-19 pandemic seemed to advance Gen Zers' connectedness with nature by increasing their appreciation of nature and, to some extent, their willingness to conserve nature and biodiversity. Future research must examine whether these effects are fleeting or lasting, while the tourism industry must respond to this trend by designing nature-based tourism experiences that, besides the appreciation of nature, also positively affect nature conservation.

Gen Z will become a powerful force in shaping tourism. Thus, tourism research must strive to understand how their lifestyle and sustainability ethos will contribute to transforming the global tourism industry. From the sustainable business perspective, an urgent need exists to integrate transformational leadership into tourism companies and understand the role of service providers in facilitating tourist transformation. The global tourism industry's challenge is to limit tourism activity to a scale that does not damage ecosystems (Sheldon, 2020), and conscious tourists are likelier to consider nature and biodiversity-respectful tourism.

References

Ateljevic, I. (2020). Transforming the (tourism) world for good and (re)generating the potential 'new normal'. *Tourism Geographies*, *22*(3), 467–475.

Capaldi, C. A., Dopko, R. L., & Zelenski, J. M. (2014). The relationship between nature connectedness and happiness: A meta-analysis. *Frontiers in Psychology*, *5*(976). https://doi.org/10.3389/fpsyg.2014.00976.

Clayton, S. (2003). Environmental identity: A conceptual and an operational definition. In S. Clayton, & S. Opotow (eds), *Identity and the natural environment: The psychological significance of nature* (pp. 45–65). Cambridge, MA: MIT Press.

Corey, S., & Grace, M. (2018). *Generation Z. A century in the making*. Routledge.

Dasgupta, P. (2021). *The economics of biodiversity: The Dasgupta Review*. HM Treasury.

Díaz, S., Settele, J., Brondízio, E. S., Ngo, H. T., Agard, J., Arneth, A., ... & Zayas, C. N. (2019). Pervasive human-driven decline of life on Earth points to the need for transformative change. *Science*, *366*(6471), 1–10.

Diener, E. (2009). Subjective well-being. In E. Diener (ed.) *The science of well-being: The collected works of Ed Diener* (pp. 11–58). Springer Science + Business Media. https:// doi.org/10.1007/978-90-481-2350-6_2.

Diener, E., Suh, E. M., Lucas, R. E., & Smith, H. L. (1999). Subjective well-being: Three decades of progress. *Psychological Bulletin, 125*(2), 276–302.

Dolnicar, S., Yanamandram, V., & Cliff, K. (2012). The contribution of vacations to quality of life. *Annals of Tourism Research, 39*(1), 59–83.

Dutcher, D. D., Finley, J. C., Luloff, A. E., & Johnson, J. B. (2007). Connectivity with nature as a measure of environmental values. *Environment and Behavior, 39*(4), 474–493.

Gössling, S., Scott, D., & Hall, C. M. (2020). Pandemics, tourism and global change: A rapid assessment of COVID-19. *Journal of Sustainable Tourism, 29*(1), 1–20.

Haanpää, S. & Laasonen, V. (2020, June 1). *Survey of Finnish nature relatedness.* MDI. Retrieved from https:// www .mdi .fi/ wp -content/ uploads/ 2022/ 05/ Luontosuhdebarometri-2020-tulokset.pdf.

Helliwell, J. F., Layard, R., Sachs, J. D., De Neve, J.-E., Aknin, L. B., & Wang, S. (Eds.). (2022). *World Happiness Report 2022.* Sustainable Development Solutions Network. Retrieved from https://worldhappiness.report/.

Howell, A. J., Passmore, H.-A., and Buro, K. (2013). Meaning in nature: Meaning in life as a mediator of the relationship between nature connectedness and well-being. *Journal of Happiness Studies, 14,* 1681–1696.

Huta, V., & Ryan, R. M. (2010). Pursuing pleasure or virtue: The differential and overlapping well-being benefits of hedonic and eudaimonic motives. *Journal of Happiness Studies, 11*(6), 735–762.

Huta, V., & Waterman, A. S. (2014). Eudaimonia and its distinction from hedonia: Developing a classification and terminology for understanding conceptual and operational definitions. *Journal of Happiness Studies, 15*(6), 1425–1456.

Jayasinghe, I., & Darner, R. (2020). Do emotions, nature relatedness, and conservation concern influence students' evaluations of arguments about biodiversity conservation? *Interdisciplinary Journal of Environmental and Science Education, 17*(1), 1–16.

Kahneman, D., Diener, E., & Schwarz, N. (Eds.). (1999). *Well-being: Foundations of hedonic psychology.* Russell Sage Foundation.

Kellert, S. R., & Wilson, E. O. (Eds.). (1993). *The biophilia hypothesis.* Island Press.

Konu, H. (2016). Customer involvement in new experiential tourism service development: Evidence in wellbeing and nature tourism contexts (Doctoral dissertation). Retrieved from https:// erepo .uef .fi/ bitstream/ handle/ 123456789/ 17152/ urn _isbn_978-952-61-2180-2.pdf.

Mayer, F. S., & Frantz, C. M. (2004). The connectedness to nature scale: A measure of individuals' feeling in community with nature. *Journal of Environmental Psychology, 24*(4), 503–515.

Nawijn, J. (2011). Determinants of daily happiness on vacation. *Journal of Travel Research, 50*(5), 559–566.

Nawijn, J., Marchand, M. A., Veenhoven, R., & Vingerhoets, A. J. (2010). Vacationers happier, but most not happier after a holiday. *Applied Research in Quality of Life, 5*(1), 35–47.

Nisbet, E. K., & Zelenski, J. M. (2013). The NR-6: A new brief measure of nature relatedness. *Frontiers in Psychology, 4,* 1–11.

Nisbet, E. K., Zelenski, J. M., & Murphy, S. A. (2009). The nature relatedness scale: Linking individuals' connection with nature to environmental concern and behavior. *Environment and Behavior, 41*(5), 715–740.

Nisbet, E. K., Zelenski, J. M., & Murphy, S. A. (2011). Happiness is in our nature: Exploring nature relatedness as a contributor to subjective well-being. *Journal of Happiness Studies, 12*(2), 303–322.

Pancer, E., & Handelman, J. (2012). The evolution of consumer well-being. *Journal of Historical Research in Marketing, 4*(1), 177–189.

Pearce, P., Filep, S., & Ross, G. (2010). *Tourists, tourism and the good life*. Routledge.

Pritchard, A., Morgan, N., & Ateljevic, I. (2011). Hopeful tourism: A new transformative perspective. *Annals of Tourism Research, 38*(3), 941–963.

Puhakka, R., Pitkänen, K., & Siikamäki. P. (2017). Health and well-being impacts of protected areas in Finland. *Journal of Sustainable Tourism, 25*(12), 1830–1847.

Ryan, R. M., & Deci, E. L. (2001). On happiness and human potentials: A review of research on hedonic and eudaimonic well-being. *Annual Review of Psychology, 52*(1), 141–166.

Ryan, R. M., Huta, V., & Deci, E. L. (2008). Living well: A self-determination theory perspective on eudaimonia. *Journal of Happiness Studies, 9*(1), 139–170.

Ryff, C. D. (1989). Happiness is everything, or is it? Explorations on the meaning of psychological well-being. *Journal of Personality and Social Psychology, 57*(6), 1069.

Ryff, C. D., & Singer, B. H. (2008). Know thyself and become what you are: A eudaimonic approach to psychological well-being. *Journal of Happiness Studies, 9*(1), 13–39.

Räikkönen, J., Grénman, M., Rouhiainen, H., Honkanen, A., & Sääksjärvi, I. E. (2021) Conceptualizing nature-based science tourism: a case study of Seili Island, Finland. *Journal of Sustainable Tourism, 31*(5), 1214–1232. https://doi.org/10.1080/09669582.2021.1948553.

Schultz, P. W. (2000). New environmental theories: Empathizing with nature: The effects of perspective taking on concern for environmental issues. *Journal of Social Issues, 56*(3), 391–406.

Schultz, P. W. (2001). The structure of environmental concern: Concern for self, other people, and the biosphere. *Journal of Environmental Psychology, 21*(4), 327–339.

Seligman, M. E. P. (2012). *Flourish: A visionary new understanding of happiness and well-being*. Simon and Schuster.

Sheldon, P. J. (2020). Designing tourism experiences for inner transformation. *Annals of Tourism Research, 83*, 1–12.

Skinner, H., Sarpong, D., & White, G. R. T. (2018). Meeting the needs of the Millennials and Generation Z: Gamification in tourism through geocaching. *Journal of Tourism Futures, 4*(1), 93–104.

Smith, M. K., & Diekmann, A. (2017). Tourism and wellbeing. *Annals of Tourism Research, 66*, 1–13.

Smith, M., & Puczkó, L. (2008). *Health and wellness tourism*. Routledge.

Voigt, C., Brown, G., & Howat, G. (2011). Wellness tourists: In search of transformation. *Tourism Review, 66*(1/2), 16–30.

Waterman, A. S. (2008). Reconsidering happiness: A eudaimonist's perspective. *The Journal of Positive Psychology, 3*(4), 234–252.

White, J. E. (2017). *Meet Generation Z: Understanding and reaching the new post-Christian world*. Baker Books.

Wilson, E. O. (1984). *Biophilia*. Harvard University Press. https://doi.org/10.4159/9780674045231.

Zelenski, J. M., & Nisbet, E. K. (2014). Happiness and feeling connected: The distinct role of nature relatedness. *Environment and Behavior, 46*(1), 3–23.

PART III

FACILITATING WELLBEING EXPERIENCES IN TOURISM

7   Nature connection and wellbeing in tourism experiences

Emma Pope and Henna Konu

7.1   Introduction

Due to their busy and stressful everyday lives, people are looking for possibilities to find balance, slow down, find meaning, and develop themselves. Wellness and wellbeing services are seen as a possibility for achieving these goals (Sheldon & Bushell, 2009; Smith & Puczkó, 2009). It is noted that experiences in natural environments or the observed wildlife can bring meaningful tourist experiences and also trigger extraordinary and transformative experiences (e.g., Arnould & Price, 1993; Kirillova et al., 2017). It is also noted that nature and rural settings may enhance tourists' wellbeing, but further qualitative studies are required to increase understanding of the deeper meanings of nature and rural areas to the wellbeing of tourists (Konu & Pesonen, 2018).

The positive outcomes of nature for wellbeing have been studied from diverse perspectives and disciplines such as environmental psychology, environmental education, human geography, benefits-based management and outcomes-focused management, outdoor recreation and adventure tourism, wellbeing tourism, and therapeutic landscapes (e.g., Hanna et al., 2019; Houge MacKenzie & Brymer, 2020; Konu & Pesonen, 2018; Lea, 2008; Little, 2012; Wolf et al., 2015). Nature has an important role in wellbeing tourism, as people travel to certain destinations and natural settings to improve or enhance their health and wellbeing (e.g., Smith & Puzckó, 2009; Voigt et al., 2011). Many wellbeing tourism offerings are also built around natural resources such as mountains (Pechlaner & Fisher, 2006), lakes (Konu et al., 2010) and mineral water or hot springs (Erfurt-Cooper & Cooper, 2009). From this perspective, nature is more seen as a resource that can be instrumentally utilised to support the provision of wellbeing. However, studies have indicated that nature can also have a more active role in supporting wellbeing and more appreciative tourism activities can boost the wellbeing benefits of nature (e.g., Bimonte & Faralla, 2014; Lea, 2008).

This chapter examines nature-based wellbeing experiences in tourism by increasing the understanding of the role of nature within these experiences. More specifically, it aims to explore which pathways to nature connection (Lumber et al., 2017) can be identified from qualitative data gained from a nature-based tourism trip, and how wellbeing experiences through nature connection could be facilitated by tourism service providers. This chapter provides exploration of this in the context of Finnish nature-based wellbeing tourism.

7.2   Wellbeing and Nature Connection as Parts of Meaningful Nature-based Tourism Experiences

7.2.1   Wellbeing in Tourist Experiences

There is increasing importance placed upon emotions and feelings within tourism encounters (Tucker & Shelton, 2018). Yet not all wellbeing tourists seek something extraordinary; rather, they are looking for a chance to relax, escape daily routines, and be physically active (Komppula & Konu, 2012). To better understand how nature-based wellbeing outcomes emerge in tourism, it is pertinent to explore how diverse forms of wellbeing, namely hedonia and eudaimonia, may occur through tourist experiences. Hedonic wellbeing is contributed to through the pursuit of pleasure and comfort, while eudaimonia represents feelings of authenticity, engagement, meaning, and personal growth (Huta & Ryan, 2010; Henderson & Knight, 2012). Despite their differences, the combination of hedonic and eudaimonic pursuits have reported high levels of wellbeing and can be complimentary to each other (Huta & Ryan, 2010). Therefore, they are not considered mutually exclusive, but can operate in a synergistic way (Henderson & Knight, 2012). This is reinforced by findings that activities used to achieve hedonic and eudaimonic wellbeing were paths to each other (Zuo et al., 2017). The link between wellbeing and tourism experiences is reinforced by tourists searching for services and experiences that holistically balance body, mind, and spirit (Hartwell et al., 2016). This focus on wellbeing ties into the provision of memorable experiences through the potential long-term effects beyond hedonic enjoyment within the consumption encounter (Knobloch et al., 2017). A memorable experience is more likely to happen when hedonism occurs through enjoyment and excitement, and combines with meaningfulness and learning about oneself, resulting in a positive impact on subjective wellbeing (Sthapit & Coudounaris, 2018). Thus, the role of tourism in providing both emotion and relaxation is echoed through the potential of a holiday to provide pleasure but also personal growth and discovery of one's 'true self' (Voigt, 2011).

Smith and Diekmann (2017) argued that the optimum wellbeing enhancing experiences would integrate all of these dimensions (fun, rest, relaxation; meaning, education, self-fulfilment; altruism, being environmentally friendly, benefiting local communities). Despite recognition of these elements, consumption contexts cannot be pre-classified as memorable or extraordinary, hedonic or eudaimonic, but are defined by those experiencing them (Knobloch et al., 2017). Through an understanding of onsite experiences, arguably, this can aid the understanding of how tourists may perceive aspects of the wellbeing experience.

7.2.2 Nature as a Source of Wellbeing in Tourism

Nature has been explored as a contributor to wellbeing in many disciplines and contexts. It can be argued that the sense of personal wellbeing may be achieved in nature environments that are nonconsumptive (e.g., Sorakunnas 2020), for example, compared to wellness facilities. This has been evidenced in literature associated with forest bathing, for example, where people visit forests for the health and wellbeing benefits they provide (e.g., Chen et al., 2018), and therapeutic landscapes defined as 'the physical and built environments, social conditions and human perceptions combine to produce an atmosphere which is conducive to healing' (Gesler, 1996, p. 96). Cleary et al. (2017) noted how early research into therapeutic landscapes centred on 'extraordinary' places of healing such as pilgrimage sites and spas (e.g., Gesler, 1996), yet researchers are increasingly looking at everyday settings to promote feelings of wellbeing. Gesler's (1996) early perspective considered how tourism can facilitate a sense of the 'extraordinary' through experiencing new destinations and activities, whilst also inspiring a sense of connection with nature to take back and seek out in the everyday. Furthermore, both environmental psychology and tourism research demonstrates that people partake in nature-based recreation and tourism for health and wellbeing reasons, yet whilst this confirms this relationship, they do not explore what this connection between nature and wellbeing looks or feels like from a visitor perspective (Hansen, 2018).

Recently it has been found that outdoor tourism can also provide longer-term effects in clarity and purpose, moving away from a personal indulgence to an investment in mental health (Buckley, 2019). Whilst Fredman et al. (2012, p. 290) acknowledged the literature around nature-based tourism in regard to recreation, adventure, protected areas, and destinations, the authors state that 'it is obvious that none of these leave nature behind, but the meaning of nature and how it is approached are less evident'. In terms of the wellbeing benefits derived from this contact with nature, they are stronger when more appreciative activities are undertaken and the environment is a cocreator of the experience, rather than nature as just the setting for the activity (Bimonte & Faralla, 2014). Whilst these appreciative forms of tourism allude to more respect, there is perhaps the need to consider ways of furthering this, so it is not just about appreciating the natural environment for facilitating the tourism activity, but actively developing a relationship with nature through meaningful encounters.

7.2.3   Connection with Nature as a Route to Wellbeing

Recent studies and trends show that people are seeking wellbeing from and connection with nature. Studies have recognised that nature can bring psychological and wellbeing benefits for people (e.g., Lee et al., 2009; Morita et al., 2007; Ohtsuka et al., 1998). Nature connection, defined as the feelings and behaviours individuals have towards nature (Cleary et al., 2017), has been found to provide a wide range of health and wellbeing benefits. For example, it has been associated with emotional and psychological wellbeing (e.g., Nisbet & Zelenski, 2013), and there is a strong relationship between nature connectedness and happiness (Capaldi et al., 2014). The amount of time spent in nature is less important than how time in nature is spent, with the need to notice and engage with nature for wellbeing outcomes to be felt (Lumber et al., 2017). This is significant in the context of designing tourism experiences and arguably takes consumption or appreciation of nature (Bimonte & Faralla, 2014) and furthers it to include connection, a more personal and meaningful relationship with nature.

Eudaimonic wellbeing can be generated through engagement with nature, yet a gap exists in understanding regarding how this is promoted among different individuals (Cleary et al., 2017). Understanding individual accounts of experiences can aid the development of future experiences and the likelihood of connection with nature forming, ensuring that individuals 'walk the path to connectedness' and gain the benefits of this connection (Lumber et al., 2017, p. 5). Arguably this makes the tourism encounter a potentially powerful one with which to establish a connection with nature. Nature, and specifically forests, can be ideal settings to situate wellbeing tourism, research findings demonstrating that the best activities included those connected to nature (Konu, 2015). This chapter builds on this by exploring the elements that make these experiences in nature meaningful.

Table 7.1   Nature connection pathways (adapted from Lumber et al., 2017)

Nature Connection Pathway	Pathway Definition
Contact	Engaging with nature through the senses
Beauty	Appreciating the aesthetic qualities of nature (e.g., shape, colour, form)
Meaning	Using nature to communicate something not directly expressed (e.g., through symbolism)
Emotion	An affective state that happens through engaging with nature and noticing the feeling of being in nature.
Compassion	Including nature in the self and having a moral and ethical concern for nature (e.g., how actions can benefit nature)

Lumber et al.'s (2017) pathways to nature connection provided a focus to understand how nature connection may occur in nature-based experiences. The pathways are derived from the values of biophilia (Kellert, 1993). Originally defined by Wilson (1984) as the human need and love for nature, biophilia stipulates that much of the human search for a fulfilling life is dependent on the relationship we have with nature (Kellert, 1993). The use of contact, emotion, meaning, compassion, and beauty are recommended for use by visitor attractions and organisations aiming to connect people with nature (Lumber et al., 2017, see definitions of pathways in Table 7.1). The pathways emerged as a means to operationalise indicators of nature connection, extending beyond activities that use knowledge and identification to connect people with nature (Lumber et al., 2017).

7.3   Data and Methods

This chapter takes a qualitative approach to examine nature-based wellbeing tourism experiences to gain a deeper understanding of customer perceptions of focal experiences. This case study focuses on examining the customer experiences of a forest-based wellbeing tourism trip with one of the potential target groups, Japanese tourists. A Japanese doctor who had previously visited the case area had the initial idea to create a forest-based tourism product for Japanese visitors in Finland. Japan is also one of the main target markets of Visit Finland, and before the COVID-19 pandemic, overnight stays in Finland were steadily increasing (Business Finland, 2022). The data was collected among customers testing a forest-based wellbeing tourism product by utilising an ethnographic approach. During the trip, the customers were taking part in different activities in nature, as well as activities that utilised natural resources (e.g., making handicrafts and cooking from the local ingredients). The tested product was developed for the Japanese target group hence, the test group was formed from eight Japanese customers and two representatives of a tour operator that offers trips to Finland for Japanese tourists. The data collection took place in North Karelia, Finland.

The data was collected by participant observation, group interviews, and customer feedback surveys. By applying ethnographic approaches and multiple data collection methods, a more comprehensive picture of the examined phenomenon is gained and the different realities and experiences of the participants revealed (e.g., Eriksson & Kovalainen, 2016). The participant observations were made by a Finnish researcher, and the observations focused on service environments (e.g., natural environments and facilities of the service providers), the test customers and their behaviour and emotional responses, and interaction between the customers, environment, and service providers. In addition, the researcher reported her own experiences of diverse situations. The participant observation started at the airport when the test group arrived at the destination and continued until their departure. During the visit the researcher took part in all the activities with the test customers. The data from participant observation comprise field notes (including both emic and etic perspectives) and a number of pictures taken from different situations and activities.

Test customers were also asked to fill feedback surveys daily, which included questions such as: what activities and/or things were the best during the day, what could be improved, and what is your overall assessment of the day? There was also an additional questionnaire used to get an overall assessment of the whole trip. The third data set was collected by conducting two group interviews to supplement the information gained from participant observation and customer feedback forms, and to gain the participants perspectives and reflections of the whole trip. In one interview, two Japanese women and in the other two representatives of the tour operators were interviewed. The interviews were semi-structured and dealt with the experiences of the test customers (e.g., what was the most memorable experience, what was the best part of the trip, and what they would improve?). The semi-structured interviews helped to maintain flexibility in the wording of the questions, as well as keep the tone of the interviews informal and conversational, which helped the interviewees to bring forth their own insiders' perspective of the experiences related to the trip (e.g., Eriksson & Kovalainen, 2016).

The data was analysed by qualitative content analysis and focused on interpreting meanings, themes and patterns that are visible or latent in the data (Çakmak & Isaac, 2012). More precisely, a directed content analysis was applied as the study aimed to deductively recognise if the five pathways to nature connection could be identified from the data. To obtain more detailed information, an inductive perspective was also adapted to ground the examination of themes that may emerge from the data.

7.4   Findings and Discussion

7.4.1   Core Experiences of the Trip and the Role of the Environment and Enablers

The findings show that most customers described their central experience of the whole trip as being immersed in the forest environment and using all their senses. These experiences were recorded as extraordinary and positive and gave the participants the feeling of being empowered and taking part in therapeutic practices.

This immersion in the environment mirrored their greater aspirations to live more in tune with nature. Central customer experiences were also linked to individual activities during the trip. These were frequently connected to the forest, and often described as extraordinary in nature (i.e., as something that the customer had not experienced before). As two participants explained their central experiences in two distinct service modules/activities:

> "Nature as an energizer" tour was good. I felt really good when I was hugging a tree with my eyes closed. (woman, 54)

> This was the most beautiful and mysterious place I have visited. I had the opportunity to collect beautiful mushrooms and it was fun that you can find berries everywhere. In addition, I liked the most that I could lie down and relax anywhere [in the forest]. Also, I don't have words to tell how interesting it was having lunch in the forest. I was paddling for the first time on a lake… (woman, 20)

The focal customer experiences were predominantly confined to interactions (service encounter) with the service provider (such as the guide) or with natural elements. For example, one of the participants reported her core customer experience of the whole trip during the guided tour in the forest:

> I felt so happy being surrounded by nature and I really felt that nature gives me power. The weather and the landscape were so great, and I don't believe that I have experienced such a thing before.' (woman, 55a)

The role of a service provider or guide is central in encouraging these moments and facilitating experiences of nature connection. The guidance makes it possible to have a deeper understanding of the activities and environment, which in turn helps the customers to focus on certain issues.

> The guide who guided us to the place where we had lunch was extremely good. Walking without talking is wonderful. (woman, 47)

> In addition I had the opportunity to get in touch with nature and refresh myself with the help and the guidance of the guide. (woman, 20)

The core experiences were thus formed during the service encounter, but also beyond this temporal scope. For example, one participant emphasised both the past (referring to previous trips) and the feeling of being in the moment (during the trip) when describing her experience of relaxation, and makes sense of her experience when reflecting over her history as a traveller:

> No matter what the sight or mountain is in Japan there are always people. In destinations [domestic and places abroad] I have fun and there is a possibility to relax, but during the trip this week I could relax so much better, extract myself from reality more than I could realise and was able to live just that particular moment. (woman, 20)

The experience with nature during this trip was also reflected upon compared to previous experiences and reinforces how different natural environments influence how nature is experienced. Hence, it seems that this trip that aimed to bring nature-based wellbeing for customers, was indeed recognised as enhancing wellbeing in different ways compared to previous nature-based experiences.

7.4.2   Identified Pathways to Nature Connection

To gain a deeper understanding of the nature-related core experiences, the analysis investigated the content of the experiences through the pathways to nature connection (Lumber et al., 2017). The positive emotions that the customers reported also indicate the sense of wellbeing that connection with nature brings to people. Whilst it is recognised that multiple pathways occur within the excerpts presented, the pathways are explored individually with data that represents the main interpretation.

7.4.2.1   Contact

The *contact* pathway was evident through experiencing nature with different senses, for instance, contact with natural elements (e.g., touch by laying down in a forest, on moss, or on rock), the smells of nature, and taste by trying berries and having lunch outdoors. Touch was also described as feeling the breeze and the softness of the moss. One Japanese man describes his experience as follows:

> When I had the possibility to lay down, bathe in the sunlight and feel the lovely breeze, I could spend luxurious time there. (man, 53)

The idea of nature providing luxury suggests the value assigned to nature. It suggests that rest, considering a more hedonic aspect (e.g., Smith & Diekmann, 2017), can become meaningful through appreciating the opportunity to feel rested. The ability to connect with nature and be in the moment appears to an important aspect of the experience and supports Arnould and Price's (1993) harmony with nature as a key component of an extraordinary experience. The notion of having the 'possibility' alludes to how tourism can provide opportunities to experience nature and wellbeing.

Sense of hearing reinforces this and had two different perspectives: the natural sounds, such as hearing the wind, and emphasising the silence. Being able to hear or be in a silence also helped people have deeper experiences with nature and also helped the person to turn into themself:

> There I could feel silently through all senses the life force of nature and it conveyed to me empowerment. (woman, 60)

This closeness to nature is expressed as it almost becomes part of the person through the empowerment it brings. This again suggests the potential for nature-based tourism experiences to provide eudaimonic outcomes.

The participants also referred to the senses more generally, as they emphasised that experiencing nature with diverse senses helped to be in the moment, and allowed a kind of active relaxation by sensing everything around them. These experiences therefore provided time to connect with nature and as a result forget about time, facilitating mindfulness, quiet, and reflection.

7.4.2.2   Beauty

The pathway of *beauty* was recognised from the descriptions of appreciating natural beauty on several occasions during the trip. This was emphasised by describing the beauty of landscapes in different places and different times of the day (e.g., appreciating the possibility to see the sky with stars and a shooting star, or admiring particular natural elements, such as lakes, forests, islands, trees, moss, lichen, or the northern lights).

> The landscape during sunrise was magnificent! (woman, 60)
> Japanese felt that walking in dark was very interesting and experiential. They admired the bright starry sky and discussed about diverse constellations. Three Japanese also saw a shooting star which brought them delight. (Field notes)

This event was also emphasised by one of the participants when she stated that

> after the dinner the starry sky and the shooting star were so beautiful and touching. (woman, 55a)

The tourism experience therefore becomes a significant way of encountering a variety of natural settings at different times of the day. If notions of beauty are more akin to hedonic elements of pleasure and enjoyment (Kim, 2014), seemingly it has potential to become eudaimonic through this appreciation, reflection, and discussion with other participants.

7.4.2.3   Emotion

The pathway of *emotion* was clearly identifiable from the data. This included immersion into the forest environment, discussing nature, experiencing the spirit of the forest, and having feelings of belonging and empowerment. This suggests both inward emotions felt by being in the forest, and how outwardly discussing nature can also generate emotions. Contact with nature was also even felt as therapeutic and it was mentioned that being able to experience nature increased the feeling of wellbeing:

> It made me feel really good, when I was hugging a tree with my eyes closed (woman, 54), [and] It was more like forest therapy than hiking in the forest. (man, 50)

Emotion was also emphasised when this experience was compared to previous ones:

> Hiking was nothing like I have experienced before, heading from one place to another, but pure happiness as I was able to walk quietly and at the same time feel the forest around me. (woman, 55a)

This reinforces how previously experienced activities can be more emotional through how the tourism experience is delivered. *Feeling the forest* also relates the *contact* pathway, but also suggests this participant feels part of nature around them, rather than just being in the environment. This was also recognisable from the participant observation field notes, which highlighted that being in the moment and experiencing nature raised powerful feelings for some tourists:

> The first exercise raised strong feelings among the Japanese guests. One of the women said that she felt being part of nature and felt that it was much easier to breathe in that situation. Another woman said that she felt very relaxed hugging a tree and she almost fell asleep while doing it. (Field notes)

During particular activities, some participants were very emotional, touched, and even shed tears. Emotions that participants emphasised were relaxation, calmness, being refreshed, gratefulness, fun, enjoyment, happiness, relief, belonging, and surprise. Hedonic and eudaimonic outcomes are all evidenced here and are reinforced as being complimentary to each other (Huta & Ryan, 2010), integrative (Smith & Diekmann, 2017), and synergistic (Henderson & Knight, 2012).

Almost all emotions were positive. The only negative emotion, sadness, was connected to the notion that the person was leaving soon and was not able to experience this kind of nature for a while. This acknowledges the powerful role of tourism in introducing people to things that they may not otherwise experience and suggests a connection to nature was developed through a desire to return to it.

7.4.2.4   Compassion

Compassion was not clearly evident from the data as such but how participants talked about nature indicated their appreciation of it. For instance, in addition of reflecting one's own emotions, one participant also reflected on 'feelings of nature'. While visiting a place that included several wood sculptures with a nature theme, a participant stated that:

> I had no expectations, and I went to the place by wondering a bit what it is about, but it was stunning. I think that the trees were also happy that she [the artist] selected them. I was touched by the art and her [the artist's] life. (woman, 55b)

This reflects the pathway of compassion through consideration of the happiness of trees. This acknowledges the intertwined nature of the pathways; in this case how an appreciation of the *beauty* of the nature-inspired artwork can create a sense of *compassion* and result in the creation of *meaning* by communicating the artists life through natural symbolism.

As well as considering the perspective of nature, the pathway of *compassion* was demonstrated through appreciation of how nature was used during the experience. Participants appreciated that food was locally produced or gathered from the wild. The appreciation of nature and respect towards how Finnish utilise natural resources was stated by one participant:

> I'm pleased that I was able to make a souvenir from a birch bark. I can feel that [Finnish] care for their forests, as they utilize diverse parts of the tree, not just the wood, and nothing goes to waste. (woman, 55b)

The participants were also interested in nature-related knowledge, which was linked to the ways Finnish people take care of their environment. Recognising the significance of nothing goes to waste suggests an awareness of actions and an ethical concern (Lumber et al., 2017). They were also interested in hearing more about human–nature relationships and what the meaning of nature is for Finnish people. This sense of gratitude and awareness of kindness towards nature again reflects aspects of eudaimonia (e.g., Huta & Ryan, 2010), whilst retaining the traditional role of tourism in providing a 'souvenir'. In this case, the souvenir is from nature and suggests a changing role of tourism consumption, from goods to symbolic elements that reflect the meaning of the experience.

7.4.2.5 *Meaning*

Meaning was less explicitly evidenced than the other pathways. Yet, one example of using nature to communicate an idea (Lumber et al., 2017) was demonstrated by the guide, and encompasses many of the discussed pathways.

The following guiding situation was very memorable for most of the participants of the trip (field notes):

> We were having a break on top of ridge, and we were surrounded by water from two sides. While having a little snack our guide started to talk about his own experience of nature and how he feels that nature is a place for calming down. He emphasised that it is important to experience "small moments" that help a person to relax and evolve. He continued that because of the hectic everyday life, human's life is not a full cycle anymore, but it consists of small separate pieces (he was highlighting this by putting small wooden sticks one after another).

Here the meaning pathway is demonstrated through utilising nature to communicate what nature means to the guide. Using the sticks to visual this idea shows how the guide inspires the participants to consider the meaning of nature:

> He said that with small moments of stopping and calming down these pieces can be unified and the cycle of life can become whole again. Japanese were listening to the guide very carefully and many of them were nodding while listening. One Japanese woman (the one that shed into tears also in Koli) seemed to react very strongly to the situation and shed into tears. When our guide asked people to share their experiences, some of the Japanese said that there are many Japanese that are very busy and who don't have time, or even can, to calm down and relax. They also felt that natural environment like this was an ideal place to find their own moments. (Field notes)

This excerpt shows that a skilful guide can help the participants to find ways to understand the role of nature and how it may enhance people's wellbeing. Here the simultaneous idea of relaxing and evolving echoes the idea of the synergistic way hedonia and eudaimonia can be experienced (Henderson & Knight, 2012); relaxation given more meaning as it allows a person to develop through this sense of being at ease. The guide and the participants recognise nature's ability to allow people to 'find their own moments' and reinforce that this connection can make lives richer and meaningful (Nisbet et al., 2011).

Data analysis shows that diverse pathways of nature connectedness (Lumber et al., 2017) can be identified. From the five pathways, three, namely contact, beauty and emotion, were easily recognisable and occurred the most. It can be seen from the data that the pathways are linked to each other and occur together within individual accounts of experiences. This is perhaps due to the customers of the forest-based wellbeing tourism trip describing the core experience as being able to immerse into the forest environment in a variety of ways.

7.5   Conclusion

The data acknowledges the powerful role of nature in creating meaningful experiences though the landscape, natural elements, and activities. These experiences were described as extraordinary and novel. The findings demonstrate tourism's potential to incorporate the pathways to nature connection (Lumber et al., 2017) into the design and delivery of experiences, and the significant role of the guide in facilitating this. This reinforces that emotional outcomes are rooted in the relationship between consumer and provider (Arnould & Price, 1993). Hence, the findings give insight into what makes nature-based wellbeing tourism experiences meaningful and memorable for customers.

The findings of this study also support the findings of Buckley (2019) by indicating that nature-based tourism services can bring diverse wellbeing benefits for customers, and hence, open up new business opportunities for nature-based tourism service providers in the future. This chapter considers how to operationalise nature connection and incorporate activities into the design and delivery of tourism experiences that focus on the wellbeing benefits of connecting with nature. The data also demonstrated that many of these experiences can be considered eudaimonic, furthering the understanding of how eudaimonia is researched and created through tourism experiences (e.g., Filep, 2016).

Future research should consider how to incorporate the pathways of nature connection directly into the design and delivery of tourism experiences, to further explore their effectiveness. Doing so would allow one to evaluate how tourists' experience and interpret these pathways. More targeted questions regarding how far participants believed a connection with nature had formed would also help map the pathways to an overall sense of connection with nature because of the tourism experience. This could also be explored in different destinations and activities to consider the role of different natural environments and contexts, and how the pathways could be applied to them.

Further studies could also consider how to incorporate lesser evidenced pathways in this research, for example, the pathway of compassion. Although this was evident in the data through tourists' appreciating the role of nature, and the Finnish attitudes and behaviours towards it, specific activities that allow tourists' to directly contribute to environmentally friendly practices (Smith & Diekmann, 2017) would help the pathway of compassion to be realised. Much in the way tourists appreciated how the Finnish respect nature, it could be communicated how their own actions outside of the tourism setting can provide this in their home environments. This suggests the service provider has an important role in communicating ways to engage and connect with nature, so a positive relationship continues outside of the tourism setting.

This chapter aimed to explore how pathways to nature connection occur in wellbeing tourism experiences, and how connection with nature can be facilitated by tourism providers. The main theoretical contribution of this chapter lies in exploring Lumber et al.'s (2017) pathways to nature connectedness in tourism research, acknowledging the recommendation for the use of these pathways by organisations to connect people to nature (Lumber et al, 2017). This holds particular promise within the tourism and wellbeing discourse as it considers how nature connectedness can build upon existing wellbeing theories to act as a bridge between experience provision and wellbeing outcomes. Its practical contribution lies in considering how to operationalise nature connectedness to incorporate this into the design and delivery of tourism experiences that focus on the wellbeing benefits of connecting with nature.

References

Arnould, E. J., & Price, L. L. (1993). River magic: Extraordinary experience and the extended service encounter. *Journal of Consumer Research, 20*(1), 24–45.

Bimonte, S., & Faralla, V. (2014). Happiness and nature-based vacations. *Annals of Tourism Research, 46*, 176–178. https://doi.org/10.1016/j.annals.2014.02.002.

Buckley, R. C. (2019). Therapeutic mental health effects perceived by outdoor tourists: A large-scale, multi-decade, qualitative analysis. *Annals of Tourism Research 77*, 164–167. https://doi.org/10.1016/j.annals.2018.12.017.

Bushell, R., & Sheldon, P. J. (Eds.). (2009). *Wellness and tourism: Mind, body, spirit, place.* Cognizant Communication.

Business Finland. (2022). Matkailu Japanista Suomeen [Travelling from Japan to Finland]. https:// www .businessfinland .fi/ suomalaisille -asiakkaille/ palvelut/ matkailun-edistaminen/toiminta-markkinoilla/japani. Accessed 24.10.2022.

Cakmak, E., & Isaac, R. K. (2012). What destination marketers can learn from their visitors' blogs: An image analysis of Bethlehem, Palestine. *Journal of Destination Marketing & Management, 1*(1–2), 124–133.

Capaldi, C. A., Dopko, R. L., & Zelenski, J. M. (2014). The relationship between nature connectedness and happiness: A meta-analysis. *Frontiers in Psychology, 5*, 1–28.

Chen, H.-T., Yu, C.-P., Lee, H.-Y., Chen, H.-T., Yu, C.-P., & Lee, H.-Y. (2018). The effects of forest bathing on stress recovery: Evidence from middle-aged females of Taiwan. *Forests, 9*(7), 403. https://doi.org/10.3390/f9070403.

Cleary, A., Fielding, K. S., Bell, S. L., Murray, Z., & Roiko, A. (2017). Exploring potential mechanisms involved in the relationship between eudaimonic wellbeing and nature connection. *Landscape and Urban Planning, 158*, 119–128. https://doi.org/10.1016/j .landurbplan.2016.10.003.

Eriksson, P., & Kovalainen, A. (2016). *Qualitative methods in business research*, 2nd Edition. SAGE Publications.

Filep, S. (2016). Tourism and positive psychology critique: Too emotional? *Annals of Tourism Research, 59*, 113–115. https://doi.org/10.1016/j.annals.2016.04.004.

Fredman, P., Wall-Reinius, S., & Grundén, A. (2012). The nature of nature in nature-based tourism. *Scandinavian Journal of Hospitality and Tourism, 12*(4), 289–309.

Gesler, W. M. (1996). Lourdes: Healing in a place of pilgrimage. *Health & Place, 2*(2), 95–105.

Hanna, P., Wijesinghe, S., Paliatsos, I., Walker, C., Adams, M., & Kimbu, A. (2019). Active engagement with nature: outdoor adventure tourism, sustainability and wellbeing. *Journal of Sustainable Tourism, 27*(9), 1355–1373.

Hansen, A. S. (2018). The visitor: Connecting health, wellbeing and the natural environment. In I. Azara (ed). *Tourism, health, wellbeing and protected areas* (pp. 125–137). CABI.

Hartwell, H., Fyall, A., Willis, C., Page, S., Ladkin, A., & Hemingway, A. (2016). Progress in tourism and destination wellbeing research. *Current Issues in Tourism, 21*(16), 1830–1892.

Henderson, L. W., & Knight, T. (2012). Integrating the hedonic and eudaimonic perspectives to more comprehensively understand wellbeing and pathways to wellbeing. *International Journal of Wellbeing*, 2(3), 196–221. doi:10.5502/ijw.v2i3.3.

Houge Mackenzie, S., & Brymer, E. (2020). Conceptualizing adventurous nature sport: A positive psychology perspective. *Annals of Leisure Research, 23*(1), 79–91.

Huta, V., & Ryan, R. M. (2010). Pursuing pleasure or virtue: The differential and overlapping well-being benefits of hedonic and eudaimonic motives. *Journal of Happiness Studies, 11*(6), 735–762.

Kellert, S. H. (1993). The biological basis for human values of nature. In S. H. Kellert & E. O. Wilson (eds), *The biophilia hypothesis*. Island.

Kim, J. (2014). The antecedents of memorable tourism experiences: The development of a scale to measure the destination attributes associated with memorable experiences. *Tourism Management, 44*, 34–45. https://doi.org/10.1016/j.tourman.2014.02.007.

Kirillova, K., Lehto, X., & Cai, L. (2017). Tourism and existential transformation: An empirical investigation. *Journal of Travel Research, 56*(5), 638–650.

Komppula, R., & Konu, H. (2012). Do wellbeing tourists expect memorable experiences? In M. Kozak & N. Kozak (eds), *Proceedings of 6th World Conference for Graduate Research in Tourism, Hospitality and Leisure, Ankara, Turkey* (pp. 462–474).

Konu, H. (2015). Developing a forest-based wellbeing tourism product together with customers - An ethnographic approach. *Tourism Management, 49*, 1–16. https://doi.org/10.1016/j.tourman.2015.02.006.

Konu, H., & Pesonen, J. (2018). Rural well-being tourism in Northern Europe - Providing opportunities to enhance quality of life. In M., Uysal, J. M. Sirgy, & S. Kruger (eds). *Managing quality of life in tourism and hospitality* (pp. 119–137). CABI.

Konu, H., Tuohino, A., & Komppula, R. (2010). Lake wellness – a practical example of a new service development (NSD) concept in tourism industry. *Journal of Vacation Marketing, 16*(2), 125–139.

Knobloch, U., Robertson, K., & Aitken, R. (2017). Experience, emotion, and eudaimonia: A consideration of tourist experiences and well-being. *Journal of Travel Research, 56*(5), 651–662.

Lea, J. (2008). Retreating to nature: Rethinking 'therapeutic landscapes.' *Area, 40*(1), 90–98.

Lee, J., Park, B. J., Tsunetsugu, Y., Kagawa, T., & Miyazaki, Y. (2009). Restorative effects of viewing real forest landscapes, based on a comparison with urban landscapes. *Scandinavian Journal of Forest Research, 24*, 227–324.

Little, J. (2012). Transformational tourism, nature and wellbeing: New perspectives on fitness and the body. *Sociologia Ruralis, 52*(3), 257–271.

Lumber, R., Richardson, M., & Sheffield, D. (2017). Beyond knowing nature: Contact, emotion, compassion, meaning, and beauty are pathways to nature connection. *PloS One, 12*(5), e0177186.

Nisbet, E. K., & Zelenski, J. M. (2013). The NR-6: a new brief measure of nature related-ness. *Frontiers in Psychology, 4*, 813.

Nisbet, E. K., Zelenski, J. M., & Murphy, S. A. (2011). Happiness is in our nature: Exploring nature relatedness as a contributor to subjective well-being. *Journal of Happiness Studies, 12*, 303–322. https://doi.org/10.1007/s10902-010-9197-7.

Morita, E., Fukuda, S., Nagano, J., Hamajima, N., Yamamoto, H., & Iwai, Y. (2007). Psychological effects of forest environments on healthy adults: Shinrin-yoku (forest-air bathing, walking) as possible method of stress reduction. *Public Health, 121*, 54–63.

Ohtsuka, Y., Yabunaka, N., & Takayama, S. (1998). Shinrin-yoku (forest-air bathing and walking) effectively decreases blood glucose levels in diabetic patients. *International Journal of Biometeorol, 41*, 125–127.

Pechlaner, H., & Fischer, E. (2006). Alpine wellness: A resource-based view. *Tourism Recreation Research, 31*(1), 67–77.

Smith, M., & Puczkó, L. (2009). *Health and wellness tourism*. Butterworth-Heinemann.

Smith, M. K., & Diekmann, A. (2017). Tourism and wellbeing. *Annals of Tourism Research, 66*, 1–13.

Sorakunnas, E. (2020). Dimensions and drivers of national park experiences: A longitu-dinal study of independent visitors. *Journal of Outdoor Recreation and Tourism, 31*, 100311. https://doi.org/10.1016/j.jort.2020.100311.

Sthapit, E., & Coudounaris, D. N. (2018). Memorable tourism experiences: Antecedents and outcomes, *18*(1), 72-94, https://doi.org/10.1177/0047287510385467.

Tucker, H., & Shelton, E.J. (2018). Tourism, mood and affect: Narratives of loss and hope. *Annals of Tourism Research, 70*, 66–75. https://doi.org/10.1016/j.annals.2018 .03.001.

Voigt, C., Brown, G., & Howat, G. (2011). Wellness tourists: In search of transforma-tion. *Tourism Review, 66*(1/2), 16–30. https://doi.org/10.1108/16605371111127206.

Wilson, E. (1984). *Biophilia*. Harvard University Press.

Wolf, I. D., Stricker, H. K., & Hagenloh, G. (2015). Outcome-focused national park experience management: Transforming participants, promoting social well-being, and fostering place attachment. *Journal of Sustainable Tourism, 23*(3), 358–381. https://doi.org/10.1080/09669582.2014.959968.

Zuo, S., Wang, S., Wang, F., & Shi, X. (2017). The behavioural paths to wellbeing: An exploratory study to distinguish between hedonic and eudaimonic wellbeing from an activity perspective. *Journal of Pacific Rim Psychology, 11*, 1–13. https://doi.org/10.1017/prp.2017.1.

8 Why blue spaces and wellbeing matter for tourism and leisure businesses

Catherine Kelly

8.1 Introduction

Blue spaces, defined simply as all natural surface waters, form a vital part of the human–nature interface in the tourism and leisure sectors. Much research has been conducted on green spaces in nature-based tourism, but the work on blue spaces lags behind somewhat. While often taken for granted as a backdrop to tourism, oceans, seas, lakes, and rivers are, in fact, often pivotal in tourist destination decision-making. This chapter explores how blue spaces are linked to wellbeing, and how they can be framed as 'therapeutic landscapes', where physical, psychological, and social wellbeing parameters are improved for visitors. Furthermore, tourism businesses and DMOs (destination management organisations) are encouraged to learn about the wellbeing benefits of their own nearby blue spaces, in order to better position their services and destination to a wider range of visitors. Thinking innovatively and collaboratively is critical to the effective delivery of visitor experiences that merge the expertise of the worlds of health, wellbeing, and natural environments within the realm of tourism.

This chapter takes a UK focus and presents a saltwater, coastal blue space example of the city of Brighton in southern England to assess blue space wellbeing tourism. Wider sectoral policy and tourism business practice recommendations are made for centralising wellbeing and blue spaces in product, service, and destination offerings. As such, this work therefore offers a unique moment-in-time analysis of opportunities for the sector to capitalise on the post-Covid human need to reconnect with self, others and our blue environment. It is through understanding the tenets of wellbeing, blue space offerings in conjunction with the interplay of stakeholders and policy imperatives, that beneficial leverage of the current world context can be applied. Tourism businesses are in a unique position to develop creative, collaborative wellbeing tourism experiences, grounded in research-informed approaches.

8.2 Blue Spaces and Wellbeing

Humans love, need, and will save their money to spend holidays beside or in water. The coast and other water environments account for 71% of the planet's surface, 96% of which are made up of saltwater oceans and seas (US Geological Survey, 2019). Blue space is a term used to describe all natural surface waters (Volker & Kistemann, 2011), although some would argue for the inclusion of manmade features such as canals, swimming pools, spas, thermal baths, and fountains as part of a wider definition. In essence, 'blue space' denotes the presence of water.

For several decades, research has focused on the importance of nature, or green spaces, for human wellbeing (Mitchell & Popham, 2007; Maas et al., 2008; White, Alcock et al., 2013), and blue spaces were implicitly included as part of this wider nature setting. Indeed, Britton et al. (2020) noted that blue space is often assumed under the umbrella concept of green space or green infrastructure where the assumption is that these spaces will 'improve environmental conditions and therefore citizens' health and quality of life' (p. 52). Historically, specific blue spaces have gained long-standing reputations for healing or wellness, including 'sacred' springs, holy wells, Eastern European *terme*, Greek, Roman and Turkish baths, Japanese *onsen*, and the Scandinavian penchant for mixing hot saunas with ice water dips (Foley, 2011; Bell et al., 2015). This chapter encompasses the idea of salutogenic wellbeing, where we focus on blue space activities and behaviours that improve or maintain our general balance of physical, psychological, and social or spiritual wellbeing with the aim of prevent ill-health.

8.3 Blue Spaces, Wellbeing, and Tourism

Wellbeing, or wellness tourism, has been a growing focus of research for the last number of decades (Smith & Kelly, 2006; Kelly & Smith, 2008; Smith & Puckzo, 2008; Kelly, 2010; Pensonen et al., 2011; Chen et al., 2013; Li & Hin, 2020). Concurrently, there has been a plethora of research in the field of nature-based tourism, ecotourism, and sustainable tourism (Page & Dowling, 2002; Weaver, 2013; Mihalic, 2016; Edgell, 2016) The interface of wellbeing and nature-focused tourism dovetails smoothly into blue spaces tourism, where opportunities for both come together. It must be noted here that blue space wellbeing means different things to different tourists; for some it will encapsulate a cocktail by the pool, a slow canal boat tourism experience, or a thalassotherapy treatment in a thermal spa. Not all imply outdoor, wild, natural, or coastal experiences. Therefore, we must acknowledge this varied spectrum of need and delivery across the sector.

In recent years, new research has focused on different blue spaces and the ways in which water can improve our health and wellbeing. Poulsen et al. (2022) gathered evidence for wellbeing impacts in freshwater blue space (FBS). Furthermore, the 'healthy coast effect' is another useful example of research from the field of health and environment studies which can be applied to tourism and leisure. Data from two large nationally representative surveys of leisure visits to the coast in England suggest that restoration/stress reduction is integral to this concept (Wheeler et al., 2012; White, Pahl et al., 2013). More research is needed, however, to differentiate between coastal residents, coastal visitors, length of stay, type of activity, demographic groupings, age, and gender (Kelly, 2018) for this research to transpose usefully across to tourism policy makers and businesses. As knowledge is gathered, more informed, holistic and interdisciplinary policy and interventions can be generated in future, as we shall explore in this chapter. To date, much of this work has concentrated on studies outside of the tourism sector, and we in the tourism and leisure academy, often 'borrow the facts and evidence', applying them to blue space tourism settings (Brereton et al., 2008; White et al., 2011; Gascon et al., 2017).

In the tourism sector, we are interested in not just the presence of blue spaces themselves, but the ways in which visitors choose to engage with them. For some, blue spaces will be places to lie next to, on a beach or lakeside, to sit beside and gaze out at, to walk or run beside, or, for many, to throw themselves into with joyful abandon, to swim, surf, paddleboard, boat, dive, or snorkel through. Volks and Kistemann (2011) referred to four main categories of blue space leisure engagement: a) kinetic, b) situation-based, c) contemplative, and d) harvesting. Sequentially, these relate in turn to movement in water (kayaking or surfing for example); having a 'favourite spot' to sit next to the water, or a favourite cove, lake, or rivershore; the practice of just 'being' by water, where we direct our gaze to the horizon and breathe; and, finally, fishing or harvesting biomatter from the water or its shores. It is important to classify these activities mainly so tourism businesses are aware of the range of market segments that may be attracted to each. There may well be overlap, but culture, age, and gender specificity play a role in preferences and practices in or next to blue spaces. Juster-Horsfield and Bell (2022) examine the idea of 'blue care' through outdoor water-based activities via practitioner perspectives. An even broader perspective of water wellbeing interfaces are offered in a special issue of the *Journal of Sport and Social Issues* (2021), entitled 'Understanding Blue Spaces: Sport, Bodies, Wellbeing, and the Sea'. Outdoor swimming and surfing are examined specifically, and both are examples of a growing tourism special interest sector.

Research suggests that blue spaces impact our wellbeing in three main areas: physical, psychological, and social (Tipton et al., 2017; Harper, 2017; Denton & Aranda, 2019; Kelly, 2021). Physical wellbeing activities form a core part of tourism experiences for many. Taking a walk or run by the sea, lake, or river, swimming in turquoise waters, or surfing the perfect wave are the ingredients of pleasure for many tourists. The four categories of blue space engagement mentioned earlier (kinetic, aesthetic, contemplative, harvest) encapsulate some of the psychological benefits of being in or near water on holiday. Contemplating life and watching the horizon at a water's edge allows our breath to slow down and our bodies to release the worries of our normal lives. The very nature of 'pausing' that holidays encapsulate are important for our mental health as research shows (Chen & Patrick, 2013; Chen et al., 2016). This includes social wellbeing (Kelly, 2020).

8.3.1 Therapeutic (Tourism) Landscapes, Place Attachment, and Emotional Geographies

Three useful theoretical concepts are appropriate for the examination of how and why blue spaces matter to human wellbeing. In his work on healing places, the American sociologist Gesler (1992, 1996) coined the term 'therapeutic landscapes'. According to Attention Restoration Theory (ART), natural settings are rich in features that enhance mental functioning. Blue spaces can therefore literally help to 'restore our attention', or our ability to function and focus, and be present in our daily lives – and therefore to feel well. Bell et al. (2015) presented research on the therapeutic landscape experience 'dimensions' we can engage with at the coast, and how they make us feel well in different ways. Their research has shown that some people prioritise opportunities to use the coast to progress towards personal goals or ('achieving' experiences), such as running, walking, and even long-distance swimming or other sports-related actions; others value opportunities to lose themselves ('immersive' experiences) or connect with others ('social' experiences), and for most, blue spaces are also 'symbolic experiences' with personal senses of place, belonging, identity, or attachment.

Place attachment can be described as an emotional bond or positive connection between an individual and a particular place (Kelly, 2021). We can see this, for example, when we think about our favourite holiday beach, or our favourite spot to sit by the lake or river. Place attachment can be further divided into subcategories: 'place identity', where a place has symbolic importance as a repository for emotions (a place where someone can feel well or be themselves – for many, this in the water) and relationships that give meaning to human life (such as holidays with family or friends); and 'place dependence', which refers to how places provide the conditions that facilitate people's aspirations in life (the idea that a person can live or be well here). Both aspects of place attachment, simply framed, are considered important in individual wellbeing. We know from tourism research on 'memorable tourism experiences' (MTEs) (Kim et al., 2010; Tung & Ritchie, 2011) that blue spaces are important in this sense of place attachment, through repeat holiday visits, especially for families with children (Kelly, 2020).

The concept of *'tourism-place-legacy'* is offered here to encapsulate the generational need to 'show and share' our childhood or valued blue space tourism places. Familial performances of ritual on coastal holidays form the life story of traditions and memories that feed into psychosocial wellbeing across one's life course. The coasts, coves, lakeshores and rivers of our happy memories are powerful, evocative forces for both visitors and the tourism sector itself to tune into. Finally, 'emotional geographies' refers to the feelings and emotions that are evoked by being in, or visiting certain places of meaning (Bondi & Davidson, 2006; Davidson et al., 2007). Emotions and tourism remain an emerging aspect of the discipline (Buda et al., 2014; d'Hauteserre, 2015; Gao & Kerstetter, 2018), yet, how our favourite tourism locations *make us feel* is fundamental to our positive experiences and memories. Places that heal, how we connect to them, and how they make us feel, form a circular realm of blue space wellbeing, in our daily lives and in the tourism places we choose to visit (Figure 8.1 below).

Therefore, as we can observe in Figure 8.1, there is a strong connective relationship between places that increase our *wellbeing*, places that *matter* to us, and the feelings or *emotions* that they engender in us. Blue space wellbeing remains important in a postpandemic world and the triumvirate of therapeutic landscapes, place attachment, and emotional geographies will weave meaning and significance into our tourism experiences.

Blue spaces are, however, complex to research, regulate, and direct policy for, insofar as they fall under the remit of multiple sectors. To date, they are governed by environmental departments, marine or inland waterway agencies,

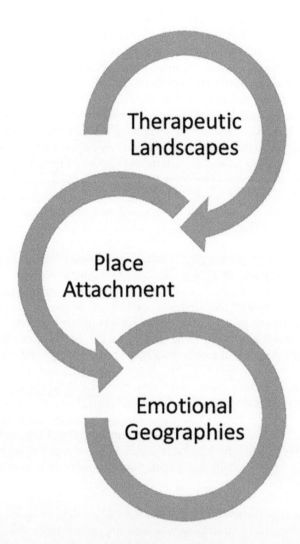

Figure 8.1   Connecting therapeutic landscapes, place attachment, and emotional geographies

tourism, leisure, and sport organisations, and, more recently, public health and wellbeing sectors. This creates difficulties in terms of a synergistic approach to their study, use, and management. The challenges lie in a cross-sectoral partnership approach to maximise their sustainable use for wellbeing and long-term inclusive engagement. We are, arguably, at a critical crossroads in our research environment, where the often taken-for-granted aspects of 'a holiday by the water', are in fact, proving to be critical for human health and wellbeing (van Tulleken, 2017; Tipton et al., 2018), the wellbeing of local/ regional blue economies, and the wellbeing of the environment itself. The role of tourism in such research and interventions is surely important, and yet, many in the tourism field do not step outside traditional research boundaries, despite the obvious centrality of both wellbeing and water in our discipline and practice. Change is therefore afoot in the research world of blue spaces – and it is important that tourism academics are at the table.

It is important to step back and consider the interrelationships between all of the themes discussed here, and how they might play out in real tourism places, with real visitors seeking to improve their wellbeing in blue spaces. We have considered the meaning of blue spaces and reviewed the emerging research agenda around them – and assessed the utility of theories of therapeutic landscapes, place attachment, and emotional geographies to show the value of such spaces for human wellbeing. We have considered the wellbeing benefits themselves, of being in or near blue spaces across a variety of dimensions. Let us turn next to examine a case study destination where blue space wellbeing tourism opportunities exist. This will be followed by an extrapolation of learning and knowledge that can be applied to tourism businesses and organisations to further promote the practical importance of these concepts.

8.4   United Kingdom Case Study: Brighton's Blue Spaces, Wellness Tourism Histories and Opportunities

8.4.1   The Past

Brighton, on the English south coast, was one of the first places in the United Kingdom to encompass the concept of coastal wellbeing for visitors. In his famous book of 1775, Dr Richard Russell, a medic with connections to royalty, exhorted the benefits of seawater for improved health. As an 18th-century remedy, it was perhaps well ahead of its time, firmly establishing Brighton as an early therapeutic landscape. However, few would encourage the actual drinking of seawater in the current environmental context of marine pollution management globally. What followed after Russell's fame was the growth of Brighton as a visitor destination, buoyed up by the escapades of the Prince Regent, George IV, and his royal entourage in the famous Royal Pavilion palace and in the Sussex coastal waters. The Victorian era saw Brighton's growth continue, with the arrival of a railway direct from London, just one hour away. Visitors continued to demand blue space wellbeing and the famous 'dipping machines' (wooden horse-drawn changing vestibules on wheels) allowed for swimming modesty to be upheld (Musgrave, 2011). Since this time, Brighton has firmly established itself as one of Britain's most visited and popular seaside tourism destinations.

8.4.2   Brighton's Contemporary Blue Space Tourism Landscape

Brighton's tourism market is diverse in nature, attracting a multitude of urban day-trippers and weekenders from the London capital nearby. The city draws an average of 10 to 12 million visitors per annum, only one million of which constitute overnight stays. Most of the visitor market looks for a fun day at the coast, with family and friend activities centred around water, food and drinks, and leisure activities (Kelly, 2020). Cultural tourism is another draw – the iconic Royal Pavilion and regency architecture are key attractions, along with the popular culture draws of independent shopping in the Laines districts, vegetarian food outlets, the Brighton festival, and a host of music and arts events across the calendar year. LGBT tourism is also key to the local economy, as the city is known fondly as the gay capital of Britain, a liberal and tolerant city for residents and visitors alike, and also hosting the largest Pride festival in the nation, although this is not without conflict and tension. Similar homogenous portrayals of Brighton and other seaside destinations as implicitly white, nonracial spaces need to be challenged (Burdsey, 2016), especially if blue space wellbeing benefits are framed as genuinely accessible to all.

Despite the historical connection to Russell's coastal wellbeing, Brighton's contemporary tourism landscape has not capitalised upon the health benefits of water in a strongly directed manner. It is an implicit tourism backdrop, rather than a unique wellbeing destination marketing anchor, which is somewhat of a missed opportunity.

The current destination management organisation, Visit Brighton's (2019) current visitor economy strategy cites wellbeing tourism as one of its key pillars. Yet, there are no flagship wellbeing attractions in the city – no spa (beyond some small offerings within a limited number of hotels) or coordinated activities or services that market wellbeing and water to tourists in a directly communicated manner. Yet, Brighton has much to offer in terms of natural resources, committed organisations, and a positive policy attitude towards the environment, nature, wellbeing, and tourism. As a liberal, alternative-lifestyle city, it is also home to a large number of individual wellbeing practitioners ranging from yoga teachers, personal trainers, complementary therapists, mindfulness instructors, nutritionists, and much more. In addition, the coast around Brighton is host to a growing number of water sports and outdoor swimming groups. These saw a surge of interest during and since the pandemic, but again, they serve mainly the local residential population and hinterland. The potential is there for collaborative, mutually beneficial cocreation of superb water and wellbeing experiences for tourists to the area.

Stakeholder analysis of the city (Morrison, 2018) shows several relevant organisations that could help the local authority to position Brighton as a unique, coastal wellbeing destination. One of only five in the United Kingdom, Brighton (and the surrounding area) holds the coveted UNESCO Biosphere designation. Its nickname, 'The Living Coast' denotes its (also unique to the United Kingdom) urban status, encompassing countryside, city, and coast (Kelly, 2016). This organisation works closely with the DMO Visit Brighton, to encourage sustainable tourism and developments that highlight the unique, cultural and environmental qualities of the area. One such successful collaboration, the 'BioCultural Heritage Tourism' project (REF online) highlighted some of the unique nature-based tourism opportunities for local enterprises and created a toolkit for implementation. Other voluntary and collaborative organisations such as the Sussex Bay project (connecting all marine organisations and interests), Sussex Underwater (an underwater kelp reforestation project, supported by Sir David Attenborough) and Leave No Trace Brighton (a beach cleaning/recycling direct action group who also target day-tripper tourists at gateway entry points to the city, to scan a litter pledge on their phone), to name a few, are already working on improving the quality of the coastal environment in Brighton.

A recent, ERDF (European Regional Development Fund) EU (European Union)-funded programme 'RISE', Research and Innovation in Sussex Excellence, involves a collaboration between both of Brighton's universities and the local authorities to encourage new growth and development in the tourism and hospitality sector. This author was part of knowledge-exchange workshops that focused on learning, capacity building, animation, and collaborative networking in the outdoor, nature, and water-based tourism sector. Participants found the sessions useful in terms of learning the key importance of wellbeing in society, the renewed importance of nature and blue spaces to customers and the opportunity to think about how to work with other, complementary small enterprises in their area. Much work remains to be done on auditing current products, services, and skill needs to ensure future collaborations and outcomes are beneficial to all. Table 8.1 assesses the current situation regarding the positioning of blue space focused wellbeing tourism in the area.

Table 8.1   SWOT analysis of blue space wellbeing tourism in Brighton

Strengths	Weaknesses
Unique seawater for wellbeing heritage Established tourism sector Popular for variety of market segments Existing wellbeing practitioners/services Breadth of interest and engagement	Disjointed approach to connecting existing operators and services across tourism, environment, wellbeing, and water interests Lack of funding for project development and marketing
Opportunities	**Threats**
Collaborative cocreation of products and experiences for tourists Huge potential for unique destination marketing focus on blue space wellbeing tourism, especially postpandemic Knowledge exchange between tourism sector, universities, and third sector	Lack of knowledge, networking opportunities and financial support Poor communication/joined up thinking from 'silos' of support agencies across tourism, public health, and environmental sectors Competition from other coastal destinations

Brighton is well placed as a coastal city within a one-hour travel distance from London to attract both day visitors and overnighters who often seek a 'short hit' of sea, culture and activities. Building upon Pine and Gilmore's (2011) model of the experience economy, Figure 8.2, below looks as aspects of 'the four Es' (entertainment, education, esthetics, and escapism), as they can be applied to the Brighton area for blue space wellbeing.

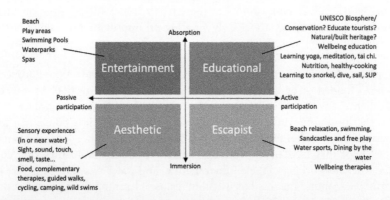

Figure 8.2   Adapted experience economy analysis for blue space wellbeing tourism in Brighton (after Pine and Gilmore, 2011)

This model can be applied to the destination in conjunction with a SWOT analysis to give both tourism organisation, stakeholders, and new or existing businesses an opportunity to think about new ways of seeing their own area and how it is currently offered to visitors.

8.5   Applying Blue Space and Wellbeing Recommendations for all Destinations and Tourism Businesses

For blue space wellbeing to be really understood in a tourism context, professionals, policymakers, organisations, and researchers in the fields of health and wellbeing, environment/sustainability, business, and the tourism and leisure sectors need to work together. It is critical that they are aware of each other's language, policies, funding structures and, most importantly, their common areas of potential overlap.

Four key themes are therefore suggested here for examining/actualising the potential of the blue space wellbeing agenda for tourism and leisure sectors:

8.5.1   Centralising Blue Spaces, Wellbeing and Nature in Marketing Messages

In terms of tourism businesses wishing to make more of the fact that they are located near water, or to emphasise a wellbeing message, the following are key takeaway points to encompass in product/service design and marketing messages:

- Being in or near blue space, and nature immersion are essential for good mental, physical health, and social wellbeing
- Green and blue spaces offer: ecosystem services, (the many economic/social/ecological benefits that nature gives to humans) carbon sequestration (reducing 'bad CO_2'), and air purity
- Contact with nature/blue space brings a sense of wellbeing and promotes an active lifestyle for tourists and locals
- Staying in touch with nature/blue space promotes calm and reduces stress
- Contact with nature/blue space strengthens the cohesion of the community by reducing social isolation, and encourages positive family holiday relationship building/repair
- Place attachment and emotional geographies therefore matter to visitors

To highlight the importance of blue space and nature for the wellbeing of its users, new and existing tourism businesses near water can actively offer guided tours and nature walks, sports activities, wellbeing experiences, education activities, conferences, and seminars that *centralise* blue space in their offering.

Ways that tourism businesses can implement this in their content and materials include:

- Highlighting aspects of the service/business activities that motivate a healthy lifestyle and personal wellbeing
- Show the natural resources the service uses, such as the sea, food, and water
- Bring people closer to environmental education (blue spaces) to make them understand how it contributes to their physical, social, and psychological wellbeing
- Explain explicitly how people can benefit from the service/product on offer
- Demonstrate how the enterprise contributes to human health and how people can make it part of their daily lives or holiday activities
- Think about the role of emotions, place, and memories in the tourism offering, bearing in mind the social wellbeing impacts that holidays by the water hold for many people
- Use a joined up/collaborative approach to get the services and expertise a single business or sole trader/practitioner are missing
- Freelance yoga, wellbeing, or lifestyle entrepreneurs can offer services to the accommodation sector for example, and to business and events tourists (fluid, flexible approach)
- A directory of blue space wellbeing therapists/providers/experts/products can be collated by local tourism authorities – especially those where there are values alignment around intended markets). For example:
  - Nutrition and physical fitness experts can collaborate with tourism accommodation and food sectors; outdoor camping sites can collaborate with arts, and water sports providers to meet the family market; therapists can block book weekend services at guest houses, self-catering accommodation or glamping sites, and much more
  - Marketing and tech freelancers can join all of the above to provide expertise and training
- All the above help to solidify or reposition nature/blue space/wellbeing more significantly to reach new tourism markets with flexible needs across different age brackets, genders, and cultures.

8.5.2   Micro-experiences, Collaboration, and Coproduction

Destinations can build on Pine and Gilmore's (2011) concept of the experience economy to meet the needs of the short-break market in particular. The need for a short holiday in an urban, stress-rich, time-poor world will always be a constant in the tourism sector. The idea of micro-experiences REF involves the visitor engaging with a collection of 'taster' products and services in a one- or two-day timeframe. Given the post-COVID renewed interest in blue spaces, nature, wellbeing, and the wider outdoors, the time is right for these facets to be presented, packaged, and marketed together by destinations. This requires stakeholder and DMO collaboration (Morrison, 2018). In some destinations, many small tourism businesses may be working with a DMO, but given the breadth of scope of blue spaces and wellbeing, many will not. Few complementary therapists or yoga teachers in a city, for example, might think to contact a hotel to offer classes to tourists. The same may be true of interactions between water-based sports operators, food experts or environmental educators. Yet, together, these pieces make up a wonderful jigsaw puzzle of sustainable, blue space wellness offerings. More creative and cross-sectoral thinking is needed if we are to do tourism differently. We need to encourage the current silos of valuable health, environment, leisure, and aquatic expertise to share their knowledge to coproduce exciting new opportunities through the correct stakeholder frameworks and processes (Perkins et al., 2020).

8.5.3   Accessibility and Participation

Blue space wellbeing matters to everyone and so it follows that our coasts, rivers, and waterways should be accessible to everyone – physically, socially, economically, and culturally. It is important that the tourism sector acknowledges its responsibility in ensuring that all visitors can participate in blue space wellbeing. Different countries will have their own legal requirements and monitoring systems for accessibility rights. However, it is no longer acceptable to disenfranchise residents/visitors with physical or sensory disabilities, or those with long-term health conditions from enjoying the huge wellbeing benefits that blue spaces offer. Several organisations and agencies in the United Kingdom are directing research towards blue spaces and access inequalities, such as the Blue Spaces Forum of the Environment Agency and the current Arts & Humanities Research Council's call for research on the reduction of health disparities (AHRC, 2022). It is always easier to assess scenarios and impacts for permanent residents, yet the need for respite for temporary access to blue spaces for tourists with special needs must also be given space in the wider health and wellbeing policy and research agendas.

8.5.4 Sustainability

Water and wellbeing are at the heart of contemporary debates about sustainability. Global media has taken the cause of the oceans to heart with the surge in popularity of documentary programmes such as *Blue Planet*, led by Sir David Attenborough. In addition, the climate crisis remains at the top of the political agenda, with the minister of Tuvalu in the Pacific Ocean famously giving his pleas for help speech 'We are Sinking', at the COP (Conference of the Parties) 26 world gathering in Glasgow in 2021. Alongside the recent G7 event in the UK, a 'Sea 7' programme was devised by some of the leading thinkers on blue spaces and ocean conservation. There were calls by Alexandra Cousteau (granddaughter of the explorer Jacques Cousteau) and W. J. Nichols, author of *Blue Mind*, among others, to consider what a healthy ocean is worth to us as a planet, not just economically, but environmentally and emotionally. These conversations hold much resonance for the tourism sector itself, as it depends hugely on clean, healthy blue spaces for much of its offering. Sea 7 (Sea 7, 2021; Finisterre, 2021) observed that exploitation of blue spaces is an outdated form of economics, and that eco-innovation using digital technology and human creativity is the way forward, where our planetary values must be aligned to our work. Cousteau calls for a new form of 'regenerative economics', where we must articulate what we want to rebuild, and how – rather than sustain what is left. She acknowledges, rightly, that there is little point in using the term 'sustainability' for blue spaces that have been damaged, polluted, and abused by all sectors – and calls instead for the '3 R's: Restoration, Regeneration and Rebuilding'. This approach is meaningful for tourism destinations that rely on the coast or other blue spaces as part of their key offering. Nichols suggests that our language of the oceans has always been related to concepts of 'resource and monetary value', but we know that since the global pandemic, nature connections have surged, and emotional values are fundamental to the wellbeing of blue spaces and the people that visit them. Encapsulating this in our tourism consumer behaviour and the destinations we engage with will be key in a regenerative economy of the future.

Collectively, these four areas need to be addressed by the tourism sector, and need to be supported with research into best practice and needs analysis for both destinations and tourists alike, on how we can move forward sustainably, innovatively, and collaboratively with blue space wellbeing as a core offering.

8.6   Conclusion

The themes covered in this chapter matter on many levels. Firstly, we are living through a unique moment in time in the world's history, where we have had perhaps the only ever 'pause and reflect' opportunity as a planet. During this pause, our very lives were under threat from a virus we struggled to curtail. And yet, amidst this were renewed engagements with Maslow's (1943) basic levels of human needs – physical health, safety, and connection. Wellbeing became a critical focus in terms of how we survived the new world that we faced – physically, emotionally, and psychosocially. It continues to be critical as we garner ways to stay connected to ourselves, to others and to our natural environment. When we could not travel to places we loved for holidays, they became even more precious to us. Many have taken to their travels again with renewed appreciation, but with a refocused desire to stay healthy and well. Blue spaces afford us an environment in which we can relax, have fun, connect, and be well on holiday.

Secondly, the themes discussed here matter in that they challenge the tourism sector to learn about and heed the call for understanding both water and wellbeing in new ways. Knowledge exchange is critical, as we have seen in the Brighton case study example, between a range of sectors that may not always have traditionally connected their policies, practices and services. Linking together businesses in the tourism sector with health and wellbeing practition-ers, environmentalists and outdoor leisure providers is critical for a joined-up approach to a future that meets the needs of visitors. Coproduction is key, but research is needed to establish levels of existing knowledge, provision, and potential collaboration at local and destination levels. From there, blue space-centred wellbeing experiences can be created in innovative, value-led ways.

Finally, this work is important because it is a call to embed our research and practices in new ways of thinking sustainably. The old economics of exploiting our natural resources in tourism commodifications of landscape and water can no longer be tolerated. Renewable economies that prioritise environmental custodianship and respond to new human values around planetary care must be taken on board by the tourism sector. Focusing on water and wellbeing is one way 'in' to this debate and new realignment. When we understand more about how visitors emotionally value the places and holidays that give them respite and a sense of existential authenticity, we can plan for how best to manage those places and develop new, value-led offerings. Humans need blue spaces, and they, in turn, need positive human custodianship. This reciprocity must be a basic premise to tourism research and practice of the future.

The impacts of thinking about these new ways forward for tourism are immense. There is an opportunity at hand in this unique moment in time, to 'do tourism business differently' and for governance structures to support such new ways of doing. Both research and financial support are needed to investigate the best ways to support a multisector informed, but wellbeing-focused tourism sector that operates in many fragile blue spaces. What we do know, is that blue spaces matter enormously to visitors and their sense of wellbeing and that they must be looked after. New ways of thinking are critical now as the world faces health, wellbeing and environmental crises in ways never before imagined. It is within our realm to cope with these challenges – based on knowledge, research, understanding, and action.

References

Arts Humanities Research Council (AHRC). (2022). *Build community research consortia to address health disparities: Call for research*. https://www.ukri.org/opportunity/build-community-research-consortia-to-address-health-disparities/.

Bell, S. L., Phoenix, C., Lovell, R., & Wheeler, B. W. (2015) Seeking everyday wellbeing: The coast as a therapeutic landscape. *Social Science and Medicine 142*, 56–67.

Brereton, F., Clinch, J. P., & Ferreira, S. (2008). Happiness, geography and the environment. *Ecological Economics, 65*(2), 386–396.

Britton, E., Kindermann, G., Domegan, C., & Carlin, C. (2020). Blue care: A systematic review of blue space interventions for health and wellbeing. *Health Promotion International, 35*(1), 50–69. https://doi.org/10.1093/heapro/day103.

Burdsey, D. (2016). *Race, place and the seaside: Postcards from the edge*. London: Palgrave Macmillan.

Chen, C. C., & Petrick, J. F. (2013). Health and wellness benefits of travel experiences: A literature review. *Journal of Travel Research, 52*(6), 709–719.

Chen, C. C., Petrick, J. F., & Shahvali, M. (2016). Tourism experiences as a stress reliever: Examining the effects of tourism recovery experiences on life satisfaction. *Journal of Travel Research, 55*(2), 150–160.

Chen, Y., Lehto, X. Y., & Cai, L. (2013). Vacation and well-being: A study of Chinese tourists. *Annals of Tourism Research, 42*, 284–310.

Davidson, J., Bondi, L., & Smith, M. (2007). *Emotional geographies*. Ashgate: Aldershot.

Denton, H. & Aranda, K. (2019) The wellbeing benefits of sea swimming: Is it time to revisit the sea cure? *Qualitative Research in Sport, Exercise and Health, 12*(5), 647-663. https://doi.org/10.1080/2159676X.2019.1649714.

D'Hauteserre, A. M. (2015) Affect theory and the attractivity of destinations. *Annals of Tourism, 55*, 77–89.

Edgell, D. L. (2016). *Managing sustainable tourism – a legacy for the future* (2nd ed.). Abingdon: Routledge.

Foley, R., (2011). Performing health in place: The holy well as a therapeutic assemblage. *Health Place, 17*, 470–479.

Gao, J., & Kerstetter, D. L. (2018). From sad to happy to happier: Emotion regulation strategies used during a vacation. *Annals of Tourism Research, 69*, 1–14.

Gascon, M., Zijlema, W., Vert, C., White, M. P., & Nieuwenhuijsen, M. J. (2017). Outdoor blue spaces, human health and well-being: A systematic review of quantitative studies. *International Journal of Hygiene and Environmental Health, 220*(8), 1207–1221.

Gesler, W. (1992). Therapeutic landscapes: Medical issues in the light of the new cultural geography. *Social Sciences and Medicine, 34*, 735–746.

Gesler, W. (1996). Lourdes: Healing in a place of pilgrimage. *Health Place, 2*, 95–105.

Harper, M. (2017). *The healing madness of sea-swimming*. YouTube. https://www .youtube.com/watch?v=0pXLF0sucDU.

Horizon 2020. (2021). Developing nature-based therapy for health and well-being. Horizon Europe – Work Programme 2021–2022. Division of Food, Bioeconomy, Natural Resources, Agriculture and Environment. European Commission. https:// ec.europa.eu/info/funding-tenders/opportunities/portal/screen/opportunities/topic -details/horizon-cl6-2022-communities-02-02-two-stage.

Journal of Sport and Social Issues. (2021). Special 'Understanding Blue Spaces: Sport, Bodies, Wellbeing, and the Sea'. *45*(1). https://journals.sagepub.com/toc/jss/45/1.

Juster-Horsfield, H. H., & Bell, S. L. (2022). Supporting 'blue care' through outdoor water-based activities: Practitioner perspectives. *Qualitative Research in Sport, Exercise and Health, 14*(1), 137–150. https:// doi .org/ 10 .1080/ 2159676X .2021 .1879921.

Kelly, C. (2010). Analysing wellness tourism provision: A retreat operators' study. *Journal of Hospitality and Tourism Management, 17*(1), 108–116.

Kelly, C. (2018). 'I need the sea and the sea needs me' – Symbiotic policy narratives for sustainability and wellbeing. *Journal of Marine Policy, 97*, 223–231. https://doi.org/ 10.1016/j.marpol.2018.03.023.

Kelly, C. (2020). Beyond 'a trip to the seaside': Exploring emotions and family tourism experiences. *Tourism Geographies, 24*(2–3), 284–305.

Kelly, C. (2021). *Blue spaces: How and 2hy 2ater dan make you feel better*. London: Welbeck.

Kelly, C. & Smith, M. (2008). Holistic tourism: Integrating body mind and spirit. In P. Sheldon & R. Bushell (eds), *Wellness tourism: Mind, body, spirit, place*. New Jersey, NJ: Cognizant.

Kim, J. H., Brent Ritchie, J. R., & McCormick, B. (2010), Development of a scale to measure memorable tourism experiences. *Journal of Travel Research, 51*(1), 12–25.

Maas, J., Verheij, R., Spreeuwenberg, P., & P.P., Groenewegen 2008). Physical activity as a possible mechanism behind the relationship between green space and health: A multi-level analysis. *Public Health, 8*, 260–273.

Maslow, A. H. (1943). A theory of human motivation. *Psychological Review, 50*(4), 430–437.

Mihalic, T. (2016). Sustainable-responsible tourism discourse – towards 'responsustable' tourism. *Journal of Cleaner Production, 111*, 461–470.

Mitchell, R., & Popham, F. (2007). Greenspace, urbanity and health: Relationships in England. *Journal of Epidemiology and Community Health, 61*, 681–683.

Morrison, A. (2018). *Marketing and managing tourism destinations*. 2nd Edition. Abingdon: Routledge.

Musgrave, C., 2011. *Life in Brighton*. London: The History Press.

Page, S. J., & Dowling, R. K. (2002). *Ecotourism*. Harlow, UK: Prentice Hall, Pearson Education.

Perkins, R., Khoo-Lattimore, C., & Arcodia, C. (2020). Understanding the contribution of stakeholder collaboration towards regional destination branding: A systematic narrative literature review. *Journal of Hospitality and Tourism Management, 43*, 250–258.

Pesonen, J. Laukkanen, T. and Komppula, R. (2011). Benefit Segmentation of Potential Well-being Tourists. *Journal of Vacation Marketing* 17(4): 303–314.

Pine, B. J., & Gilmore, J. H. (2011). *The experience economy*. Boston, MA: Harvard Business Press.

Poulsen, M. N., Nordberg, C. M., Fiedler, A., DeWalle, J., Mercer, D., & Schwartz, B. S. (2022). Factors associated with visiting freshwater blue space: The role of restoration and relations with mental health and well-being. *Landscape and Urban Planning, 217*, 104282.

Russell, R. (1755). *The oeconomy of nature in acute and chronical diseases of the glands*. London: Printed for J. and J. Rivington, J. Fletcher, Oxford, 1755. https://wellcomecollection.org/works/ebtrwjew.

Sea 7. (2021). *Securing the future of our ocean*. Podcast Video Panel. Finisterre. https://sea7.finisterre.com/workshop/panel-securing-the-future-of-our-ocean/.

Smith, M., & Kelly C. (2006). Journeys of the self: The rise of the wellness tourism sector. *Tourism Recreation Research, 31*(1), 15–25.

Smith, M., & Puckzo, L. (Eds). (2008). *Health and wellness tourism*. Oxford: Butterworth-Heinemann.

Tipton, M. J., Collier, N., Massey, H., Corbett, J., & Harper, M. (2017). Cold water immersion: Kill or cure? *Physiology, 102*(11), 1335-1355.

Tung, V. W. S., & Ritchie, J. R. B. (2011). Exploring the essences of memorable tourism experiences. *Annals of Tourism Research, 38*, 1367–1386.

US Geological Survey. (2019). *How much water is there on Earth?* www .usgs .gov. Accessed May 2022.

Van Tulleken, C., Tipton, M., Massey, H., & Harper, C. M. (2018). Open water swimming as a treatment for major depressive disorder. *British Medical Journal Case Reports*. https://doi.org/10.1136/bcr-2018-225007.

Visit Brighton. (2019). *The economic impact of tourism on Brighton and Hove*. https://www .visitbrighton .com/ dbimgs/ Brighton %20EIA %202019 .pdf. Accessed April 2022.

Volker, S., & Kistemann, T. (2011). The impact of blue space on human health and wellbeing: Salutogenic health effects of inland surface waters: A review. *International Journal of Hygiene and Environmental Health, 214*(6), 449–460.

Weaver, D. (2013). *Sustainable tourism – Theory and practice*. London: Routledge.

Wheeler, B. W., White, M., Stahl-Timmins, W., & Depledge, M. H. (2012) Does living by the coast improve health and wellbeing? *Health Place, 18*(5), 1198–1201. https://doi.org/10.1016/j.healthplace.2012.06.015.

White, M., Smith, A., Humphryes, K., Pahl, S., Snelling, D., & Depledge, M. (2010). Bluespace: The importance of water for preference, affect, and restorativeness in ratings of natural and built scenes. *Journal of Environmental Psychology, 30*, 482–493.

White, M. P., Alcock, I., Wheeler, B. W., & Depledge, M. H. (2013). Coastal proximity, health and well-being: Results from a longitudinal panel survey. *Health & Place, 23*, 97–103. http://dx.doi.org/10.1016/j.healthplace.2013.05.006.

White, M. P., Pahl, S., Ashbullby, K., Herbert, S., & Depledge, M. H. (2013). Feelings of restoration from recent nature visits. *Journal of Environmental Psychology, 35,* 40–51.

9 Cross-national analysis of wellness tourism concepts, tourists' motivations, and service preferences

Daumantas Bočkus, Elli Vento and Raija Komppula

9.1 Introduction

The COVID-19 pandemic has disrupted the global tourism market and has caused increased competition due to the decrease in the number of international tourists, and has also caused health and safety issues (Gössling et al., 2020). In contrast, the pandemic is also expected to increase the demand for wellness tourism services (Wen et al., 2020), as the behaviour of tourists is now being influenced by a desire to recover their mental, psychological, and physical wellbeing, which might have been affected during the that time (Azara & Foster, 2021).

Even before the pandemic, consumption of wellness tourism services had become common among ordinary people and are no longer regarded as the privilege of the elite or rich (Mueller & Kaufmann, 2001; Smith & Kelly, 2006). On the contrary, wellness is increasingly seen as a necessity and as a form of self-fulfilment and personal growth rather than a luxury (Denizci Guillet & Kucukusta, 2016; Thorne, 2021). Tourists are influenced to take wellness trips from numerous inner motivations connected to emotional, physical, spiritual, intellectual, social, and stimulus-avoidance dimensions (e.g., Smith & Puczkó, 2014, Bockus et al., 2022) and are attracted by wellness and spa services (e.g., Dryglas & Salamaga, 2017; Tsai et al., 2012) or factors like landscape, climate, destination image, and quality of services (e.g., Klenosky, 2002; Uysal et al., 2008). Motivation refers to the reason why customers choose a certain type of wellness holiday, while knowledge or previous experience of a certain type of holiday may define how customers expect the holiday to fulfil their needs (Bočkus, Vento et al., 2023). Services, however, may refer to the mode in which customers' needs and motivations may be fulfilled in reality and in practice (Bočkus, Tammi et al., 2023).

Destinations may have different approaches to providing wellness tourism services based on the regional conception of wellness, which is influenced by the traditions, natural resources, landscape, and legislation (Bočkus et al., 2021; Dutt & Selstad, 2022). Although the majority of previous studies on wellness tourism do not contain any cross-country or nationality group comparison in terms of wellness motivations, three earlier studies (Bočkus, Vento et al., 2023; Niinepuu et al., 2022; Tooman et al., 2013) found evidence showing that different nationality groups differ in terms of wellness motivations and service preferences. These differences may be formed by their experiences of wellness service offering to which they are accustomed in their home country.

The differences in the concept of wellness in the source markets may cause challenges for enterprises and DMOs (destination management organisations) when adjusting their marketing message and offerings to different international target groups. The internationalisation of wellness tourism has created a need to increase the understanding of businesses as to how the motivations and service preferences of customers may vary between different source markets and how destinations can materialise wellness in their product and service offerings. This kind of insight into the market may enhance the development of competitiveness of wellness destinations.

This chapter aims to understand the connection between the motivation of wellness tourists and their service preferences and the concept of wellness and wellness service offering in the tourists' home country. Hence, this chapter overviews and compares motivations, service preferences, wellness concepts and wellness service offerings in Finland, Russia (Russian Karelia and St. Petersburg area), and Lithuania. These issues are investigated from the standpoint of marketing and consumer research. From a managerial perspective, this research will provide a basis for making informed decisions by entrepreneurs, local and national policy/decision makers, and DMOs on the priorities and actions that need to be taken to improve service offerings. In addition, the results will also allow international tourists to improve their communication strategies, which will consequently advance the promotion, positioning, and competitiveness of wellness tourism businesses.

9.2   Theoretical Background

9.2.1   Wellness Tourism Categorisation

The categorisation of wellness may be based either on the perspective of the supply side or the demand side. However, the categorisation is challenging due to the complexity of the wellness concept and the definition of wellness tourism; there is also an abundance of interconnected terms such as thermal tourism, spa tourism, medical wellness tourism, and wellbeing tourism, which are often used interchangeably and in the same context (Bočkus et al., 2021; Mihók & Marčeková, 2022; Smith & Puczkó, 2014; Voigt, 2014). There is an ongoing discussion about the differences between wellness and wellbeing. This study adopts the view that wellness is an active pursuit, or an evolving process, of growth closely connected to an individual's lifestyle, consumption choices, and adoption of attitudes and that by going through a range of proactive activities, for example, exercise, healthy nutrition, and meditation, individuals seek to enhance their physical, spiritual, mental, emotional, and social wellbeing, and optimal health (Dunn, 1959; Global Wellness Institute, 2018; Grénman et al., 2019). Wellbeing, however, is a broader term which is understood as a state of being achieved when the mental, physical, and spiritual dimensions of health are well balanced (Hjalager et al., 2011), and thus may be considered a result rather than an action. Wellbeing is closely interlinked with the concepts of positive psychology, happiness, quality of life, and life satisfaction (Grénman, 2019; Smith & Diekmann, 2017). Differences in understanding and interpretation of wellness may be impacted by the existence of natural resources at the tourist destination, as well as the landscape, traditions, regulation of the industry (Smith & Puczkó, 2014; Voigt, 2014) and other comparative advantages.

Analysis of the prior literature reveals that several different regional approaches to wellness tourism can be distinguished (e.g., Smith & Puczkó, 2014; Voigt, 2014). One of the most evident factors determining the mode of wellness tourism offering are the resources that the destination possesses. The existence of natural resources (e.g., therapeutic mud, mineral water), the landscape (e.g., lakes, mountains, forests, wilderness areas), and the climate are commonly reflected in wellness tourism supply. For example, destinations in the Baltic states, Central and Eastern Europe, parts of Germany, Austria, and France exploit the possibility of experiencing balneotherapy, peloidotherapy, biotherapy, or thermal waters, including other noninvasive therapeutic procedures – most of which are provided by the medical spas or sanatoria types of enterprises.

The second type of destinations described in the prior literature are commonly referred to as wellbeing (Hjalager et al., 2011) or nature-based wellness (Pforr et al., 2014) destinations. Recent conceptualisations of wellness tourism in the Nordic European countries have emphasised the importance of nature, and the main focus is placed not on the natural resources (e.g., thermal water, curative mud) but on the elements like the landscape, scenery, wilderness, peacefulness, and quietness of the location; there is also a focus on the various activities that can be experienced in these natural surroundings, including nature walks, forest bathing, berry picking, cycling, canoeing, and watching the Northern Lights. There are region-based conceptualisations such as lake wellness (Konu et al., 2010), forest-based wellbeing (Komppula et al., 2017), and rural wellbeing (Pesonen & Komppula, 2010), which are encompassed by the Nordic wellbeing (Hjalager et al., 2011) concept and form the basis of the activities, authentic experiences, marketing, and positioning of these nature-based wellness destinations. The third type of wellness destinations in Europe may include sea- and water-based destinations, which are common in Southern Europe, or be based on leisure and recreational activities popular in Western wellness destinations (Smith & Puczkó, 2014).

Concepts like therapeutic landscapes (Gesler, 1992) or EcoWellness (Reese & Myers, 2012) suggest that simply being in natural surroundings is beneficial for an individual's wellbeing. This is an opposite approach to medical wellness, where different manual pressure techniques and the appliance of mineral water or other materials are used for the enhancement of health.

The supply and provision of wellness tourism services is also shaped by the existing legislation, government regulation and policies (Harmsworth, 2004; Konu et al., 2014), which also influence customer preferences and behaviour (Powel & DiMaggio, 1991). For example, whereas in the West, weekends at a spa were often considered a luxury, in the former Soviet Union countries like the Baltic states or other states in Eastern and Central Europe governed by communists, sanatoria and medical spas were easily accessible for ordinary people, as the state guaranteed sponsorship of these institutions. However, due to changes in the political system and legislation, these types of establishments have, for several decades, been subject to a decrease in governmental funding (e.g., Derco, 2017; Diekmann et al., 2020; Dryglas, 2020). Previously, these medical spa services were mostly used by domestic customers/patients, but since the beginning of 1990, due to the changes in funding and demand, medical spas had to rebrand and reorientate in order to acquire new foreign markets. This was achieved by including more wellness services and by catering to the needs of Western customers, who expect to receive pampering and relaxation experiences rather than therapeutic treatments when visiting a spa.

Religion, culture, and traditions are all interrelated and could be considered as another constituent factor influencing wellness tourism offerings. For example, such services as meditation, yoga, massage, and different practices in Asia are closely connected to leading philosophies or beliefs like Buddhism or Ayurveda (Laing & Weiler, 2008). In the Middle Ages, Christianity was against bathing for social, spiritual, or therapeutic purposes (Voigt, 2014), which shows how religion can impact the development of certain services at tourism destinations.

Despite the different regional approaches to the provision of wellness tourism, it has to be recognized that spas play a key role in the wellness tourism business (Global Wellness Institute, 2018). Consequently, with the globalisation of the knowledge and traditions employed in wellness (Erfurt-Cooper, 2009) certain services (e.g., massage, body scrubs, jacuzzis, saunas, swimming pools) are rather similar at many destinations, especially those provided in spas at international hotel chains. However, wellness tourism trends and service offerings are mostly region based rather than global (Health Tourism Worldwide & Wellness Tourism Association, 2021).

9.2.2 Wellness Tourism Motivations

The push-and-pull model of tourist motivation is an often-used theory when examining tourists' behaviour (e.g., Pesonen, 2012; Uysal et al., 2008). The push factors are commonly described as intrinsic and intangible needs and desires (e.g., emotional, social), whereas the pull factors are represented by external, situational, and tangible features like attractions and attributes of the destination (Crompton, 1979; Klenosky, 2002). Knowledge of these motivations may help destinations and businesses to improve their marketing campaigns and service offering.

The most commonly cited push motivations for wellness tourists include the desire to escape, relax, be pampered, be beautified, and improve physical health (e.g., Aleksijevits, 2019; Dimitrovski & Todorović, 2015; Koh et al., 2010; Kucukusta et al., 2013). These are all being provided in different wellness and spa settings. The majority of the motivations are related to hedonistic experiences as spas dominate the market regarding the provision of wellness services. However, tourists may also be motivated by the ability to attain spiritual growth, to find peace with oneself, to develop themselves, or to connect with nature (e.g., Kessler et al., 2020; Mak et al., 2009). These motivations are linked with a search for eudaimonic experiences, and could be assumed to be connected with spiritual wellness (e.g., Kelly, 2012; Lehto et al., 2006), which may take place at retreats, yoga centres, and nature-based wellness activities like forest bathing (Komppula et al., 2017) or lake wellness (Konu et al., 2010). However, the European perspective on wellness has often been connected to water (e.g., mineral, thermal); therefore, spas have played a central role (Erfurt-Cooper, 2009; Stevens et al., 2018), and the motivations tend to be more connected to the pleasure aspects, indulgence, and healing. Other commonly cited motivations among wellness tourists include novelty seeking or trying new things (Buxton & Michopoulou, 2021; Konu & Laukkanen, 2009; Mak et al., 2009).

Cultural background and nationality may have an impact on customers' decisions (Hindley & Smith, 2017) and on tourists' preferences and expectations (Weiermair, 2000). Subsequently, Hindley and Smith (2017) argue that a comparison of national characteristics may be useful when analysing a sample of the same age, gender, or religion. In addition, evidence of the impact of nationality on wellness tourism behaviour has been provided by Bočkus, Vento et al. (2023) and Tooman et al. (2013). However, two studies conducted among Finnish wellness tourism customers (Konu & Laukkanen, 2010; Pesonen et al., 2011) did not find any statistically significant connection between the sociodemographic variables and the customers' intention to go on a wellness trip.

In terms of the pull motivations in wellness tourism, the key elements attracting tourists to a wellness destination include (among others): the activities, social and cultural attributes, physical setting, the infrastructure, hospitality, cost, distance, security, image, quality of services and facilities, authenticity (Buhalis, 2000; Kucukusta et al., 2013; Uysal et al., 2008), and accessibility (Michopoulou & Hilton, 2021). In addition, wellness tourists may be pulled by the service offering itself (e.g., swimming pools, saunas), packaged services, fresh air, peacefulness, a quiet natural environment, natural sights like forests or lakes, natural resources (e.g., thermal waters), cleanliness, and spa/wellness infrastructures (Dryglas & Salamaga, 2017; Komppula et al., 2017; Konu et al., 2010; Konu & Laukkanen, 2010).

In summary, wellness tourism customers are considerably heterogenic in terms of their needs and motivations, meaning that different segments of customers may seek different benefits from the same service offering (Koh et al., 2010). Motivation, as well as several sociodemographic variables (Cain et al., 2016; Kucukusta et al., 2013) have an impact on the service preferences of wellness tourists (e.g., Tsai et al., 2012). Tourism scholars have argued that there is a need for further research on the disparity between the service preferences of tourists and the services supplied by businesses (Kisperska-Moroń, 2005; Nysveen et al., 2002).

9.3   Research Methods

This multiple case study encompasses the market perspective from the supply side and the demand side in Finland, Russia, and Lithuania. In terms of Russia, the supply side refers to the Republic of Karelia, and the demand to the St. Peterburg area. The St. Petersburg area used to be one of the key source markets generating the wellness tourist flow in the regions investigated in this study. In this chapter, from the supply side, the regions are seen as wellness destinations, and from the demand side as the source markets. These regions share similar characteristics in their nature and landscape and are geographically close to each other. Finland shares a border with the Republic of Karelia in Russia, and Lithuanian development was previously influenced by the regime governing the Soviet Union (Mole, 2012). In addition, wellness tourism has been identified as one of the priorities of the tourism development strategies in all of these regions.

The data for this study was gathered by using a mixed-method approach. The supply side data (for a detailed description of the method, see Bočkus et al., 2021) consists of semi-structured interviews, and were gathered from altogether 30 wellness tourism enterprises in Eastern Finland (11), Russian Karelia (10), and Lithuania (9) between June 2020 and September 2020. The participant enterprises were chosen using a purposeful sampling method aiming to reach a representative sample of wellness tourism enterprises: large and small, urban and rural, wellness, leisure, and medically oriented. The interviewees were either the entrepreneurs or responsible managers. The themes discussed included the interviewees' understanding of wellness, service offerings, and future prospects. Interviews were conducted in the local language and translated into English for further analysis. The study followed the process of thematic content analysis which allowed the identification, coding, categorising, comparison, and reporting of different patterns in the phenomenon of interest (Vaismoradi et al., 2013).

In addition to the interviews, the supply side study included an analysis of secondary data. The websites of the interviewed enterprises were utilised to supplement the data regarding service offering in the destinations. In order to increase the understanding of the role of governmental regulatory mechanism on the local wellness concept and service offering, a cross-country comparison of state standards, certification systems, legislations, and other official documents related to the regulation of the provision of wellness tourism services was conducted.

The demand side data (for a detailed description of the method, see Bočkus, Vento et al., 2023; and Bočkus, Tammi et al., 2023) was gathered in the form of an online panel survey among consumers who had participated in a wellness trip during the previous 24 months; the survey aimed to measure the motivations of wellness customers and their service preferences. The data consists of 1,562 responses (Finland 529, St. Petersburg [Russia] 544, and Lithuania 489). Based on the extensive analysis of previous wellness tourism literature, a list of 24 motivational items were developed and used with a seven-point Likert scale to evaluate the motivations of tourists when considering a wellness trip. In addition, the respondents' service preferences for their future wellness trips were measured with a seven-point Likert scale consisting of 15 wellness services. The scale items were developed based on the classification of services offered by Voigt (2014), and Smith and Puczkó (2014). Respondents were also asked to select which services they have used in previous wellness trips both in their home country, and abroad. Additionally, questions related to sociodemographic characteristics as well as wellness trip frequencies were included in the questionnaire.

The collected data was analysed by examining the descriptive statistics of the scale-based motivation and service preference items. The analysis included Kruskal-Wallis, and Mann-Whitney U tests. The first method allowed for the testing of statistically significant differences in the mean scores, while the second was used for pairwise comparisons to identify statistically significant differences between the nationality groups.

9.4   Results

9.4.1   The Supply Side Study: Differences Between Wellness Concepts

In the first stage of the supply side analysis, differences in the concepts of wellness between the destinations were examined. Table 9.1 is based on the analysis of interviews with the respondents.

The findings revealed that the concepts of wellness, the traditions and the wellness tourism offerings are rather different at all the analysed destinations. The Finnish interviewees emphasised the importance of privacy, individualism, peacefulness, and nature. In Russian Karelia and in Finland particularly, the focus was placed on nature-based activities like Nordic walking, forest bathing, cycling, or just simply relaxing and enjoying the quietness and peacefulness in

Table 9.1   Relative differences in the wellness concepts between the destinations

Wellness concept and service offering	Finland	Lithuania	Russia
Water-based treatments	*	***	***
Curative mud and mineral water	*	***	***
Equipment aided procedures	*	***	**
Medical wellness	*	***	***
Spa procedures	***	***	***
Relaxation	***	***	***
Sauna	***	***	***
Individualism and privacy	***	*	*
Outdoor activities	***	*	***
Education	***	*	*
Nature	***	*	***
Fitness and wellbeing	*	**	***
Nutrition	**	*	***
Wellbeing	***	*	**

Notes: * Little importance; **Average importance; *** High importance

the wilderness. Lithuanian and Russian interviewees highlighted the importance of curative resources like mud and mineral water, which are used in various spa treatments or the use of unique resources like amber in Lithuania or *shungite* in Russia. Lithuanian interviewees emphasised medical wellness and equipment-based procedures like sleep capsules or cryotherapy which could be used both in wellness and medical tourism.

In summary, the analysed data suggests that Finland and Lithuania have a rather different approach to wellness and different wellness services offerings. The Finnish wellness concept and tradition is based on nature and outdoor activities, while the Lithuanian concept is mostly connected to therapeutic recreation. The Russian concept includes both traditions common to Finland and Lithuania but with the addition of healthy nutrition and fitness – which are more important in Russia than in the other two destinations. Despite the differences, saunas, spa procedures, and relaxation were indicated by the great majority of interviewees in all three destinations as an important part of wellness and its offerings.

Analysis of the legislation, certification systems, state standards, and other governmental regulatory mechanisms disclosed that the wellness tourism industry in Lithuania and Russia is significantly more regulated than in Finland. The differences in state intervention may affect wellness concepts and service offerings in terms of how and what kind of services are provided.

9.4.1.1   Demand Side Study: Results of Analysis of the Wellness Motivations of Tourists and Their Service Preferences

Analysis of the descriptive statistics of the motivation scale items revealed significant differences in the mean scores between the source markets (see Figure 9.1).

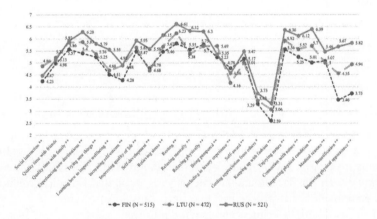

Figure 9.1   Importance of motivations when considering going on a wellness trip

Notes: 1 = not important at all, 7 = extremely important; ** p < 0.01, * p < 0.05

Respondents indicated that their main motivations for going on a wellness trip were *resting, relieving stress,* and *relaxing physically and mentally,* all of which are mostly connected to aspirations of hedonistic experiences. Nevertheless, eudemonic motivations such as enjoying *nature, experiencing new destina-*

tions, quality time with the family, and *improving the individual's quality of life* were among those with the highest rated scores in all the source markets.

The greatest differences found between the source markets were the motivations concerned with *beautification, improving physical appearance,* and *physical condition.* Finns were the least motivated in these three dimensions, whereas they were highly important to the Russian group and moderately important to the Lithuanians. *Indulging in luxury experiences* was the only motivational item where Finns had higher mean score than the other nationalities.

Figure 9.2 shows the interest of wellness tourists in using wellness related services in their future wellness trips. The data revealed that *pools, saunas(s),* and *massage and body care* were regarded as highly important in all the source markets. The least interesting services were *mind and body, meditation and/or relaxation techniques, alternative therapies,* and *educational activities.*

The greatest differences between the source markets were in *healthy nutrition services, outdoor activities, indoor exercise,* and *fitness;* the Russian group showed significantly more interest in these compared to the other nationalities. The Finns appear to be significantly less interested in *wellness-based treatments, rehabilitation and/or therapeutic recreation,* and *beauty treatment services* compared to the reference groups.

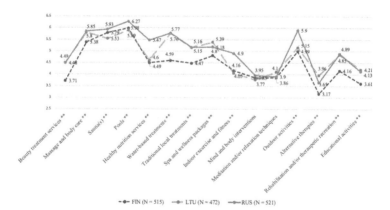

Figure 9.2   Intention of using wellness services when considering future wellness trips

Notes: 1 = not interested at all, and 7 = extremely interested; ** $p < 0.01$, * $p < 0.05$

First, the results shows that motivations and service preferences related to beauty and physical appearance are highly important to Russians, moderately important to Lithuanians, and less important to Finns. Second, relaxation and nature have considerable importance in all the source markets. Third, Lithuanians and Russians are significantly more interested in medical wellness, curative treatments, massage, and therapeutic recreation compared to Finnish tourists. Fourth, none of the source markets are interested in status. Fifth, socialisation is more important to Lithuanians compared to the other groups.

9.5   Discussion and Conclusion

This chapter aimed to contribute to the literature of wellness tourism by expanding the knowledge on different market perspectives on the concept of wellness. This was achieved by analysing the connection between wellness concepts in the home country of the tourists, the wellness motivations of tourists and their service preferences.

The findings revealed that on the supply side, the wellness concept and service offerings at the destinations are mostly dependent on natural resources, the natural environment, state regulations, traditions and culture. On the other hand, from the demand point of view, the findings indicate that consumers' motivations, needs, and preferable mode of fulfilment of expectations may differ between the source markets, which in this study was represented by three different nationality groups. Finally, our findings showed that the wellness concept in the source market may affect the expectations of wellness tourists when travelling abroad.

In line with previous wellness tourism studies (e.g., Aleksijevits, 2019; Mak et al., 2009; Voigt et al., 2011), motivations related to resting and relaxation were of key importance in all the source markets, which aligns with the high mean scores in service preferences related to swimming pools, saunas, massages, body care, and spa and wellness packages.

Generally, the wellness concepts in the destinations in the country of residence align with the motivations and service preferences of the respective wellness tourism source market. This suggests that previous experiences of wellness tourism consumption may impact customers' needs, motivations and their preferences in the way it should be fulfilled on future wellness trips. In line with Smith and Puczkó (2014), this conclusion is also supported by the findings revealing that Lithuanian and Russian respondents were significantly more interested in water-based treatments, traditional local treatments, rehabilitation and therapeutic recreation which all are important elements of wellness concept in these destinations.

An interesting difference between the source markets was found in the preference for beauty and appearance treatments, which played a significantly more important role for the female respondents from Russia compared to the two other source markets. In the post-Soviet media, a sexualised model of beauty and glamour for femininity were represented by self-indulgence and privileged leisure, which later actualised in high spending on beauty products among Russian women (Rudova, 2014), which may explain this phenomenon.

Additionally, the role of nature and the outdoors varied between the service offering at the destinations and the demand in the source markets. In Finland, the concept of wellness is based on activities in nature, which is also demonstrated by the abundance of nature-based wellness concepts like lake wellness (Konu et al., 2010), forest-based wellbeing (Komppula et al., 2017), or Nordic wellbeing (Hjalager et al., 2011). Interestingly, according to the results, the Finnish respondents plan to use outdoor activity services in their future wellness trips, even though the nature related motivation for wellness trip was relatively low. However, these results correspond with previous studies (e.g., Konu & Laukkanen, 2009) and may indicate that outdoor activities in nature for Finnish wellness tourists are considered to be more like daily exercises than a wellness holiday motivation.

Common to all the source markets, motivations related to status and recognition appeared to be the least important. As the Lithuanian and Russian wellness tourism market is medically oriented (Bočkus et al., 2021; Smith & Puczkó, 2014), and it is still state policy to subsidise part of these services, it may not be considered a luxury or something only for the elite. In Finland, in contrast, due to the higher standard of living compared to other OECD countries (OECD, 2020) wellness and spa services are more accessible to a relatively large percent of the society; thus, wellness is not seen as exclusive. Nevertheless, the results show that Finns connect wellness to luxury experiences that offer an opportunity to indulge in forms of self-development (see Konu et al., 2010), in a quiet and peaceful environment (Iloranta & Komppula, 2021).

Finally, in line with Global Wellness Institute (2018), the results indicate an increasing demand for eudaimonic and transformative experiences related to self-development and fulfilment. Therefore, wellness tourism destinations and businesses should be able to accommodate these expectations rather than focusing solely on services designed to fulfil hedonistic needs. However, service preferences like *mind and body interventions, meditation and relaxation techniques, and alternative therapies* were the least important; this suggests that customers' preferences are rather conservative, and mostly associated with more tangible and traditional services common to the European market rather than Eastern traditions.

This chapter adds to the literature of wellness tourism by demonstrating that the wellness concept in the home country, tourists' motivations, and service preferences are all interlinked. In line with previous studies (e.g., Hindley & Smith, 2017) respondents' nationality, or, more precisely, the source market of the respondents proved to be related to differences in tourists needs and expectations. The wellness concept in the source market may affect the expectations of wellness tourists when travelling abroad. In some cases, tourists from different nationality groups may be driven by the same motivation, but their preferences for services may differ, demonstrating cross-national differences in the choice of means to satisfy motivation. Due to the globalisation of competition, knowledge about the needs of customers from different cultural backgrounds and the ability to accommodate those needs has become increasingly important (Lin et al., 2007). In order to increase their competitiveness, entrepreneurs and DMOs should be able to customize their service offering, and to differentiate their positioning and communications messages for different source markets.

Funding

This work was supported by the Finnish Cultural Foundation under Grant [number 00210241 and 00220176]; European Union, Russian Federation, and Republic of Finland under Karelian Wellness project [project number: KA8022].

Declaration of Competing Interest

The authors declare that they have no known competing financial interests or personal relationships that could have appeared to influence the work reported in this chapter.

Acknowledgments

The authors thank Elisa Sulkinoja from the University of Eastern Finland and Natalia Kolesnikova from the Institute of Physical Education (Russia) for participating in research planning.

References

Aleksijevits, K. (2019). Consumer motivation and behaviour when selecting a wellness holiday destination. *International Journal of Spa and Wellness, 2*(2), 78–97. https://doi.org/10.1080/24721735.2020.1771017.

Azara, I., & Foster, C. (2021). Editorial: Re-imaging a life after Covid-19. *International Journal of Spa and Wellness, 4*(2–3), 114–117. https://doi.org/10.1080/24721735.2021.2015142.

Bočkus, D., Sulkinoja, E., Kolesnikova, N., & Komppula, R. (2021). Differences in the concept of wellness and its materialisation in service offering: a multiple case study from Eastern Finland, Russian Karelia, and Lithuania. *Tourism Recreation Research*, 1–16. https://doi.org/10.1080/02508281.2021.1984693.

Bočkus, D., Tammi, T., Vento, E., & Komppula, R. (2023). Wellness tourism service preferences and their linkages to motivational factors: a multiple case study. *International Journal of Spa and Wellness, 6*(1), 78–108.

Bočkus, D., Vento, E., Tammi, T., Komppula, R., & Kolesnikova, N. (2023). Comparing the motivations behind wellness tourism in three source markets. *European Journal of Tourism Research, 33*, 3303. https://doi.org/10.54055/ejtr.v33i.2786.

Buhalis, D. (2000). Marketing the competitive destination of the future. *Tourism Management, 21*(1), 97–116. https://doi.org/10.1016/S0261-5177(99)00095-3.

Buxton, L., & Michopoulou, E. (2021). Value co-creation and co-destruction: Considerations of spa servicescapes. *Tourism Planning & Development, 18*(2), 210–225. https://doi.org/10.1080/21568316.2021.1873837.

Cain, L. N., Busser, J., & Baloglu, S. (2016). Profiling the motivations and experiences of spa customers. *Anatolia, 27*(2), 262–264. https://doi.org/10.1080/13032917.2015.1076729.

Crompton, L. (1979). Motivations for pleasure vacation. *Annals of Tourism Research, 6*(4), 408–424. https://doi.org/10.1177/004728758001900185.

Denizci Guillet, B., & Kucukusta, D. (2016). Spa market segmentation according to customer preference. *International Journal of Contemporary Hospitality Management, 28*(2), 418–434. https://doi.org/10.1108/IJCHM-07-2014-0374.

Derco, J. (2017). Impact of health care funding on financial position of Slovak medical spas. *Tourism, 65*(3), 376–380.

Diekmann, A., Smith, M. K., & Ceron, J.-P. (2020). From welfare to wellness: European spas at the crossroads. In A. Diekmann & S. McCabe (Eds), *Handbook of social tourism* (pp. 108–122). Edward Elgar Publishing.

Dimitrovski, D., & Todorović, A. (2015). Clustering wellness tourists in spa environment. *Tourism Management Perspectives, 16*, 259–265.

Dryglas, D. (2020). Wellness as a new direction of development of Polish spa resorts. *International Journal of Spa and Wellness, 3*(2–3), 69–81. https://doi.org/10.1080/24721735.2020.1857207.

Dryglas, D., & Salamaga, M. (2017). Applying destination attribute segmentation to health tourists: A case study of Polish spa resorts. *Journal of Travel & Tourism Marketing, 34*(4), 503–514. https://doi.org/10.1080/10548408.2016.1193102.

Dunn, H. L. (1959). High-level wellness for man and society. *American Journal of Public Health and the Nation's Health, 49*(6), 786–792. https://doi.org/10.2105/AJPH.49.6.786.

Dutt, B., & Selstad, L. (2022). The wellness modification of yoga in Norway. *International Journal of Spa and Wellness, 5*(1), 33–49. https://doi.org/10.1080/24721735.2021.1948274.

Erfurt-Cooper, P. (2009). The health and wellness concept: A global overview. In P. Erfurt-Cooper & M. Cooper (Eds), *Health and wellness tourism: Spas and hot springs.* Channel View Publications.

Gesler, W. (1992). Therapeutic landscapes – Medical issues in light of the new cultural-geography. *Social Science & Medicine, 34*(7), 735–746. https://doi.org/10.1016/0277-9536(92)90360-3.

Global Wellness Institute. (2018). *Global wellness tourism economy.* https://globalwellnessinstitute.org/wp-content/uploads/2018/11/GWI_GlobalWellnessTourismEconomyReport.pdf.

Gössling, S., Scott, D., & Hall, C. M. (2020). Pandemics, tourism and global change: a rapid assessment of COVID-19. *Journal of Sustainable Tourism, 29*(1), 1–20. https://doi.org/10.1080/09669582.2020.1758708.

Grénman, M. (2019). *IN QUEST OF THE OPTIMAL SELF. Wellness consumption and lifestyle – A superficial marketing fad or a powerful means for transforming and branding oneself?* [Doctoral dissertation]. University of Turku.

Grénman, M., Hakala, U., & Mueller, B. (2019). Wellness branding: Insights into how American and Finnish consumers use wellness as a means of self-branding. *Journal of Product & Brand Management, 28*(4), 462–474. https://doi.org/10.1108/JPBM-04-2018-1860.

Harmsworth, S. (2004). *The latest trends and developments in the health and spa market.* Tourism Insights. http://www.insights.org.uk.

Health Tourism Worldwide, & Wellness Tourism Association. (2021). *Wellness travel 2030 post-COVID19: A pioneering study.* https://htww.life/download/wellness-travel-2030-a-pioneering-study-full-report.

Hindley, C., & Smith, M. K. (2017). Cross-cultural issues of consumer behaviour in hospitality and tourism. In S. K. Dixit (Ed.), *The Routledge handbook of consumer behaviour in hospitality and tourism* (pp. 86–95). Routledge.

Hjalager, A.-M., Konu, H., H Huijbens, E., Björk, P., Flagestad, A., Nordin, S., & Tuohino, A. (2011). *Innovating and re-branding Nordic wellbeing tourism.* Nordic Council of Ministers. http://www.diva-portal.org/smash/record.jsf?pid=diva2:70721.

Iloranta, R., & Komppula, R. (2021). Service providers' perspective on the luxury tourist experience as a product. *Scandinavian Journal of Hospitality and Tourism,* 1–19. https://doi.org/10.1080/15022250.2021.1946845.

Kelly, C. (2012). Wellness tourism: Retreat visitor motivations and experiences. *Tourism Recreation Research, 37*(3), 205–213. https://doi.org/10.1080/02508281.2012.11081709.

Kessler, D., Lee, J.-H., & Whittingham, N. (2020). The wellness tourist motivation scale: A new statistical tool for measuring wellness tourist motivation. *International Journal of Spa and Wellness, 3*(1), 24–39. https://doi.org/10.1080/24721735.2020.1849930.

Kisperska-Moroń, D. (2005). Logistics customer service levels in Poland: Changes between 1993 and 2001. *International Journal of Production Economics, 93–94,* 121–128. https://doi.org/10.1016/j.ijpe.2004.06.047.

Klenosky, D. B. (2002). The "pull" of tourism destinations: A means-end investigation. *Journal of Travel Research, 40*(4), 396–403. https://doi.org/10.1177/004728750204000405.

Koh, S., Yoo, J. J-E., & Boger, C. A. (2010). Importance-performance analysis with benefit segmentation of spa goers. *International Journal of Contemporary Hospitality Management, 22*(5), 718–735. https://doi.org/10.1108/09596111011053828.

Komppula, R., Konu, H., & Vikman, N. (2017). Listening to the sounds of silence: Forest-based wellbeing tourism in Finland. In J. S. Chen & N. K. Prebensen (Eds.), *Nature tourism* (1st ed., pp. 132–142). Routledge. https://doi.org/10.4324/9781315659640–19.

Konu, H., & Laukkanen, T. (2009). *Roles of motivation factors in predicting tourists' intentions to make wellbeing holidays – a Finnish case.* ANZMAC 2009 – Sustainable Management and Marketing Proceedings. Available at: http://www.duplication.net.au/ANZMAC09/papers/ANZMAC2009-376.pdf.

Konu, H., & Laukkanen, T. (2010). Predictors of tourists' wellbeing holiday intentions in Finland. *Journal of Hospitality and Tourism Management, 17*(1), 144–149. https://doi.org/10.1375/jhtm.17.1.144.

Konu, H., Tuohino, A., & Björk, P. (2014). Wellbeing tourism in Finland. In M. K. Smith & L. Puczkó (Eds), *Health tourism and hospitality. Spas, wellness and medical travel* (pp. 345–349). Routledge.

Konu, H., Tuohino, A., & Komppula, R. (2010). Lake wellness — a practical example of a new service development (NSD) concept in tourism industries. *Journal of Vacation Marketing, 16*(2), 125–139. https://doi.org/10.1177/1356766709357489.

Kucukusta, D., Pang, L., & Chui, S. (2013). Inbound travelers' selection criteria for hotel spas in Hong Kong. *Journal of Travel & Tourism Marketing, 30*(6), 557–576. https://doi.org/10.1080/10548408.2013.810995.

Laing, J., & Weiler, B. (2008). Mind, body and spirit: Health and wellness tourism in Asia. In J. Cochrane (Ed.), *Asian tourism: Growth and change.* Elsevier.

Lehto, X. Y., Brown, S., Chen, Y., & Morrison, A. M. (2006). Yoga tourism as a niche within the wellness tourism market. *Tourism Recreation Research, 31*(1), 25–35. https://doi.org/10.1080/02508281.2006.11081244.

Lin, C. C. J., Tu, R., & Tu, P. (2007). *The changing expectations of consumers in cross-cultural service encounters. International Management Review, 3*(3), 27–35.

Mak, A. H. N., Wong, K. K. F., & Chang, R. C. Y. (2009). Health or self-indulgence? The motivations and characteristics of spa-goers. *International Journal of Tourism Research, 11*(2), 185–199. https://doi.org/10.1002/jtr.703.

Michopoulou, E., & Hilton, S. J. (2021). Accessibility to spa experiences. In C. Eusébio, L. Teixeira, & M. J. Carneiro (Eds), *ICT tools and applications for accessible tourism* (pp. 146–168). IGI Global. https://doi.org/10.4018/978-1-7998-6428-8.ch007.

Mihók, P., & Marčeková, R. (2022). Considerations on spa, spa tourism and some related terms definitions and positioning. *International Journal of Spa and Wellness, 5*(3), 320–329. https://doi.org/10.1080/24721735.2022.2107819.

Mole, R. (2012). *The Baltic States from the Soviet Union to the European Union: Identity, discourse and power in the post-communist transition of Estonia, Latvia and Lithuania* (1st ed.). Routledge. https://doi.org/10.4324/9780203121498.

Mueller, H., & Kaufmann, E. L. (2001). Wellness tourism: Market analysis of a special health tourism segment and implications for the hotel industry. *Journal of Vacation Marketing, 7*(1), 5–17. https://doi.org/10.1177/135676670100700101.

Niinepuu, T., Tooman, H., & Smith, M. K. (2022). Customer delight and implications for spa management: examples from Estonian and Finnish day spas. *International Journal of Spa and Wellness, 5*(1), 101–111. https://doi.org/10.1080/24721735.2021.1961113.

Nysveen, H., Methlie, L. B., & Pedersen, P. E. (2002). Tourism web sites and value-added services: the gap between customer preferences and web sites' offerings. *Information Technology & Tourism, 5*(3), 165–174. https://doi.org/10.3727/109830503108751117.

OECD. (2020, March 9). *How's life? 2020: Measuring well-being.* https://doi.org/10.1787/9870c393-en.

Pesonen, J. A. (2012). Segmentation of rural tourists: Combining push and pull motivations. *Tourism and Hospitality Management, 18*(1), 69–82. https://doi.org/10.20867/thm.18.1.5.

Pesonen, J., & Komppula, R. (2010). Rural wellbeing tourism: Motivations and expectations. *Journal of Hospitality and Tourism Management, 17*(1), 150–157. https://doi.org/10.1375/jhtm.17.1.150.

Pesonen, J., Laukkanen, T., & Komppula, R. (2011). Benefit segmentation of potential wellbeing tourists. *Journal of Vacation Marketing, 17*(4), 303–314. https://doi.org/10.1177/1356766711423322.

Pforr, C., Hughes, M., Dawkins, M., & Gaunt, E. (2014). Nature-based wellness tourism: The case of the Margaret River region in Western Australia. In C. Voigt & C. Pforr (Eds), *Wellness tourism: A destination perspective* (pp. 176–187). Routledge. https://researchrepository.murdoch.edu.au/id/eprint/25575/.

Powel, W. W., & DiMaggio, P. J. (1991). Introduction. In W. W. Powell & P. J. DiMaggio (Eds), *The new institutionalism in organizational analysis* (pp. 1–38). University of Chicago Press.

Reese, R. F., & Myers, J. E. (2012). EcoWellness: The missing factor in holistic wellness models. *Journal of Counseling & Development, 90*(4), 400–406. https://doi.org/10.1002/j.1556-6676.2012.00050.x.

Rudova, L. (2014). "Who's the fairest of them all?" Beauty and femininity in contemporary Russian adolescent girl fiction. *The Russian Review, 73*(3), 389–403. https://doi.org/10.1111/russ.10737.

Smith, M., & Diekmann, A. (2017). Tourism and wellbeing. *Annals of Tourism Research, 66*, 1–13. https://doi.org/10.1016/j.annals.2017.05.006.

Smith, M., & Kelly, C. (2006). Wellness tourism. *Tourism Recreation Research, 31*(1), 1–4. https://doi.org/10.1080/02508281.2006.11081241.

Smith, M., & Puczkó, L. (2014). *Healh, tourism and hospitality: spas, wellness and medical travel.* Routledge.

Stevens, F., Azara, I., & Michopoulou, E. (Elina). (2018). Local community attitudes and perceptions towards thermalism. *International Journal of Spa and Wellness, 1*(1), 55–68. https://doi.org/10.1080/24721735.2018.1432451.

Thorne, S. (2021). Are spas and wellness still considered luxurious in today's world? *Research in Hospitality Management, 11*(1), 9–14. https://doi.org/10.1080/22243534.2020.1867379.

Tooman, H., Tomasberg, K., & Smith, M. (2013). Cross-cultural issues in health and wellness services in Estonia. In J. Kandampully (Ed.), *Service management in health and wellness services* (pp. 347–361). Kendall Hunt Publishing Company. https://www.etis.ee/Portal/Publications/Display/83c929f7–30e1–4eb5-b583–52040f44e0e6.

Tsai, H., Suh, E., & Fong, C. (2012). Understanding male hotel spa-goers in Hong Kong. *Journal of Hospitality Marketing & Management, 21*(3), 247–269. https://doi.org/10.1080/19368623.2012.624295.

Uysal, M., Li, X., & Sirakaya-Turk, E. (2008). Push–pull dynamics in travel decisions. In H. Oh (ed.) *Handbook of Hospitality marketing management* (pp. 412–439). Butterworth-Heinemann.

Vaismoradi, M., Turunen, H., & Bondas, T. (2013). Content analysis and thematic analysis: Implications for conducting a qualitative descriptive study: Qualitative descriptive study. *Nursing & Health Sciences, 15*(3), 398–405. https://doi.org/10.1111/nhs.12048.

Voigt, C. (2014). Towards a conceptualisation of wellness tourism. In C. Voigt & C. Pforr (Eds.), *Wellness tourism: A destination perspective.* Routledge.

Voigt, C., Brown, G., & Howat, G. (2011). Wellness tourists: In search of transformation. *Tourism Review, 66*(1/2), 16–30. https://doi.org/10.1108/16605371111127206.

Weiermair, K. (2000). Tourists' perceptions towards and satisfaction with service quality in the cross-cultural service encounter: Implications for hospitality and tourism management. *Managing Service Quality: An International Journal, 10*(6), 397–409. https://doi.org/10.1108/09604520010351220.

Wen, J., Kozak, M., Yang, S., & Liu, F. (2020). COVID-19: Potential effects on Chinese citizens' lifestyle and travel. *Tourism Review, 76*(1), 74–87. https://doi.org/10.1108/TR-03-2020-0110.

PART IV

EFFECTS OF TOURISM ON WELLBEING

10 Wellbeing outcomes of social tourism: evidence from Finland

Elli Vento, Scott McCabe and Raija Komppula

10.1   Introduction

Traditionally, researchers have conceived tourism as part of discretionary consumer activity and therefore focused on middle- and upper-class consumers, those individuals and families with the disposable income to enjoy the recognized benefits and wellbeing outcomes of taking holiday on a regular basis (see e.g., Cole & Morgan, 2010; Schänzel & Yeoman, 2014). These benefits and outcomes include, for instance, increased quality and satisfaction with life, emotional refreshment and recreation, improved social and family relationships, and the creation of memorable experiences (e.g., Durko & Petrick, 2013; Gilbert & Abdullah, 2004; Kelly, 2020; Neal et al., 2004). In advanced societies, a holiday away from home is considered as an important aspect of social life (McCabe & Diekmann, 2015), providing special leisure opportunities and quality time outside the everyday life environment, responsibilities, and routines (Durko & Petrick, 2013).

Although in many countries holiday taking has become possible for a large proportion of society, less well-off and disadvantaged groups are often excluded from participation due to economic and/or social factors (e.g., Cole & Morgan, 2010; McCabe & Diekmann, 2015; McCabe & Qiao, 2020). However, it has been argued that these are the very groups within society that would benefit most from holiday opportunities (Cole & Morgan, 2010; Smith & Hughes, 1999), particularly since the positive effects of a holiday can be very short-lived among the more affluent, frequent travellers (see e.g., deBloom et al., 2010). In some countries and societies, social tourism has been developed specifically to create opportunities for disadvantaged individuals and families to participate in tourism (McCabe & Diekmann, 2015; Minnaert et al., 2011). Commonly, the primary goal of social tourism initiatives is to enhance societal wellbeing and inclusion (Minnaert et al., 2009).

In general, social tourism can be seen as a special form of tourism aiming to generate wellbeing outcomes and reduce inequality through targeted social interventions. Whereas commercial tourism offerings are geared towards market needs and motivations, and normally determined by customers willingness to pay, the objectives of social tourism are, in part, determined by or in conjunction with the objectives of a funding organization, often through the public or charity sectors. So-called visitor-related social tourism primarily aims to benefit disadvantaged people, which can lead to additional societal benefits, such as savings in healthcare and social support costs (Minnaert et al., 2011). However, there is a lack of understanding of how publicly funded social tourism programs meet their objectives from the suppliers' perspective and what kind of wellbeing outcomes they actually generate from the customer's perspective, which is particularly important in enabling credible evaluation of public spending. Currently, many countries are struggling with tightening budgets and economic uncertainty (Lima & Eusébio, 2020), mainly because of the COVID-19 pandemic and, more recently, the war in Ukraine. However, social tourism has been identified as providing possible opportunities to stimulate domestic tourism recovery after the pandemic (McCabe & Qiao, 2020). In these debates, social tourism has been presented as a positive alternative to commercial mass tourism, which has been often criticized due to some associated negative consequences (overcrowded destinations, unsustainability, ecological and cultural damage) (McCabe & Qiao, 2020).

This chapter outlines and synthesizes findings from a longitudinal, multitimethod study, which has been published in three separate research articles (Vento & Komppula, 2020; Vento et al., 2020; Vento, 2022). The research aimed to enhance understanding of the wellbeing outcomes of social tourism from different stakeholder perspectives. Additionally, the study sought to determine how a social holiday, which is the most typical social tourism product and type of social tourism experience, affects customer's subjective wellbeing by examining both the outcomes for customers, holiday providers perspectives on the wellbeing outcomes derived from social holiday experiences and funders perspectives on the organization and management of the social tourism system in achieving higher levels of wellbeing.

Subjective wellbeing can be conceived variably: as the level of satisfaction people feel with the way their lives are going in general; an all-encompassing construct covering different aspects of life, including mental and physical health, social life, family, financial wellbeing, leisure time, and work; and as a broader concept that includes people's perceptions on the extent they have the resources to lead a good and meaningful life (c.f. Diener et al., 1999; European Social Survey, 2013). Wellbeing has often been linked to the concept of social inclusion. People's experience of inclusion is associated with social belonging and membership, feelings of equality and as having a meaning and purpose in life, for example (Nivala & Ryynänen, 2013). Wellbeing and inclusion are often considered at the level of the individual. Yet, holidays, and particularly social tourism provisions are often targeted towards disadvantaged families (Komppula & Vento, 2021; McCabe, 2009), and supporting disadvantaged families has been identified as being particularly beneficial from the societal perspective (Schänzel & Yeoman, 2014). Hence, in this study, special attention was also paid to family outcomes of social tourism in addition to the individual level.

This research was conducted in the Finnish context, where visitor-related social tourism is a long-established, publicly funded and regulated social policy program designed to improve wellbeing (see Komppula & Vento, 2021). In Finland, a social holiday is normally a five-day domestic holiday. Guided activities with voluntary participation and full board accommodation are offered to eligible applicants. Finnish social holidays are designed for different target groups, such as people with illnesses and disabilities, pensioners, unemployed individuals, and families with children. People must apply for a social holiday, which are assessed by one of five holiday associations based on social, financial, and health-related criteria.

Finnish social holidays aim to promote opportunities for participation, strengthen social networks, support life management, strengthen intrafamily relationships, create a sense of community, develop life patterns conducive to health and emotional wellbeing, and prevent problems (Hyvinvointilomat ry, 2018). The Funding Centre for Social Welfare and Health Organisations (STEA, 2022), which is a public operator under the Ministry of Social Affairs and Health, allocates funding to social tourism and sets guidelines that shape the programs offered. The funding is derived from the profits of Veikkaus Oy, which is a gaming monopoly owned by the Finnish state. In Finland, the profits of Veikkaus Oy have been traditionally allocated to 'good purposes', such as culture, social welfare and health, sports, and science. In recent years, the profits of Veikkaus Oy have fallen due to the COVID-19 pandemic and some new regulations that have been implemented mainly to combat gambling addiction (Veikkaus Oy, 2021).

10.1.1 Research on Wellbeing Outcomes of Social Tourism

Recently, there has been growing research interest in social tourism, although it can be characterized as an emergent field of research. The research contexts and settings still lack diversity as many previous studies in the English language have focused on UK and European experiences (e.g., Diekmann et al., 2020; Eusébio et al., 2016; Ferrer et al., 2016; Kakoudakis, McCabe & Story, 2017; McCabe et al., 2010; McCabe & Johnson, 2013; Minnaert et al., 2009; Smith & Hughes, 1999). Additionally, since the range of social tourism programs is as diverse as the types of consumer contexts studied, it is difficult to generalize about the outcomes associated from participation in social tourism activities. Most studies have, however, focused on the demand side perspective and attempted to understand how people and/or families benefit from the experience (e.g., Minnaert et al., 2006). Much of that research has adopted qualitative approaches (e.g., Bos et al., 2015). There are still not many quantitative studies based on large databases, with an exception being Diekmann et al.'s (2020) study on seniors' holiday practices. Most previous quantitative studies, particularly in tourism journals, have utilized somewhat basic methods (McCabe et al., 2010: McCabe & Johnson, 2013; Pyke et al., 2019) that may, for instance, lead to a lack of generalizable conclusions regarding the outcomes (e.g., Austin, 2011).

Previous quantitative studies have often adopted a two-stage approach to measure any differences in wellbeing states before and after a holiday to try to link changes to the outcomes (McCabe & Johnson, 2013; Pyke et al., 2019). These have indicated that social tourism initiatives can lead to positive outcomes in terms of general satisfaction with life, social and family relationships, and leisure. A positive effect on material wellbeing (Pyke et al., 2019) or employment status (Kakoudakis et al., 2017) has also been recognized. However, a large natural experiment conducted in South Korea did not capture any wellbeing outcomes as a result of receiving a travel voucher (Park et al., 2018), leading to some uncertainty about the true nature of the relationship between social tourism and wellbeing. Even the quantitative studies that did register positive wellbeing outcomes (McCabe & Johnson, 2013; Pyke et al., 2019), found little effect on some elements, such as emotional (i.e., the balance between positive and negative feelings) and/or psychological wellbeing derived from social tourism participation.

Despite these equivocal findings, much research has highlighted very positive and important benefits derived from social tourism initiatives. Qualitative studies have identified the importance of emotional outcomes as a benefit of a social holiday (Hazel, 2005; McCabe, 2009; Smith & Hughes, 1999). Many researchers found that a social holiday also offers beneficiaries a much-needed escape from routine, worries, and responsibilities of everyday life (Hazel, 2005; McCabe, 2009; Smith & Hughes, 1999). For people struggling with, for example, a severe illness in a family, opportunities to experience 'a normal life' during a holiday can also be highly meaningful (Chung & Simpson, 2020;

Hunter-Jones et al., 2020). For those facing difficult life situations, a holiday away from home can lead to feelings of optimism, hope, and a more positive outlook on life (McCabe, 2009; Minnaert et al., 2009). Additionally, a holiday can increase people's confidence and motivation to make positive life changes, such as more active job-searching and social networking (Kakoudakis et al., 2017; Minnaert et al., 2009).

Among families with children, nurturing family relationships, creating happy childhood memories for children, and spending quality time together are often the most important components of a social holiday (Hazel, 2005; McCabe, 2009; McCabe et al., 2010). Overall, the results of previous research indicate that a social holiday can enhance intrafamily communication and encourage families to spend quality family time outside a home environment (Minnaert et al., 2009). For children, seeing new places and experiencing new things can support learning and broaden social worlds (Bos et al., 2015; Minnaert, 2012). For parents, learning outcomes may actualize as improved life management or parenting skills (Minnaert 2012).

The results of previous studies demonstrate that socialization with other holiday makers is particularly crucial for seniors, the unemployed and people with illnesses and disabilities (Eichhorn, 2020; Kakoudakis, 2020; Morgan et al., 2015). In their daily life, these groups often struggle with social isolation. Especially for people with health issues, meeting others suffering from the same medical condition, peer support, can be important (e.g., Komppula et al., 2016). If a social tourism initiative is conducted in a form of a group holiday, it may enhance group working skills, socialization, and participation in organized activities (Bos et al., 2015; Komppula et al., 2016). In the context of a Finnish social holiday, Komppula et al. (2018) and Komppula et al. (2016) have found that social interaction, physical activities, and spending time in nature are the most crucial elements of a social holiday experience for the customers suffering from a heart disease or unemployment.

Although several benefits related to social tourism initiatives have been identified in previous research, also some critical aspects have been noted. If customers receive solely financial support and go on an independent holiday, they may feel insecure about their ability to cope without the support of des-tination staff or a holiday representative (Minnaert et al., 2009). Sometimes, feelings of stress and insecurity can be associated with certain health problems (Hunter-Jones, 2004), a lack of previous vacationing experience, or a situation, where parents go on a holiday with special needs children or a large family (Minnaert et al., 2009). On a group holiday, heterogeneous holiday groups may jeopardize social networking and group formation among other participants

(Komppula et al., 2016). In addition, in the Finnish context, all customers may not participate in guided activities (e.g., crafting, physical exercise in different forms, games for children, lectures and peer support discussions) (Komppula & Vento, 2021). Nonparticipation could jeopardize achieving the funding organizations' stated aims and objectives. Therefore, while our understanding of the possible linkages between social tourism participation and wellbeing is quite advanced, there remains much to be discovered on the nature of those relationships.

10.2   Methodology

This study was undertaken in cooperation with the largest social holiday association in Finland, Hyvinvointilomat ry. All participants were either cooperation partners, applicants, or accepted customers of the association. The mixed-methods study utilized both quantitative and qualitative data and methods. This enabled a holistic approach including the customer, service provider, and funding authority's perspectives. Briefly, the quantitative analyses provided information of the outcomes of a social holiday for a customer, which was deepened and complemented by qualitative analyses focusing on the service providers' views of the wellbeing outcomes and the funders' perspectives on way the system is regulated and managed to meet the objectives, opportunities, and challenges of the Finnish social tourism system. In the following sections, the data collection and analysis are briefly described. More detailed descriptions are included in the related research articles (Vento & Komppula, 2020; Vento et al., 2020; Vento, 2022).

10.2.1 Quantitative Data and Methods

The quantitative data of this study was collected in 2018 to 2019 by a two-stage questionnaire survey targeted at social holiday applicants and customers. The applied scales and target groups are visible in Table 10.1.

The two waves of data collection took place during the general application periods of Finnish social holidays in November 2018 (winter holidays 2019) and March 2019 (summer holidays 2019). All applicants of Hyvinvointilomat ry received the first-stage questionnaire before any holidays had been allocated. The first-stage questionnaire included general scales that measured subcomponents of subjective wellbeing. Additionally, scales measuring family wellbeing were included in the questionnaire that was sent to the applicants

Table 10.1   Survey composition and target groups

	1st-stage survey	2nd-stage survey	Control group survey
Target group	All social holiday applicants	Those who had been accepted in the social holiday application process	Those who had been rejected in the social holiday application process when applying a summer holiday
Composition	1) General-level scales measuring subjective wellbeing and experience of inclusion 2) Scales measuring family wellbeing among the applicants of a family holiday	1) General-level scales measuring subjective wellbeing and experience of inclusion 2) Scales measuring family wellbeing among the family holiday applicants 3) Additional scale directly measuring respondent's social holiday experience	1) General-level scales measuring subjective wellbeing and experience of inclusion 2) Scales measuring family wellbeing among the family holiday applicants 3) Additional questions to ensure that a respondent had not been on a self-paid holiday away from home after filling the 1st-stage survey

Note: All respondents included in this study were applicants and/or customers of the holiday association Hyvinvointilomat ry.

of a family holiday (family holiday takers). This ensured that family outcomes were measured in the right target group.

For those respondents who were accepted on a holiday, a second-stage survey was distributed one month after their trip. This questionnaire included the same scales as the first-stage survey, as well as an additional scale that directly measured customers' social holiday experience, either from the individual perspective (adult groups) or from the perspective of a family (customers of a family holiday). This scale was based on the Finnish social tourism objectives and was designed together with the holiday association representatives.

Among those applicants who had applied for a summer holiday in 2019 but had not been funded, a survey was conducted in mid-August 2019 to form a control group. The control group questionnaire included the same scales as the first-stage questionnaire. Additionally, we asked if respondents had been on a self-paid holiday away from home after completing the first-stage survey.

To ensure a sufficient sample size, those respondents who had not been on a holiday during the study period and those who had been on a holiday of one to three nights were included in the control group.

Apart from the control group survey, for which the response rate was only 10% for obvious reasons, the response rates of the surveys varied from 25% to 36%. Eventually, the amount of longitudinal data (combined responses of the first- and the second-stage questionnaires), was after data cleaning (N = 299 in the holiday-taking group and N = 72 in the control group). Additionally, the amount of nonlongitudinal data (responses to the extra scale of the second-stage survey) was after data cleaning (N = 796; family holiday takers, N = 326, adult groups, N = 470).

The longitudinal data of this study was analysed using several methods, namely, two kinds of data matching techniques (case-control matching and inverse probability weighting [IPW]) combined with a Mixed ANOVA analysis and an average treatment effect on the treated (ATET) estimation. This analysis strategy, which has been previously applied, for instance, in econometrics and the behavioural and medical sciences, enabled consideration of possible selection bias and confounding factors more effectively than other approaches (Austin, 2011). The nonlongitudinal data were analyzed using descriptive statistics of the scale items and a Mann-Whitney U test to compare the means of the family and holiday takers, allowing statistically significant differences between the groups to be identified.

10.2.2 Qualitative Data and Methods

Insight into service provider and funding authority perspective was sought by semi-structured interviews. Firstly, in September 2018, five interviews were conducted with four representatives of Finnish holiday associations, as well as two representatives of the funding organization STEA (Funding Centre for Social Welfare and Health Organisations). During the interviews, the policies, practices, opportunities, and challenges of Finnish social tourism were discussed. Second, six interviews were conducted with four holiday instructors, who each had long experience of working with social tourism customers at the four biggest resorts (two spa resorts, a sports centre, and a holiday village) where Hyvinvointilomat ry organizes social holidays. Two of the informants were interviewed twice, pre-COVID in 2019 and post-COVID, and two were interviewed only post-COVID, in November 2021, before the omicron variant wave. The themes of the interviews included the benefits and challenges associated with Finnish social holidays and social tourism, social tourism target groups and the impacts of COVID-19. Overall, the interviews were from 1 h 45 min to 13 min in length. Six interviews were performed face-to-face and five remotely by telephone, Microsoft Teams, or Skype. Interviews were recorded and transcribed. The data were analyzed with qualitative theme-based content analysis. The social tourism stakeholders' interview data and the holiday instructors' interview data were treated as separate entities.

10.3 Findings

The findings are briefly described below. A more detailed presentation of the findings is included in the related research articles (Vento & Komppula, 2020; Vento et al., 2020; Vento, 2022).

10.3.1 Quantitative Findings

10.3.1.1 Longitudinal Data

In this study, the results of the quantitative two-stage survey (Vento et al., 2020) indicated *a clear positive relationship* (i.e., a significant positive effect) between a social holiday and overall satisfaction with life as well as satisfaction with economic situation, employment situation, social life, and quality of the leisure time. Regarding family outcomes, the results demonstrated that a holiday encouraged families to spend more family time outside home. A holiday also strengthened experiences of equality among family holiday customers.

Some of the aspects measured indicated *signs of a positive relationship* (i.e., a positive effect) between a social holiday and the variables. Satisfaction with mental health, family, amount of leisure time, and calmness of daily life and life management fell in this category, as well as positive affect, social wellbeing, and individual-level social comparison (i.e., the feelings of equality). Concerning family outcomes, family cohesion, family expressiveness, and family conflict also indicated signs of a positive effect as a result of a holiday. However, these variables were associated with skewness, which suggests that the families with low levels of family wellbeing may not apply for a social holiday.

Additionally, some aspects indicated *no relationship* (i.e., no effect) between a social holiday and the variables. Satisfaction with physical health, societal status, and learning and self-development, as well as negative affect, fell in this category.

Finally, some of the variables indicated negative (e.g., individual-level social comparison, social wellbeing, satisfaction with physical health) or positive (e.g., positive affect, negative affect, satisfaction with calmness of daily life and life management) effect in the control group. These *confounding factors* may demonstrate that, for instance, a general holiday period has affected the measurement of these items in the control group.

10.3.1.2 Nonlongitudinal Data

The results of the nonlongitudinal quantitative study (Vento, 2022) indicated that emotional recreation and increased mental wellbeing are the most crucial outcomes of a social holiday for both adult customers and families. A social holiday had also encouraged both groups to increase physical activity levels and participation and inspired them to exercise more. Regarding a positive effect on social relationships, guidance towards new hobbies and improvement of eating habits, the individual holiday takers' item scores were higher than the scores of the family holiday takers, thus demonstrating a stronger effectiveness. The biggest differences between the two groups were associated with the items measuring whether a holiday had offered tips for calmer daily life or tools for better life management, as well as the items asking if the customers had had new friends or received peer support during a holiday. Regarding these items, the scores of the adult groups were significantly higher than those of family respondents. Finally, the results indicated that among families with children, a social holiday had encouraged families to spend time together and strengthened intrafamily relationships. Among families, these aspects turned out to be the second most important benefits of a holiday after the emotional and mental outcomes.

10.3.2 Qualitative Findings

10.3.2.1 Holiday Instructors' Interviews

In the holiday instructors' interview findings (Vento, 2022), all informants identified the mental and emotional benefits as the most important outcome of a Finnish social holiday. Particularly, the notion of escapism was underscored, as providing a break from difficult life situations and everyday life. In the findings, a social holiday was described as 'vitally important' if it leads to a more positive outlook on life for people in a severely difficult life situation. Generally, the informants thought that if a holiday group includes customers with similar life situations, it engenders social networking between the customers.

According to the interview findings, families commonly enjoy quality time together either individually or in the context of guided activities. For children, fun activities are typically more important than for parents, who primarily seek rest and relaxation. For individuals with health problems, peer support, which may actualize as a need for mental health support or concrete advice for coping better with a condition, is often crucial. However, one informant pointed out that peer support can also be problematic as, while being on a holiday, some customers do not want to think about their issues and conditions.

The interview findings illustrated that holiday groups are highly different from one another, and participation rates in holiday activities can vary significantly, for instance, between two family holidays. One informant described there being three types of customers: those who participate in activities, those who are active on their own, and those who may struggle with holiday taking (e.g., scheduling and/or social isolation). These customers would need extra support during a holiday, for instance, organized support with a holiday instructor. For holiday instructors, heterogeneous holiday groups are problematic when planning programs such as guided activities – particularly when the preliminary information available about the groups is very limited. Finally, the importance of, and the need for, Finnish social tourism were emphasized in the findings, particularly when the COVID-19 pandemic has had negative impacts on the lives of disadvantaged populations. The informants also recognized the complexity of monitoring wellbeing outcomes especially in a situation where Veikkaus funding is decreasing and competition for the remaining funding is increasing.

10.3.2.2 Social Tourism Funding Organization Interview Findings

In the social tourism stakeholders' interview findings (Vento & Komppula, 2020), constructs such as equalization, empowerment, caring, and the welfare state ideology were related to the Finnish social tourism system. Already in 2018, the interviewees highlighted the issue of widening inequality gaps between different groups of society when discussing the purpose and the meaning of the Finnish social tourism. Increasing societal inequality was seen as a harmful development particularly from the perspective of disadvantaged children. Certain contradictions were also included in the findings, when, on the one hand, the importance of voluntary participation and so-called low threshold ideology were underscored. However, on the other hand, the interviewees described how the guided holiday activities aim to engender different kinds of positive developments, such as physical activity, spending time in nature, socialization and being in a group, learning healthy life habits and fostering family relationships, that are related to the social tourism objectives.

Although social tourism has long traditions in Finland, the activities and programs have become highly regulated, particularly since the 2010s, which was reflected in the interview findings. The funding organizations had developed strategies to ensure that the holiday associations work together to broaden participation and ensure access amongst the most vulnerable in society, and to counteract the perception that social resources and services were too heavily concentrated on some individuals. Additionally, the representatives of the funding organization stated that the holiday associations should improve the quality of their impact evaluation, measurement and reporting, so that there is better evidence of the effectiveness of social holidays, which would strengthen the justification for allocating funding to social tourism. Although the holiday association representatives criticized the increasing workload and bureaucracy, all interviewees believed that the Finnish social tourism generally has deeper-level positive impacts on the lives of the customers – they are just extremely challenging to capture and measure.

10.4   Discussion and Conclusion

Overall, it is noteworthy that despite some complexities and limitations related to the research setting, various wellbeing outcomes associated with Finnish social tourism were identified in this study. When the research problem was approached from different perspectives and by mixed methods, diverse insights were gained, leading to both theoretical and managerial contributions.

The mixed-methods, longitudinal research process, involving both beneficiary, as well as service provider perspectives, led to novel insights into the outcomes of social tourism initiatives. The results of the quantitative two-stage analysis correspond with previous two-stage studies examining the wellbeing effects of social tourism initiatives, indicating positive outcomes in terms of satisfaction with life, social relationships, family, leisure, economic wellbeing, and employment situation (McCabe & Johnson, 2013; Pyke et al., 2019). However, similar to previous two-stage survey approaches, we found no effects on emotional or mental aspects, but these were clearly identified both in our qualitative findings and the nonlongitudinal quantitative results, as well as in the earlier qualitative social tourism studies (Hazel, 2005; McCabe, 2009; Smith & Hughes, 1999). This signals that when the outcomes of a social tourism initiative are examined, the methods chosen, measures, and research strategies can have an impact on the results. Some deeper-level, transformational outcomes, such as the potential of a social holiday to provide some relief from extremely difficult – even desperate – life situations could be difficult to capture solely by quantitative research methods.

Our results demonstrated how sharing holiday experiences with peers can be particularly important for disadvantaged children, who may not normally have much to contribute when their classmates and friends talk about their own holiday trips. Additionally, it is noteworthy that the experiences of equality and satisfaction with societal status weakened significantly in the control group. This also emphasizes the meaning of a holiday away from home during a general summer holiday season. Overall, these findings are novel and valuable, for instance, in the field of (social) tourism research, poverty research, and sociology.

Whereas our results demonstrate that some benefits of a social holiday, such as emotional outcomes, increased activity levels, and a temporal escape from everyday life and the domestic environment, were witnessed among all social tourism customers, they also bring forth the divergent needs and motivations of different target groups. Some of these differences are somewhat obvious, as the life situations of families with children, seniors, caregivers and disabled individuals differ significantly. However, the differences have not been considered in social tourism objectives, which are generic for all target groups. This may lead to a situation in which certain objectives are systemically not met among particular beneficiary groups – for instance, the meaning of peer support can be lower on family holidays than on the holidays of illness-based groups. Hence, we suggest that matching social tourism objectives to the actual needs and motivations of target groups could improve the effectiveness of the activity (McCabe & Qiao, 2020). Additionally, the internal heterogeneity of some 'broad' target groups, such as a disadvantaged family, could be considered more efficiently while planning the aims and contents of social tourism offerings (McCabe & Qiao, 2020). If personalized holidays were to be organized, for example, for different family types, it would contribute to the problem of heterogeneous holiday groups (Komppula et al., 2016). We recommend that future research should investigate the needs of different family types to ensure that those who require greater active intervention can be differentiated from those who have greater capacity to build their own family experiences independently.

When the holiday instructors, who represent grassroots workers in the context of social tourism, were included in the study, some practical tips to combat certain problems currently related to Finnish social holidays were identified.

First, the results indicate that holiday taking can be problematic for some customers, for instance, due to social exclusion, passiveness, and/or the inability to structure and build routines in daily life. These customers, who may not have much experience of vacationing, would need some extra support, but currently, holiday instructors do not have resources to provide it to them (see Minnaert et al., 2009). An obligatory meeting with a holiday instructor was suggested as a potential solution to this issue. Additionally, more preholiday information about the makeup of a holiday group would help holiday instructors to consider the characteristics of a group while planning the contents of guided activities.

Finally, it can be stated that in many societies, social tourism is currently in a challenging situation, when the need for the activity is increasing, but the available funding resources declining. The COVID-19 pandemic (see Save the Children Finland, 2021), followed by the war in Ukraine, have typically complicated the lives of disadvantaged populations who are currently struggling with, for instance, rising prices and the cost of living. Potentially, this development will lead to a situation, in which fewer people will have access to holiday taking in the future (Cole & Morgan, 2010). This underscored the urgency of analyzing the outcomes of social tourism in different contexts, so that the meaning and the value of the activity can be better evidenced and justified. With respect to this, the role of cooperation between the academic world and the operational field of social tourism is even more important going forward.

References

Austin, P. C. (2011). An introduction to propensity score methods for reducing the effects of confounding in observational studies. *Multivariate Behavioral Research*, *46*(3), 399–424.

Bos, L., McCabe, S. & Johnson, S. (2015). Learning never goes on holiday: an exploration of social tourism as a context for experiential learning. *Current Issues in Tourism*, *18*(9), 859–875.

Chung, J. Y. & Simpson, S. (2020). Social tourism for families with terminally ill parent. *Annals of Tourism Research*, *84*(C), 10.1016/j.annals.2019.102813.

Cole, S. & Morgan, N. (2010). Introduction: Tourism and inequalities. In S. Cole & N. Morgan (Eds), *Tourism and inequality: Problems and prospects* (pp. xvii–xxv). Wallingford: CABI.

Diekmann, A., Vincent, M., & Bauthier, I. (2020). The holiday practices of seniors and their implications for social tourism: A Wallonian Perspective. *Annals of Tourism Research*, *85*, 103096. https://doi.org/10.1016/j.annals.2020.103096.

Diener, E., Suh, E. M., Lucas, R. E. & Smith, H. L. (1999). Subjective well-being: Three decades of progress. *Psychological Bulletin*, *125*(2), 276–302.

Durko, A. & Petrick, J. (2013). Family and relationship benefits of travel experiences: A literature review. *Journal of Travel Research, 52*(6), 720–730.

Eichhorn, V. (2020). Social tourism to overcome social exclusion: towards a holistic understanding of accessibility and its users. In A. Diekmann & S. McCabe (Eds), *Handbook of social tourism* (pp. 177–194). Cheltenham, UK: Edward Elgar Publishing Ltd.

European Social Survey. (2013). Round 6 module on personal and social well-being – Final module in template. Centre for Comparative Social Surveys. City University London, London, UK. https:// www . europeanso cialsurvey .org/ docs/ round6/ questionnaire/ESS6_final_personal_and_social_well_being_module_template.pdf.

Eusébio, C., Carneiro, M. J., Kastenholz, E., & Alvelos, H. (2016). The impact of social tourism for seniors on the economic development of tourism destinations. *European Journal of Tourism Research, 12*, 5–24.

Ferrer, J. G., Sanz, M. F., Ferrandis, E. D., McCabe, S., & García, J. S. (2016). Social tourism and healthy ageing. *International Journal of Tourism Research, 18*(4), 297–307.

Gilbert, D. & Abdullah, J. (2004). Holidaytaking and the sense of well-being. *Annals of Tourism Research, 31*(1), 103–121.

Hazel, N. (2005). Holidays for children and families in need: An exploration of the research and policy context for social tourism in the UK. *Children & Society, 19*, 225–236. https://doi.org/10.1002/chi.838.

Hunter-Jones, P. (2004). Young people, holiday-taking and cancer – an exploratory analysis. *Tourism Management, 25*(2), 249–258. https:// doi .org/ 10 .1016/ S02615–177(03)000943–.

Hunter-Jones, P., Sudbury-Riley, L., Al-Abdin, A., Menzies, L., & Neary, K. (2020). When a child is sick: The role of social tourism in palliative and end-of-life care. *Annals of Tourism Research, 83*, 102900, https://doi.org/10.1016/j.annals.2020 .102900.

Hyvinvointilomat ry. (2018). Toimintakertomus 2017. [Annual report 2017 of Hyvinvointilomat association] Hyvinvointilomat ry, Helsinki, Finland.

Kakoudakis, K. I. (2020). Counterbalancing the effects of unemployment through social tourism. In A. Diekmann & S. McCabe (Eds), *Handbook of social tourism* (pp. 195–208). Cheltenham, UK: Edward Elgar Publishing Ltd.

Komppula, R. & Ilves, R. (2018) Social tourism as correlates of QoL: The case of disadvantaged people. In M. Uysal, M. J. Sirgy, & S. Kruger (Eds). *Managing quality of life in tourism and hospitality* (pp. 54–69). Wallingford: CABI.

Komppula, R., Ilves, R., & Airey, D. (2016). Social holidays as a tourist experience in Finland. *Tourism Management, 52*, 521–532.

Kakoudakis, K. I., McCabe, S., & Story, V. (2017). Social tourism and self-efficacy: Exploring links between tourism participation, job-seeking and unemployment. *Annals of Tourism Research, 65*, 108–121.

Komppula, R., & Vento, E. (2021). Challenges and opportunities for development of social tourism in Finland. In J. Lima & C. Eusébio (Eds). *Social tourism: Global challenges and approaches* (pp. 30–40). Wallingford: CABI.

Kelly, C. (2020). Beyond 'a trip to the seaside': Exploring emotions and family tourism experiences. *Tourism Geographies, 24*(2–3), 284–305.

Lima, J., & Eusébio, C. (2020). Economic benefits of social tourism: Theoretical reflections and insights for management. In A. Diekmann & S. McCabe (Eds), *Handbook of social tourism* (pp. 43–58). Cheltenham, UK: Edward Elgar Publishing Ltd.

McCabe, S. (2009). Who needs a holiday? Evaluating social tourism. *Annals of Tourism Research*, 36(4), 667–688.

McCabe, S., & Diekmann, A. (2015). The rights to tourism: Reflections on social tourism and human rights. *Tourism Recreation Research*, 40(2), 194–204.

McCabe, S., & Johnson, S. (2013). The happiness factor in tourism: Subjective well-being and social tourism. *Annals of Tourism Research*, 41, 42–65.

McCabe, S., Joldersma, T., & Li, C. (2010). Understanding the benefits of social tourism: Linking Participation to subjective well-being and quality of life. *International Journal of Tourism Research*, 12(6), 761–773.

McCabe, S., & Qiao, G. (2020). A review of research into social tourism: Launching the Annals of Tourism Research Curated Collection on Social Tourism. *Annals of Tourism Research*, 85, 103103, https://doi.org/10.1016/j.annals.2020.103103.

Minnaert, L. (2012). Social tourism as opportunity for unplanned learning and behavior change. *Journal of Travel Research*, 51(5), 607–616.

Minnaert, L., Maitland, R., & Miller, G. (2006). Social tourism and its ethical foundations. *Tourism Culture & Communication*, 7(1), 7–17.

Minnaert, L., Maitland, R. & Miller, G. (2009). Tourism and social policy. The value of social tourism. *Annals of Tourism Research*, 36(2), 316–334.

Minnaert, L., Maitland, R., & Miller, G. (2011). What is social tourism? *Current Issues in Tourism*, 14(5), 403–415.

Morgan, N., Pritchard, A., & Sedgley, D. (2015). Social tourism and well-being in later life. *Annals of Tourism Research*, 52, 1–15, https://doi.org/10.1016/j.annals.2015.02.015.

Neal, J. D., Sirgy, M. J., & Uysal, M. (2004). Measuring the effect of tourism services on travelers' quality of life: Further validation. *Social Indicators Research*, 69, 243–277.

Nivala, E., & Ryynänen, S. (2013). Kohti sosiaalipedagogista osallisuuden ideaalia. *Sosiaalipedagoginen aikakauskirja*, 14, 10–41, https://doi.org/10.30675/sa.122317.

Park, S., Park, C., & Kang, C. (2018). Effects of a holiday trip on health and quality of life: Evidence from a natural experiment in South Korea. *Applied Economics*, 50(42), 4556–4569.

Pyke, J., Pyke, S., & Watuwa, R. (2019). Social tourism and well-being in a first nation community. *Annals of Tourism Research*, 77, 38–48. https://doi.org/10.1016/j.annals.2019.04.013.

Save the Children Finland. (2021). Lapsen ääni 2021: Lasten ja nuorten kokemuksia koronapandemian ajalta. Available at: https:// pelastakaalapset .s3 .eu -west -1 .amazonaws .com/ main/ 2021/ 05/ 21110913/ lapsen -aani -2021 _raportti1 _fi .pdf. Accessed 3.2.2023.

Schänzel, H. A., & Yeoman, I. (2014). The future of family tourism. *Tourism Recreation Research*, 39(3), 343–360.

Smith, V., & Hughes, H. (1999). Disadvantaged families and the meaning of the holiday. *International Journal of Tourism Research*, 1(2), 123–133.

STEA. (2022). Funding Centre for Social Welfare and Health Organisations. https:// www.stea.fi/en/. Accessed 8.5.2022.

Veikkaus Oy. (2021). Veikkauksen tulos laski viime vuonna merkittävästi koronaepidemian vuoksi. [The profit of Veikkaus declined significantly last year due to the corona epidemic] https://www.veikkaus.fi/fi/yritys#!/article/tiedotteet/yritys/2021/03-maaliskuu/01_vuositulostiedote. Accessed 15.6.2022.

Vento, E. (2022). Exploring the effectiveness of social holidays in the Finnish context. *Tourism Recreation Research*, https://doi.org/10.1080/02508281.2022.2067954.

Vento, E., & Komppula, R. (2020). Social tourism practices and implementation in Finland. In A. Diekmann & S. McCabe (Eds), *Handbook of social tourism* (pp. 244–255). Cheltenham, UK: Edward Elgar Publishing Ltd.
Vento, E., Tammi, T., McCabe, S., & Komppula, R. (2020). Re-evaluating well-being outcomes of social tourism: evidence from Finland. *Annals of Tourism Research, 85,* 103085, https://doi.org/10.1016/j.annals.2020.103085.

11 African diaspora tourists' experiences of wellbeing

Xavier Matteucci, Sebastian Filep, Jerram Bateman and J. A. (Tony) Binns

11.1 Introduction

The body of knowledge on diaspora tourism is now well established in tourism studies (Duval, 2003; Marschall, 2017; Scheyvens, 2007). Despite the significant attention devoted to diaspora tourism and visiting friends and relatives (VFR) research in the literature (Backer, 2008; Hing & Dimmock, 1997; O'Leary & Morrison, 1995), most of the studies in this area have focused on understanding tourism activities, expenditures, information sources, and classifications of diaspora tourists (Shani, 2013). The literature on both diaspora tourism and VFR tourism stresses the economic value of visits back to the homelands (Marschall, 2017). It is established that when a country's nationals return home for a holiday and/or family gathering, they bring foreign currency, as well as enduring economic ties with their country (Coles & Timothy, 2004). In this way, diaspora tourism serves as an important source of foreign direct investment. Asiedu (2005) claimed that leakages out of economic systems through diaspora tourism have been low compared with other forms of tourism. This is because of the extensive use of local resources and services (for example, local transportation and hospitality services).

Contributions from people returning to their home country for a holiday can be significant, and can include 'financial remittances, technology and skills transfer, material and equipment donations' (Asiedu, 2005, p. 1). King and Gamage (1994), Lew and Wong (2004), and Barkin (2001) demonstrated that when expatriates returned to Sri Lanka, China, and Mexico (respectively) for holidays, their actions had significant developmental benefits. As well as giving money and gifts to family members and spending in the local area, expatriates often supported community organisations such as schools and religious groups. Asiedu (2005) found that Ghanaian nationals returning home for visits spent £2,769 on average, including international travel, but a significant £585 was spent on incidentals such as contributions to community development funds and expenses for funerals, and another £433 was used to purchase food and entertainment for friends and relatives. Overall, these studies show the potential of diaspora tourism as a source of community development through remittances and financial contributions.

On the other hand, relatively little consideration has been given to the social (noneconomic) facets of diaspora tourism particularly with regard to developing countries (Scheyvens, 2014). This chapter, therefore, explores how a sense of psychological wellbeing is experienced by diaspora tourists adding to an understanding of the sociopsychological facets of diaspora visits. For the purposes of the chapter, psychological wellbeing broadly encompasses a reflection on emotions experienced in diaspora tourist experiences, as well as meanings derived from such visits.

11.2   Theoretical Background

Although there is a dearth of research on psychological wellbeing in diaspora tourist experiences (Filep et al., 2022), there are studies that have examined related topics. For example, in the VFR tourism literature, some studies have addressed the experiences of migrants visiting their relatives back home. In this context, Uriely (2010) draws from the seminal work of sociologist George Simmel (1949) on the notion of *sociability* to emphasise the essential role of interactions with loved ones in fostering the warm feeling of being 'at home'. Social relationships are an important domain of quality of life; it is therefore not surprising that perceived quality of life tends to be improved after visiting friends and relatives (Backer, 2019). A number of social and psychological benefits have been associated with migrants' visits to their ancestral homeland. For instance, in a recent African diaspora study, Otoo, Kim and King (2021) found that tourists travelling to Ghana felt a sense of pride, a sense of belonging and shared heritage with their loved ones. Trips to Ghana also allowed the diaspora tourists to fulfil social obligations, which bestowed significant meaning upon them.

Other wellbeing dimensions that have been linked to the return travel of the African diaspora include a coherent sense of self and the emotion of love. In her study with African transnational migrants residing in South Africa, Marschall (2017) found that encounters with traces of the person's autobiographical past (spaces, objects, social relations) could positively lead to reconnecting with their own cultural self. Filep et al. (2022) have linked wellbeing to the emotion of love, which, they argue, permeates the multiple stages of the African diaspora tourists' experiences. These authors remarked that, for example, love manifests itself in terms of a deep attachment to the land and a strong desire to provide intimate care to their dear ones. Likewise, in an analysis of diaspora travel by the Caribbean communities, Chamberlain (2017) suggested that tourists' visits back to the Caribbean from the United Kingdom explain the commitment of the British diaspora to providing ongoing, intimate, support to their friends and relatives in their homelands.

Beyond the African context, similar wellbeing outcomes have been reported in studies with Chinese diaspora tourists. For instance, travel back home allows diaspora tourists to develop their cultural identification with China and to embrace their multicultural identities (Li & Chan, 2017). As a result of their visit, Chinese tourists felt a heightened purpose in life (Li & Chan, 2017), and they felt physically and spiritually more connected with their ancestral homeland (Huang et al., 2018). This short review has highlighted the link between diaspora trips and a number of wellbeing dimensions. Yet, it would be naive to believe that returning home is only associated with positive outcomes. In fact, some studies have reported some challenges broadly subsumed under the term *reverse culture shock* (AlSaleh & Moufakkir, 2019). However, here our focus is set on the wellbeing outcomes experienced by members of the African diaspora.

11.3   Context

To meet the aim of exploring how a sense of psychological wellbeing is experienced in diaspora tourism by tourists during and after their trip, this chapter reports on research carried out in collaboration with the Sierra Leonean diaspora community in London, United Kingdom (UK). Sierra Leone is one of the world's poorest countries and is ranked 181 out of 189 countries according to United Nations Human Development Index (UNDP, 2019). Sierra Leonean migration to the UK has a long history, with many Sierra Leonean elite sending their children to Britain to be educated since the mid-19th century (Binns & Binns, 1992). More recent migration from Sierra Leone to the UK was driven by poor governance and a downturn in the economy in the 1970s and 1980s, and the devastation caused by the Sierra Leone Civil War (1991–2002), with some stating that as many as 17,000 Sierra Leonean refugees migrated to the UK over the duration of the war (Rutter, 2003). Postwar migration from Sierra Leone to the UK has primarily consisted of people seeking study or work opportunities, or to rejoin family who had already arrived (Rubyan-Ling,

2013). In 2011, it was estimated that 23,000 Sierra Leoneans were living in the UK, with the majority of them having settled in London (UK Office for National Statistics, 2013). While this community may not have a history of significant travel experience to international destinations, there has been a steady flow of diaspora tourism to Sierra Leone, largely driven by the members of this community regularly travelling between London and Sierra Leone (Filep et al., 2022). Recognising the lack of research with this community, we aimed to explore how a sense of psychological wellbeing is experienced in diaspora trips, as reported by the community members.

11.4   Methodology

To address the aim of the study, 12 in-depth interviews with Sierra Leonean tourists (representatives of the Sierra Leonean diaspora) were conducted in London in January 2019, before the global pandemic. We recruited participants from the Sierra Leone diaspora who reside in London, and who had been to Sierra Leone in the last five years to visit friends and relatives. We obtained the contact details of potential participants (telephone numbers and/ or WhatsApp) from their friends and relatives in Sierra Leone who were well known to us from previous research projects. This convenience sampling approach allowed participants to be selected on the basis of access (Bradshaw & Stratford, 2000). Our sample consists of eight males and four females between 27 and 61 years of age. On average, our participants had been living about 24 years in London.

The interviews lasted between 50 and 60 minutes and were held in places convenient to participants, such as their homes or local coffee shops. Each interview included some general questions about visits to Sierra Leone (such as, 'When did you go?' or 'Whom did you go with?'), followed by questions on their trip experiences (such as, 'Tell us about your friends and family, and how did the visit contribute to your sense of wellbeing?'). The research was inductive, allowing for follow-up questions and probes. Interview questions were open-ended to facilitate in-depth responses and allow rich, nuanced data to emerge. It is recognised that prior experiences of researchers can affect the way studies are designed and framed, so researchers' positionalities are important to acknowledge. Although none of the four authors is of Sierra Leonean ethnicity, two of the interviewers (third and fourth author) have a good knowledge of Sierra Leone, in one case going back 46 years, so it proved relatively easy to develop rapport with the interviewees. There was a level of empathy between the researchers and interviewees, and issues relating to Sierra Leone figured prominently in the informal discussions. The interviews were recorded on a digital audio recorder and were transcribed verbatim by the authors. Member checking was completed by the authors by asking participants to review transcripts, confirm data accuracy, and clarify any comments as necessary.

Thematic analysis was completed on both semantic and latent levels to evaluate and record the themes within the data (Braun & Clarke, 2006). Analysis involved coding of repeated words and phrases; evaluating relationships between codes; identifying patterns, commonalities and differences; and creating a set of higher-order themes (Braun & Clarke, 2006), following the processes in other relevant qualitative studies in tourism (e.g., Matteucci & Aubke, 2018). Emergent themes were then analysed by the first three authors (see Table 11.1). Due to time and budget constraints, the authors ceased to collect data after 12 interviews. Due to the richness of the data obtained, the narrow focus of the study, and the homogeneous nature of the research participants, it was deemed that this sample of informants held substantial information power (Malterud et al., 2016). In other words, while saturation of information may not have been reached after 12 interviews, the excellent interview dialogues generated data that offer rich insights and sufficient variation of findings. Data and discussions of each theme are integrated in the following section to provide a cohesive interpretation for readers.

11.5   Findings

The diaspora tourists' accounts were replete with descriptions of positive emotions felt in Sierra Leone, which reveals substantial psychological benefits of those trips. We identified four main themes from these accounts, of which three themes represent positive psychological wellbeing outcomes: isolation and estrangement (1), intimacy and togetherness (2), attachment to the land and a sense of belonging (3), and satisfaction in fulfilling social obligations (4). The positive outcomes felt in the country of origin, however, can be better understood by exposing the Sierra Leoneans' emotional states before their trips. Our account, therefore, begins with descriptions of the diaspora tourists' feelings of isolation and estrangement in London before their visit to Sierra Leone.

11.5.1 Isolation and Estrangement

To situate the diaspora tourists' experiences in their country of origin, it is worth noting that about half of our Sierra Leonean informants reported feel-

Table 11.1   Example of coding

	Coding	Initial themes	Revised themes
Foday: 'Sierra Leoneans are very very helpful. Even though they're expecting, there's that expectation from them; when we are there they always want to help. Want to help with the kids, um, whatever I'm doing they will, they want to help with it. And there's a concern. Here in the UK people don't care about, even the elderly. When they are, if they're sick, they'll just send them to an elde- um- um- old people's home. In Sierra Leone we don't do that. As soon as, if someone is old, or sick, they will come and look after you. So, I've been telling my wife that if I'm old, and can't look after myself, that she'll send me back to Sierra Leone, instead of leaving me here. Yeah, and so ... there is the concern. Sierra Leoneans they're warm, warm-hearted. That's one thing I miss most when I'm here'.	Sierra Leoneans (SLs) are helpful / SLs expect favors / SLs care about people / British people don't care about people / SLs behave differently / Identifying with SL mode of being Wishing to be in SL when too old to look after himself / SLs are kind / Missing warm-heartedness in the UK	SL kindness SL expectations Caring / mattering Relating to SL mentality Comfort in SL Alienation	Attachment to the land Experiencing care (positive emotions) Identification with SL culture (sense of belonging) Comfort (positive emotions) Estrangement

ings of isolation and estrangement before their travel to their ancestral land. Isolation is interpreted as being far away from the cherished homeland and the loved ones. Isolation is, therefore, closely linked to feelings of deprivation of something dear and needed. A number of informants, like Komba below, have articulated missing and worrying about their relatives who live in Sierra Leone.

> I was also very homesick, I was unsettled. I wasn't sleeping properly, I was just thinking of Sierra Leone [...] and my dad for me is what makes me look, think hard, most of his friends they've died. Or they've got serious illnesses. So, one of my big motivations is to be going regularly to see them now.

Komba's mental wellbeing seems to be subject to his longing for home. His malaise is epitomised by the reference he makes to his homesickness and poor sleep. Similar to Komba, in the subsequent excerpt, Kai discloses feeling depressed and eager to reunite with his mother and siblings he had not seen for 10 years.

> My first visit was because I had been 10 years in the UK. 10 years outside my birth-place, 10 years not seeing my mom, 10 years not seeing my brothers, my sisters. It was a very depressing, frustrating ... I mean, it's beyond imagination that I can live even six months without seeing my mom, especially [...] and I became very frustrated in this country. Regardless of whatever you call it the saying, we have good health here, we have food, we have this. But to me, it's not all that. It's about my mom in particular. Not enjoying that motherhood, not enjoying my mom, being together with her, seeing her. It depressed me to an extent. I sat here thinking when am I going to see my mom? So that was why I went to go and see her, and I spent four good weeks with her. Those weeks or those times, I really treasure it as I'm talking to you. So that was why I went.

Some informants, such as Foday below, also expressed feeling lonely in London, or lacking the physical and emotional warmth of their home country, which suggests that regular trips back to Sierra Leone are essential to the informants' psychological wellbeing.

> We are lonely most of the time. In the UK. So I've said, ah yeah, it's me and my family. Lonely, yeah. And, so if you compare that to how I was in Sierra Leone, growing up. Because I came from a family of, of 13. They were always around me. My friends, my cousins. So the loneliness here [in London] at times causes you to think back. And think, oh, our life was in Sierra Leone. It was fun, it was exciting. So you start calling them, they'll call you. So when you go back, you try to help them, because you've missed them.

These findings are concordant with the diaspora tourism literature, which indicates that travel to one's ancestral home may serve as a means of escaping alienation in the country of residence (Otoo, Kim & Choi, 2021; Shuval, 2000). This sense of estrangement or alienation in London is felt more deeply by the first-generation immigrants – the vast majority of our informants – who have maintained a stronger attachment to their ancestral home (Hay, 1998).

11.5.2 Intimacy and Feelings of Togetherness

Unlike the sense of isolation and melancholy felt in London, the tourists' trips to their homeland were punctuated by uplifting moments. Through their return visits to Sierra Leone, the members of the diaspora were able to reunite and socialise with their beloved friends and relatives in places that had meaning for them. In order to emphasise these pleasurable moments of family encounters, Sahr metaphorically associates his everyday experience in Sierra Leone to 'Christmas time':

> You haven't seen them for a while. You are living with your relatives. You're bringing memories, smiles, that's what it's about, really. Yeah. You feel part of life. The familiar feeling which you miss for quite a while. Because here in London we never have our relatives around. Yeah, it's just that feeling of being with family members. Any time I visit, I feel like it's Christmas time with them.

Diasporic travel presents an ideal space to experience quality intimate relationships. The members of the Sierra Leonean diaspora particularly enjoy the physical closeness to their loved ones, which reinforces emotional bonds between the tourists and their relatives. Our African diaspora data support the positive psychology literature (e.g., Seligman, 2011) that ascertains the positive contribution of human relationships to wellbeing. Indeed, the positive emotions felt in the company of meaningful others help to recover from negative psychological states (e.g., loneliness felt in London) and to feel rejuvenated. To illustrate this point said:

> We are lonely most, most of the time. Yeah, it's me and my family in the UK. Well, the thing that I like most is to wake up in the morning and they're there. Your friends, people you grew up with. It makes me feel better.

The subsequent excerpt from Kai reveals feelings of happiness through physical closeness and shared moments of togetherness:

> When they know you are there, they come home in the morning, in the afternoon, in the evening. We eat together. They cook, we eat together. We sit down and talk a lot of things. Like old things like when you went to school together, what happened? You bring all these stories up. You laugh and laugh and laugh. You grew up with each other. Oh, you remember when we were in sixth form and all that kind of thing. What we used to do. It helps them. It makes them feel happy, it makes me feel happy. And this is why a person like me goes there now often. And I need to go there often. Yeah.

The diaspora tourists' accounts point to the significance of experiences of intimate sociality with their loved ones as constitutive elements of their wellbeing. Intimacy is experienced through talks, recalling shared life experiences, and laughter. These simple moments of closeness and togetherness are conducive to bonding and are highly valued by the diaspora tourists. The literature also provides some evidence that diaspora tourists feel positive emotions and derive pleasure from partaking in the mundane activities of their relatives. For instance, in her recent study with ancestral tourists visiting Sweden, Prince (2022) noted that tourists derive deeply positive experiences through family encounters and through partaking in the everyday activities of the current Swedes. The words articulated by Aiah below point to the psychological health benefits of return travel to Sierra Leone:

> I love the shared experiences with family and friends, you know, about how life is going on. And you share ideas, you know [...] Yeah, I mean, they [visits to Sierra Leone] are always helpful [for my wellbeing]. Um. Maybe I'll say, you know, they are therapeutic in a sense, after staying here [in the UK] for a long time...So once I'm there, you know, and I'm just gonna relax; chill out. Enjoy myself [laughter]... It's like takin' a body off your head. You're there...the lifestyle is just different. People are more relaxed there. It's a bit therapeutic... You go to the countryside, to the village; it's just basic. No complexities, you know, life is just simple. Hmm, that kind of thing, basically. So, uh, it can be really helpful, mentally.

As Aiah unambiguously articulates, the visits were therapeutic in nature. They were therapeutic, in the sense that they assisted the diaspora community to break their usual routines and feel more refreshed as a result of the strong companionships.

11.5.3 Attachment to the Land and Belonging

A sense of psychological wellbeing manifested itself among Sierra Leoneans also as an attachment to their ancestral land. Attachment to the land is intricately linked to the Sierra Leoneans' fond childhood memories, which are brought back through everyday activities during their holiday. The following excerpt from Sahr illustrates this aspect:

> Sometimes I go, I go walking. I'll go to my village where we have got over 200 acres of land, sometimes I go to just to, to, to take a walk in the bush. It brings back memories of when I was growing up. I feel very at home.

As in the case of Sahr, childhood memories are revived through walks in nature; that is a sensual re-encounter with textures, colours, sounds, and smells. These sensory cues give Sahr a sense of who he is and where he belongs to. The walks in nature allow Sahr to reconnect with his own cultural self. In other words, through ubiquitous activities in long known environments, the diaspora tourists are able to embody their cultural identity. For Sahr, family is equated to Sierra Leone. It is where his heritage lies and where his true connections are. These bonds acts as a powerful motivator for him to travel there. The next account similarly highlights the link between memories of one's past, emotions, and feelings of comfort.

> We all have fun, we go to places, we eat, we chat and we have fun. So we all feel good. And it brings emotions when I'm about to come back [to London]. Emotions

rise but these are good emotions […] Like when I go to Kono, I enjoy eating my traditional food, things I don't eat here. We go to places. I like going around, we go to places. In the bush, you know, just to visit the farmers and the garden. I used to do a lot of gardening when my mum was alive.

Sia's testimony above intimates a feeling of comfort when she refers to 'good emotions' and 'eating my traditional food'. Beyond comfort, the reference to 'her' traditional food points to the relevance of food for the construction of her cultural self. This comment about 'her' traditional food resonates with Jackson's (2002) remark that our choice of food reflects our cultural identities. Attachment to the land and its cultural manifestations (such as food) may contribute to sustain the informants' sense of self. A number of other members of the diaspora have also expressed this feeling of comfort, belonging, and profound attachment to place. For instance, Yai commented:

I started going to the villages to see those that I have not seen for a very long time. And every time I went that's what I do. I stay in the village, with no lights, just to feel what they feel. To be a part of them. It gives me some sense of uh, belonging. It gives me uh, I reconnect. It takes me right back to my childhood. Mostly like the people that I grew up with, to sit down and then we snap pictures. That for me, you know, and the, the way they accept me. You know, most of them will say, you never changed […] I love Sierra Leone. Here, England, it's my second home. But I will never want to grow old here. I will never want to die here. I want to be at home. Because there's a connection there.

In the subsequent quotation, Kumba employs the words 'emptiness' and 'gap' to refer to her estrangement as a Sierra Leonean living in the UK. Beyond loneliness, for some like Kumba, regular visits to the homeland help Sierra Leoneans sustain a sense of adequacy with who they feel they are. Our data suggest that return visits to the homeland enable tourists to indulge in therapeutic self-authenticity.

Like Sierra Leone is my home, I can't compromise it. Even if none of my friends or my siblings are there I was still gonna ...Yeah something about the place. I'm from there and I think for me personally I think it's my role to do something here [...] I need to associate. I need to talk to people… It does make me feel like I'm part of Sierra Leone and I'm connected yeah [...] the British government have been very nice to us. Like I have my own flat. I have my own career. I have, there's nothing I'm worried about here as compared to other people. But there you fill that gap. That emptiness that, there's home… It's difficult to fill. I don't think any, whatever I get from here will always feel Sierra Leone is home.

Expressions of a profound sense of belonging to Sierra Leone were frequent in the informants' accounts. A sense of belonging and attachment to the land are prominent themes in diaspora studies (Otoo et al., 2021). Li and McKercher

(2016) noted that through diasporic travel, individuals are able to strengthen their bond with their homeland. These authors also remark that the closer the diaspora tourists' ties are with their ancestral land, the more their travel experiences are endowed with significant meaning. In the same vein, Li and Chan (2017) associated return travel to the ancestral homeland with an influential family event that contributes to the feeling that life is worth living. In the following section, the sense of belonging to Sierra Leone is shown to be intricately connected with a sense of obligation towards the country.

11.5.4 Satisfaction in Fulfilling Social Obligations

Another positive outcome of the diaspora tourist experience is the satisfaction derived from maintaining family ties alive and fulfilling social obligations. Like other participants, in the following quotation, Finda expresses her satisfaction with her regular trips to Sierra Leone. Nurturing family ties gives Finda not only satisfaction, but also a sense of belonging to her reference group; her Sierra Leonean identity is, therefore, cultivated by a strong emotional connection to her African roots.

> To go back home and people turned their back on you because you, you know, you didn't keep in contact. So, if you don't establish those family ties, and that connection, it's like you've lost your heritage. And you know, for us, it's not just your family, it's your ancestors, and then it goes quite deep. So, it's like if you lose your family, it's like you lose your identity. You know. You lose the essence of who you are.

Finda's words intimate a eudaimonic dimension to diasporic travel. Eudaimonia relates to a higher state of flourishing that is formed through personal growth and self-realisation of the individual (Ryff & Singer, 2008). Because Finda feels spiritually connected to her ancestral land, she feels the need to remain connected to her roots; this bond is achieved through return visits, which gives meaning to her life. Li and Chan (2017) similarly suggested that relatedness and meaning in life are two eudaimonic dimensions underpinning diaspora tourists' experiences. Most members of the Sierra Leonean diaspora expressed a strong sense of obligation towards their family. The fulfilment of this sense of obligation is the source of much satisfaction as clearly articulated by Komba in the following excerpt:

> I feel great. Um, I feel great. I have this, um, cousin who was like down and at my dad's so I found out in his village and I kind of helped her to start a business. So when I went this time she called the whole village and they were dancing. It was, it's hard to describe. She said this is the guy that saved me and so on. So it's, it does feel good to like support others. Um, I get a lot of, um, happiness from that.

Acts of kindness in the form of financial help provided to friends and relatives in the country of origin were often reported by members of the diaspora. Acts of kindness allow the Sierra Leonean tourists not only to support their relatives in need but these acts also help tourists to remain connected to their home community. The following quotation from Yai further illustrates this sense of social obligation:

> Well, I come from that background where we believe in uh, you know, helping one another. If you, you are fortunate, you share. That is what I grew up with, it makes me happy when I can put a smile on somebody's face. It makes me happy when I can make a difference in somebody's life. Yeah, I feel good. Uh, it's not just giving for giving's sake. I give when, like I said, people who need, I give for that, and I give for good work. There are certain kids that do, somebody will do well. You know, kind of for, to motivate them... Yeah. But I don't give to expect. I give because ... that's the way it's supposed to be.

11.6   Conclusion

This exploratory study aimed to uncover how a sense of psychological wellbeing was perceived by the British Sierra Leonean diaspora in relation to their travel experiences between the UK and Sierra Leone. Powerful experiences of intimacy, belongingness and togetherness were revealed by the travelling diaspora while interacting with their family and friends and the land itself. The findings also point to the role of diaspora tourism in nurturing one's own cultural identity and building a sense of self, as demonstrated by the participants' accounts.

The study findings add to nascent research on diaspora tourism and wellbeing (Filep et al., 2022; Li & Chan, 2020). Li and Chan's (2020) study explained that diasporic return shaped tourists' subjective wellbeing over life courses. Our study has similarly revealed the intrinsic value of diasporic relationships to tourist wellbeing. In particular, our investigation shows how social ties are sustained through tourism, and in turn how relationships contribute to eudaimonic wellbeing dimensions such as meaning and purpose in life. Our findings are in line with recent studies, which highlight the centrality of intimate socialities in fostering a sense of wellbeing in individuals (e.g., Kong et al., 2022; Matteucci et al., 2022). Perspectives of the African travelling community were investigated. A follow up investigation to understand the perspectives of the hosts or of non-African diaspora communities would be valuable.

While the diaspora tourists in our study mostly reported positive experiences, a few anecdotes also revealed some frustration felt in relation to expectations from friends and relatives who stayed in Sierra Leone. Assuming that 'life is easier in London' the Sierra Leoneans often expected gifts and money from their diasporic relatives. Also, Uriely (2010) remarked that being a noncommercial guest staying with relatives may be a constraint to bonding with significant others. Further research may explore the tension and ambivalence within the extended family remittance relationships and how this tension impinges upon the diaspora tourists' sense of wellbeing. By and large, the study suggests that diaspora community provides a utilitarian function in assisting the loved ones financially, but the visits have a therapeutic effect on the travelling community, which diaspora tourism provides. A resounding conclusion based on the study is clear. Diaspora tourism acts as a facilitator of connections to significant places and to significant people and therefore as a vehicle for enhancing psychological wellbeing.

References

AlSaleh, D., & Moufakkir, O. (2019). An exploratory study of the experience of VFR tourists: A culture shock perspective. *Tourism Geographies, 21*(4), 565–585.

Asiedu, A. (2005). Some benefits of migrants' return visits to Ghana. *Population, Space and Place, 11*(1), 1–11.

Backer, E. (2008). VFR travellers – Visiting the destination or visiting the hosts? *Asian Journal of Tourism and Hospitality Research, 2*(1), 60–70.

Backer, E. (2019). VFR travel: Do visits improve or reduce our quality of life? *Journal of Hospitality and Tourism Management, 38*, 161–167.

Barkin, D. (2001). Strengthening domestic tourism in Mexico: Challenges and opportunities. In K. Ghimire (Ed) *The native tourist: Mass tourism within developing countries* (pp. 30–54). Oxfordshire: Earthscan.

Binns, M., & Binns, T. (1992). *Sierra Leone, world bibliographical series*, Vol. 148. Oxford: Clio Press.

Bradshaw, M., & Stratford, E. (2000). On research design and rigour. In I. Hay (Ed), *Qualitative research methods in geography* (pp. 37–49). Melbourne: Oxford University Press.

Braun, V., & Clarke, V. (2006). Using thematic analysis in psychology. *Qualitative Research in Psychology, 3*(2), 77–101.

Chamberlain, M. (2017). *Family love in the diaspora: Migration and the Anglo-Caribbean experience*. New York: Routledge.

Coles, T., & Timothy, D. (Eds). (2004). *Tourism, diasporas and space*. London: Routledge.

Duval, D. T. (2003). When hosts become guests: Return visits and diasporic identities in a Commonwealth Eastern Caribbean community. *Current Issues in Tourism, 6*(4), 267–308.

Filep, S., Matteucci, X., Bateman, J., & Binns, T. (2022). Experiences of love in diaspora tourism. *Current Issues in Tourism, 25*(16), 2547–2551.

Hay, R. (1998). Sense of place in developmental context. *Journal of Environmental Psychology, 18*(1), 5–29.

Hing, N., & Dimmock, K. (1997). Contemporary tourism issues in Asia Pacific journals 1989–1996: A thematic perspective. *International Journal of Contemporary Hospitality Management, 9*(7), 254–269.

Huang, W.-J., Hung, K., & Chen, C-C. (2018). Attachment to the home country or hometown? Examining diaspora tourism across migrant generations. *Tourism Management, 68,* 52–65.

Jackson, P. (2002). Commercial cultures: Transcending the cultural and the economic. *Progress in Human Geography, 26*(1), 3–18.

King, B., & Gamage, A. (1994). Measuring the value of the ethnic connection: Expatriate travellers from Australia to Sri Lanka. *Journal of Travel Research, 32*(2), 46–50.

Kong, S., Guo, J., & Huang, D. (2022). The girlfriend getaway as an intimacy. *Annals of Tourism Research, 92,* 103337.

Lew, A. A., & Wong, A. (2004). Sojourners, guanxi and clan associations: Social capital and overseas Chinese tourism to China. In T. Coles & D. J. Timothy (Eds) *Tourism, diasporas and space* (pp. 202–214). London: Routledge.

Li, T. E., & Chan, E. (2017). Diaspora tourism and wellbeing: A eudaimonic view. *Annals of Tourism Research, 63,* 205–206.

Li, T. E., & Chan, E. (2020). Diaspora tourism and well-being over life-courses. *Annals of Tourism Research, 82,* 102917.

Li, T. E., & McKercher, B. (2016). Developing a typology of diaspora tourists: Return travel by Chinese immigrants in North America. *Tourism Management,* 56, 106–113.

Malterud, K., Siersma, V. K., & Guassora, A. D. (2016). Sample size in qualitative interview studies: Guided by information power. *Qualitative Health Research, 26*(13), 1753–1760.

Marschall, S. (2017). *Tourism and memories of home: Migrants, displaced people, exiles and diasporic communities.* Bristol: Channel View.

Matteucci, X., & Aubke, F. (2018). Experience care: Efficacy of service learning in fostering perspective transformation in tourism education. *Journal of Teaching in Travel and Tourism, 18*(1), 8–24.

Matteucci, X., Volić, I., & Filep, S. (2022). Dimensions of friendship in shared travel experiences. *Leisure Sciences, 44*(6), 697–714.

O'Leary, J. T., & Morrison, A. M. (1995). The VFR – visiting friends and relatives – market: Desperately seeking respect. *Journal of Tourism Studies, 6*(1), 2–5.

Otoo, F. E., Kim, S. S., & King, B. (2021). African diaspora tourism – How motivations shape experiences. *Journal of Destination Marketing & Management, 20,* 100565.

Otoo, F. E., Kim, S. S., & Choi, Y. (2021). Developing a multidimensional measurement scale for diaspora tourists' motivation. *Journal of Travel Research, 60*(2), 417–433.

Prince, S. (2022). Affect and performance in ancestral tourism: Stories of everyday life, personal heritage, and the family. *Journal of Heritage Tourism, 17*(1), 20–36.

Rutter, J. (2003). *Supporting refugee children in 21st century Britain: A compendium of essential information.* London: Trentham Books.

Ryff, C., & Singer, B. (2008). Know thyself and become what you are: A eudaimonic approach to psychological well-being. *Journal of Happiness Studies, 9,* 13–39.

Scheyvens, R. (2007). Poor cousins no more: Valuing the development potential of domestic and diaspora tourism. *Progress in Development Studies, 7*(4), 307–325.

Scheyvens, R. (Ed.). (2014). *Development fieldwork: A practical guide.* London: Sage.

Seligman, M. (2011). *Flourish*. New York: Free Press.

Shani, A. (2013). The VFR experience: 'Home' away from home? *Current Issues in Tourism*, *16*(1), 1–15.

Shuval, J. T. (2000). Diaspora migration: Definitional ambiguities and a theoretical paradigm. *International Migration*, *38*(5), 41–56.

Simmel, G. (1949). The sociology of sociability. *The American Journal of Sociology*, *55*(3), 254–261.

UK Office for National Statistics. (2013). *Immigration patterns of non-UK born populations in England and Wales in 2011*. London: UK Office for National Statistics. https://www.bl.uk/collection-items/immigration-patterns-of-nonuk-born-populations-in-england-and-wales-in-2011.

UNDP (United Nations Development Programme). (2019). *Human development report, 2019*. New York: UNDP. https://hdr.undp.org/content/human-development-report-2019.

Uriely, N. (2010). 'Home' and 'away' in VFR tourism. *Annals of Tourism Research*, *37*(3), 854–857.

12 Smells like my vacation: attenuating the fadeout effect

Ondrej Mitas and Marcel Bastiaansen

12.1 Introduction

Vacations provide a host of wellbeing benefits, including health, longevity (Eaker et al., 1992; Gump & Matthews, 2000), social cohesion (Mitas et al., 2012; Shahvali et al., 2021), and greater quality of life in general (Chen & Yoon, 2018). A number of review papers have synthesized the many empirical works and theoretical perspectives on the topic (Mitas et al., 2017; Smith & Diekmann, 2017; Vada et al., 2020). From the research it is evident that vacations are enjoyable and have an important role in many individuals' quality of life. The change in environment and routine seems to affect many valuable outcomes through a variety of mechanisms. Findings on these wellbeing pathways are often directly linked to researchers' disciplines, with public health researchers focusing on physical health (Strauss-Blasche, Riedmann, et al., 2004), while organizational psychologists focus on recovery from work demands (Fritz & Sonnentag, 2006; Westman & Etzion, 2001), for example.

Buoyed by compelling findings from positive psychology (Lyubomirsky et al., 2005), some researchers have posited that positive emotions are an alleged mechanism of vacation benefits (Mitas, 2010). The broaden-and-build theory offers a robust, empirically supported explanation of how momentary experiences of positive emotions accrue to longer-term changes in wellbeing (Fredrickson, 2001). Vacations can create many positive emotions (Ito et al., 2023; Lin et al., 2014; Mitas, Yarnal & Chick, 2012), and a higher frequency of vacationing contributes to year-to-year wellbeing (Mitas & Kroesen, 2019), consistent with the broaden-and-build theory.

Unfortunately, numerous studies also show that positive emotions decline to baseline levels within days of the end of a vacation (de Bloom et al., 2010; Mitas et al., 2012). This "fadeout" effect, the topic of this chapter, is considered one of the main experience design issues facing tourism providers. Many destinations, hotels, airlines, and tour operators have considered interventions to make the "holiday feeling" – by which they usually mean the vacation-driven boost in positive emotions – last for weeks or months after returning home. The emotional effects of daily hassles, routine, obligation, and boredom appear stubborn, however, and both popular media, as well as academic discourse, seem rather accepting of the fadeout effect to date.

Considering biological linkages between smell and memory, the sense of smell could be a promising and underexplored pathway to extend emotions associated with vacationing to the days after return home. While the sense of smell in tourism experience is acknowledged and occasionally researched, it is not widely used to combat the fadeout effect. Therefore, we attempted to investigate this in a small-scale experiment at two vacation parks in the Netherlands. Specifically, we present here an experimental intervention using a scented postcard to trigger memories of a recent vacation.

12.2 Theoretical Background

12.2.1 Tourism Experience and Wellbeing

It is widely understood that tourism experiences contribute to individuals' wellbeing. People who vacation are happier (Nawijn et al., 2010) and healthier (Eaker et al., 1992) than those who do not, and increases in vacation frequency are associated with increases in wellbeing in subsequent years (Mitas & Kroesen, 2019). Affective components of wellbeing, such as positive emotions (Mitas, Yarnal, Adams, et al., 2012) and moods (Strauss-Blasche, Muhry et al., 2004) are often improved in the short term, while improvements in cognitive components such as life satisfaction are most evident in multiyear studies (Kroesen & Handy, 2014; Mitas & Kroesen, 2019). A variety of eudaimonic wellbeing dimensions such as relationship quality are also improved by vacationing (Shahvali et al., 2021). The relationship between different wellbeing components in tourism literature is somewhat dependent on scholars' theoretical orientations.

While some conceptualizations of wellbeing, such as Diener and Seligman's (2002) subjective wellbeing framework or Seligman's (2011) PERMA framework, view a healthy balance of positive and negative affect as a *component* of wellbeing, others, such as the broaden-and-build theory, view affect as a *mechanism* which contributes to other, more significant outcomes (Fredrickson et al., 2008). These views are not incompatible. It is possible to see an optimal mix of positive and negative emotion as indicative of wellbeing in its own right, but also to acknowledge processes by which it contributes to, for example, life satisfaction (Garland et al., 2010). In any case, the role of affect and especially its distilled form, emotion, in wellbeing outcomes of vacations is undeniable. According to the peak model of tourist emotion, tourism experiences usually feature positive emotions elevated above day-to-day levels (Mitas, Yarnal, Adams et al., 2012). This "peak" pattern of positive emotion also holds over longer time scales, with measurements over an entire year being highest closest to a vacation (Nawijn et al., 2010) and over just the vacation itself, with the middle of the vacation being more positive than its very early and final moments (Nawijn et al., 2013).

Not all vacations are emotionally positive, nor should they be. In fact, there is a limit above which the ratio of positive to negative emotions is seen as no longer beneficial (Fredrickson, 2010). Our lives include many contexts in which specific negative emotions are appropriate and adaptive. One such context in tourism are concentration camps from the Second World War, which have been managed as museums and are open to visitors. Here, it is a particular mix of positive and (intense) negative emotions that predicts how these experiences are evaluated (Nawijn et al., 2017; Nawijn & Fricke, 2015; Nawijn et al., 2016). A similar mix of emotion was found among visitors of a museum exhibit about the war (Mitas et al., 2020). Such experiences are present in a minority of vacations, however, and when they are, they comprise only a brief segment of the overall vacation.

12.2.2 Fadeout of Vacation Emotions

It is, therefore, a rather frustrating but recognizable finding that the positive emotion boost from most vacations fades out within days (de Bloom et al., 2010). This finding appears in studies of winter sport vacations (de Bloom et al., 2010), vacations related to participants' hobbies (Mitas, Yarnal, Adams et al., 2012), brief Easter and Pentecost breaks (Kühnel & Sonnentag, 2011), and health resort stays (Strauss-Blasche, Muhry et al., 2004). The graphs in Mitas, Yarnal, Adams et al. (2012) showed a dip in emotions to baseline in the two days after returning home, while weekly measurements by Strauss-Blasche, Muhry et al. (2004) and de Bloom et al. (2010) showed a similar decline in the first survey after return home. The fadeout effects documented by Kühnel and Sonnentag (2011) were abrupt but not absolute in the first two weeks after return home, and led more gradually to near-baseline levels two weeks after that. The patterns visible in these data differ in time scale but are otherwise remarkably consistent, considering the widely differing study contexts and populations.

The fadeout effect is usually explained in terms of psychological mechanisms which operate in working life, such as daily hassles or time pressure (de Bloom et al., 2010; Kühnel & Sonnentag, 2011). The general tone of studies on the topic is to understand and accept the fadeout effect, and is only occasionally presented as a problem. Potential solutions are even less frequent. While de Bloom et al. (2010) suggested that the duration or timing of vacations could be fine-tuned for minimum fadeout, Kühnel and Sonnentag (2011) emphasize the importance of favorable working conditions upon return to work. These suggestions, however, do not address the fadeout effect, but provide best practices of organizational management in general. Thus, there remains a gap in research and design around this phenomenon. As de Bloom et al. (2010) asked, "Is it possible to conserve positive vacation effects, and if so, which strategies can be used to slow down fade-out processes and prolong vacation relief?" In this chapter, we propose coupling an olfactory stimulus to vacation enjoyment as one such possible strategy. Thereby, we test the argument that memory recall driven by smell can create positive emotions related to the vacation after returning home, thus reducing the fadeout effect.

12.2.3 The Effect of Smell on Memory

It has been a long-standing folk belief that odors are particularly powerful at eliciting memories. The phenomenon has been termed the Proust phenomenon, after the French literary author who brilliantly described how a certain odor evoked a strong memory of dipping a madeleine biscuit in his tea as a child (Proust, 1922). Contemporary empirical science has confirmed the existence of the Proust phenomenon by demonstrating that olfactory perception is an effective way of retrieving experientially rich, episodic, past memories. For example, olfactory-evoked memories are reported to be more emotional (Herz, 2004), more vivid (Chu & Downes, 2002), and more pleasant (Rubin et al., 1984) than memories retrieved through retrieval cues in other sensory modalities. Also, odor-evoked memories produce a stronger feeling of being brought back in time compared to visually evoked memories (Herz & Schooler, 2002). The neural basis for these phenomena is most probably that the olfactory neural structures (olfactory bulb and piriform cortex) directly connect with the amygdala or hippocampal complex, which is the neural substrate for emotional memories (Cahill et al., 1995; Herz et al., 2004). How these effects play out in a socially complex milieu such as everyday life – or vacationing – is not well understood.

In a tourism context, it is thought that experiences are remembered when they elicit strong emotions (Bastiaansen et al., 2019; Duerden, et al., 2015). In other words, emotions are key in triggering the mind to remember an experiential episode (Kim et al., 2012; Strijbosch et al., 2021), as the mind only remembers the emotional (Bastiaansen et al., 2019; Duerden et al., 2015). In the case of smell, such emotional memories are likely to be most vividly retrieved by the specific scents that were present during the encoding (i.e., during the tourism experience). Indeed, it has been shown that, in addition to other factors, olfactory stimulation led to more vivid recall of a cultural festival experience (Kim & Jang, 2016). Besides the above study, research related to smell in tourism has been largely confined to written descriptions of smell (Dann & Jacobsen, 2003; Magnini & Karande, 2010; Pan & Ryan, 2009), rather than the subjective experience of smell itself (Kim & Fesenmaier, 2015).

Furthermore, it is important to note that while emotions are key in encoding memories, recalling them does not mean necessarily reexperiencing an emotion. Thus, processes of memory encoding and affective fadeout from a vacation are partly independent. Potential connections between these processes have not been studied in a tourism context, making it all the more urgent to test how a smell-based intervention designed to evoke memories might affect the fadeout effect.

12.2.4 Hypotheses

Existing knowledge shows that 1) vacations increase positive emotions, but only temporarily, embodying a *fadeout effect*; 2) smell empowers encoding of emotions in memory, enabling emotion recall; and 3) emotions are an important component of subjective wellbeing and predict its other component, life satisfaction. With this in mind, we posit that:

H1. A perfume-based intervention will cause improved subjective wellbeing after a vacation compared to baseline.

H2. A perfume-based intervention will reduce the emotional fadeout effect after a vacation.

12.3 Methods

The goal of the present empirical study was to determine the causal effect of a perfume-based intervention on vacation fadeout and subjective wellbeing.

Thus, a true experimental design, in which participants are randomly assigned to receive either the intervention or a comparable placebo, was called for. A smell stimulus in the form of perfume spray was self-administered by tourists randomly assigned to a treatment group with the instruction to "spray the perfume during a highlight of the vacation." The same scent was applied to a postcard participants received one to two weeks after returning home. The logic of this design was coupling an emotional episode during the vacation, with the assumption that a "highlight" would be interpreted as a strongly emotional moment by participants, with a specific smell. The same smell would then be presented at a moment when, according to previous research, effects of the vacation were likely to have faded out. Finally, subjective wellbeing (including emotions) was assessed immediately afterward.

12.3.1 Sample

The study used a convenience sample based on two bungalow parks in the Netherlands. These accommodation facilities include bungalows or huts which are usually rented for one or two weeks, or for a long weekend. They both also include general recreational facilities such as swimming pools, playgrounds, restaurants, and game rooms for residents. Furthermore, both are deliberately located near attractive public natural areas used for hiking, running, and cycling. One of the vacation parks was located just behind a beach on the Zeeland coast, while the other was in a forest and moor area in the southeast of the country. While the coastal park offers various bungalows as accommodations, the inland park also rents grounds for tents in addition to permanent accommodations. The data collection period was determined by peak vacation booking periods in the Netherlands around the Ascencion and Pentecost holiday weekends in May and June of 2021. Park management sent a recruitment message to all customers who booked a stay for this period, preceding the stay itself by three to 14 days. Ten gift certificates of €20 each were offered as an incentive to be raffled off at each park at the end of the data collection. Ultimately, 45 participants completed the study.

12.3.2 Data Collection

The initial recruitment message based on participants' bookings included an intake questionnaire which measured demographics and baseline subjective wellbeing. We then used the random number function in Excel to assign participants to either the treatment or the control condition. Upon check-in, participants in the treatment condition received a small bamboo keychain meant to function as a smartphone stand. Attached to it was a small organza drawstring bag just large enough to hold a spray tester filled with a "unisex" perfume, Calvin Klein One. It is worth noting that, due to the exploratory nature of this research, a generally pleasant scent was chosen, rather than a smell specific to the destination or accommodation setting.

Also attached to the keychain was a card that 1) thanked participants for their cooperation, 2) instructed them to fill out a questionnaire using the provided QR code every evening of their vacation, and 3) instructed them to spray and smell the provided perfume "during a highlight of the vacation." No specific instructions about the physical or social context of the highlight were given. Participants in the control condition received an identical keychain, but no perfume was attached. They received a similar card with instructions as well, but the instruction to use perfume was omitted.

In the intake questionnaire, participants were invited to express a preference for being contacted by email or WhatsApp. Based on their choice, they received a message or email every evening reminding them to fill out the questionnaire. Daily questionnaires measured emotions and, for participants in the treatment group, asked whether they had actually used the perfume that specific day or not. There was also a filter question asking if it had been the last day of their vacation. If so, a measurement of life satisfaction was also displayed.

One to two weeks after returning home, participants received a postcard provided by the vacation park. The postcards varied but always showed the landscape surrounding the park. On the back of the postcard was a message that once again 1) thanked participants for their cooperation and 2) instructed them to immediately fill out a final questionnaire using the provided QR code. The final questionnaire assessed subjective wellbeing. For participants in the treatment group, the postcard was sprayed with the same perfume that had been given to participants earlier. For participants in the control group, the postcard was unscented. Postcards were sent inside envelopes to preserve the strength of the scent. The speed of domestic post (usually within 24 to 48 hours) further gave us confidence that postcards would arrive at participants' homes with the smell still obvious and recognizable. We verified this by sending one postcard to ourselves, then waiting an extra day to open it.

12.3.3 Measures

The present study adopts the common subjective wellbeing conceptualization of Diener and colleagues (2010), which comprises three components, namely positive affect, negative affect, and satisfactions with life domains, chiefly life satisfaction. To assess long-term or stable subjective wellbeing, positive and negative affect are usually measured at the trait level (Rosenberg, 1998) but may also be summed or averaged from daily emotion scores (Diener & Seligman, 2002). We chose the former approach before and after the questionnaires, asking participants *how often* they felt each affect in a list of emotions in "the past three days." For the vacation itself, we instead asked participants daily *to what extent* they felt each of them in a list of emotions that day.

The list of emotions we used is a slight modification of the Scale of Positive and Negative Experience (SPANE; Diener et al., 2010). The SPANE is based on a logic of six basic emotion items (*angry, afraid, sad, joyful, happy, content*) and six valence items (*positive, negative, pleasant, unpleasant, good, bad*), with equal numbers of positive and negative items, so that half of the "weight" in averaging together positive and negative emotion indices comes from valence as a whole, and half from basic emotions. We reduced the valence items from six to two (namely, *positive* and *negative*), as the distinction about weight appeared to make little difference to psychometric properties and could be implemented by weighing items after the fact (but was not in the present study). We also substituted a positive basic emotion, *positive surprise,* for *happy*, as the novelty inherent to vacationing gives positive surprise a potentially more important role in this context than in daily life (Mitas et al., 2018). With these adjustments we felt we struck the best balance of covering the emotional experience of vacationing, as well as daily life, while keeping participant burden low. Participants rated their experience of each emotion on a five-point Likert-type scale.

12.3.4 Attrition

Of 74 participants that provided responses to daily questionnaires during the vacation, 33 were in the control condition, 20 reported using the perfume during at least one day of their vacation, and 19 received the perfume but did not report using it. Further analyses omit the latter group and focus on participants who received and used perfume compared to participants who did not receive perfume. Because the intervention focused on experiences after returning home from vacation, the effective sample size was reduced by attrition between the questionnaires on vacation and the follow-up questionnaire. Of 45 participants that responded to both, 22 were in the control group, 13 reported using the perfume, and 10 received the perfume but did not report using it. These group sizes are less than the recommended absolute minimum for between-group comparisons (Hair et al., 2009), and the findings should thus be seen as an indication of possible effect sizes and directions, rather than conclusive in terms of inference.

12.3.5 Data Analysis

As the present study featured a two-group between-persons experiment, the analyses are based on independent T-tests implemented within a linear regression framework. The outcomes were in terms of change over time. Our first hypothesis concerned the effect of the perfume intervention on subjective wellbeing after a vacation compared to baseline. Thus, for outcome variables (positive trait affect, negative trait affect, and life satisfaction) we subtracted the prevacation baseline from the final measurement one week after the vacation. Our second hypothesis touched on the fadeout effect, that is, the change from during to after vacation. Once again, we used difference scores, but this time focused on the final scores minus the scores during the vacation. The scores during this period for life satisfaction were recorded on the last day of vacation. Affect was measured during vacation as daily emotion, and averaged over the course of the vacation.

12.4   Findings: Describing Participant Experiences

Participants reported moderately positive experiences on vacation. Positive emotions averaged 2.9 (sd=0.56), just below the scale midpoint of 3. Negative emotions were low (mean=1.28, sd=0.32). Life satisfaction on the last day of their vacation averaged 5.75 on a 1-to-7 scale (sd=1.05). Participants evaluated their vacations favourably on their last day, giving the overall experience a grade of 8.22 (sd=1.13) on a 0-to-10 scale, where 10 was best. On the same 0-to-10 scale, they tended to recommend the region (mean=8.38, sd=0.98) and their accommodation (mean=8.30, sd=1.39).

Changes in subjective wellbeing from before vacation, to during, to after were extremely small. Positive emotion barely decreased from before the vacation to after (mean=−0.05, sd=0.65) and from during the vacation to after (mean=−0.05, sd=0.63), indicating a nearly nonexistent fadeout effect (Figures 12.1 and 12.2). Negative emotion change was in the opposite direction but similarly small – both from before vacation to after (mean=0.07, sd=0.36) and from during vacation to after (mean=0.10, sd=0.35; Figures 12.3 and 12.4). Like positive emotion, life satisfaction also showed a negligible decline from before vacation to after (mean=−0.08, sd=0.94) and from during vacation to after (mean=−0.04, sd=0.63; Figures 12.5 and 12.6).

Independent T-tests implemented by linear regression showed that none of these effects differed meaningfully between the control group and treatment

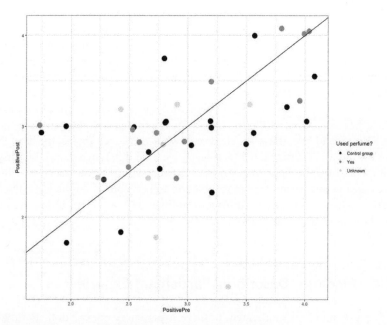

Figure 12.1   Positive affect change from baseline

Note: Points above diagonal black line represent participants who experienced an increase in positive affect from before to after vacation

group participants who complied with the intervention, actually using the perfume. All p-values were above 0.4 and all R-square values were less than 0.02, except for the change in negative emotion from baseline to after the vacation. Participants in the control group reported negative emotion 0.29 higher on a five-point scale after the vacation compared to before. Participants who used the perfume reported negative emotion 0.08 *lower* after the vacation compared to before. This difference explained 7.4% of the between-person variation in negative emotion change, and approached significance with a p-value of 0.119.

12.5 Discussion

Our empirical study assessed the effect of a scent-based experiment on subjective wellbeing after vacation and on the vacation fadeout effect. While differences between the control group and treatment group members who complied

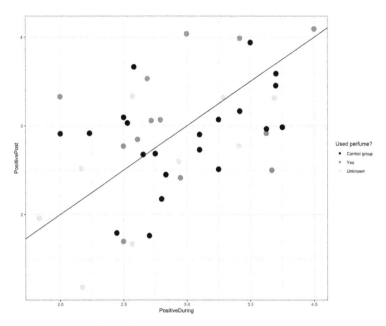

Figure 12.2 Positive affect fadeout

Note: Points below diagonal black line represent participants who experienced fadeout in positive affect after vacation

with the intervention were in the hypothesized direction, effects were very small and not statistically significant. Furthermore, small sample size and high attrition reduced statistical power to the point that all but substantial effects could not be detected. While somewhat ambiguous, these findings nevertheless contribute to our understanding of how vacation benefits to wellbeing fade out, and how this effect may be mitigated. First, we refute the universality of a large, drastic fadeout effect. Second, we show that an incremental intervention leads, not surprisingly, to an incremental (or no) improvement. Finally, we speculate if the unique conditions of vacationing in mid-2021 could mask both fadeout and intervention effects, leaving our research questions partly unanswered.

Many of the studies cited in our literature review reported fadeout effects that reflected large differences between vacation experiences and daily life. For example, de Bloom et al. (2010) found a decline of nearly 10% in mood, similar to the 8% decline in mood in Strauss-Blasche, Muhry et al. (2004). Kühnel and Sonnentag (2011) further reported a 19% increase in emotional

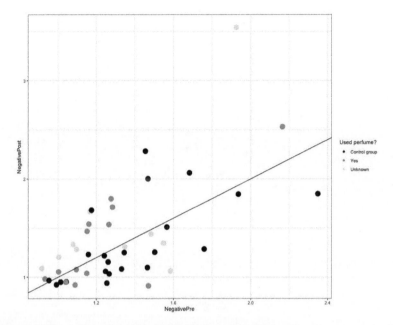

Figure 12.3   Negative affect change from baseline

Note: Points above diagonal black line represent participants who experienced an increase in negative affect from before to after vacation

exhaustion. These studies focused on somewhat different dimensions of affect than the present study. Another study which measured affect more like the present study found a similar 8% decline; however, this was even larger when not accounting for the effect of weekends (Mitas, Yarnal, Adams et al., 2012). In contrast, the present study showed a decline of approximately 1% to 2% in affect and life satisfaction variables, even in the control group. Thus, it is possible that certain people are less affected by fadeout. For example, Kühnel and Sonnentag (2011) deliberately chose to study teachers as individuals who experience high work stress. The fadeout effect may also differ by vacation type. While Strauss-Blasche, Muhry et al. (2004) studied a health resort stay, Mitas, Yarnal, Adams et al. (2012) focused on vacations around very specific hobby interests. Compared to these, a stay at a rural camping in the Netherlands may be described as a more routine experience – a ritual that one repeats annually, perhaps in a different park or season, but the experience itself is more of a mild break in one's routine than something truly "special." It is then reasonable to expect less fadeout upon return to one's work. Intensely emotional, extraordinary vacations may not only feature higher fadeout but also higher material

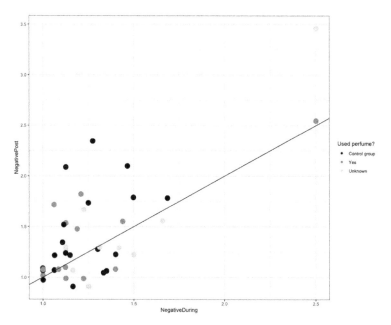

Figure 12.4   Negative affect fadeout

Note: Points below diagonal black line represent participants who experienced fadeout in negative affect after vacation

costs. However, it is hard to imagine that people would pass up the chance for an intensely enjoyable vacation just because readjustment to daily life afterward would be unpleasant. Further research is needed on what sort of vacation motivations, destinations, and experiences best blend with one another into a life well lived.

Not only did the studied experiences feature little vacation fadeout, but it differed little – albeit in the hypothesized direction – between experimental and control groups. The effect was not large enough to be detected statistically in a sample which was simply too small. The question remains on whether a larger effect could be reasonably expected. Existing literature on olfaction and memory suggested that smell could be powerfully coupled to experience, with subsequent exposure to the same smell producing intense recall of that experience (Herz, 2004; Herz & Schooler, 2002). It is questionable, however, if spraying perfume during an apparent vacation highlight sufficiently couples this specific smell with the memory of that moment. It is possible that the use of a smell more specifically related to the vacation or accommodation context,

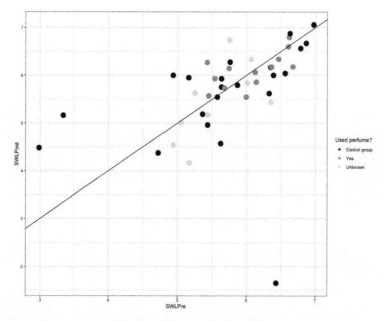

Figure 12.5   Life satisfaction change from baseline

Note: Points above diagonal black line represent participants who experienced an increase in life satisfaction from before to after vacation

for example, related to the plants growing in the nature around each park, would have been more powerful.

It is also not known if sensing the same smell on a postcard later is a sufficiently immersive olfactory experience to trigger recall. It is possible that the intervention tested was simply too brief and unsurprising to induce a strong emotional reaction. Supporting this conclusion, there was also rather low compliance with the intervention, with only slightly more than half of treatment-group participants reporting using their perfume during the vacation. A future version of the present study could feature more striking and elegantly designed delivery of scent to enhance both compliance and emotional impact. Furthermore, as social interaction is a well-known driver of emotion in the context of vacations (Mitas et al., 2017; Mitas, Yarnal, & Chick, 2012), an intervention that included social interaction around the perfume might have been more powerful.

It is also worth noting that a small experimental effect is perhaps to be expected when intervening on a small fadeout effect. Experimental and fadeout effects in

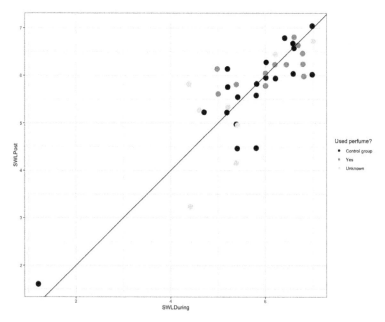

Figure 12.6   Life satisfaction fadeout

Note: Points below diagonal black line represents participants who experienced fadeout in life satisfaction after vacation

the present study were on the same (very low) order of magnitude. By extension, it is actually possible that a similar intervention would have a greater impact in case of a more substantial fadeout effect. The use of a distinct scent during and after the vacation was not likely and not hypothesized to substantially elevate subjective wellbeing above vacation levels, but rather merely to mitigate the decline back to baseline. Thus, any possible impact of the perfume was limited by the ceiling effect of minimal fadeout in the average participant.

The findings of this study also point to context of the data collection for an explanation. After the 2020 to 2021 winter in pandemic-related lockdown, people in the Netherlands were looking forward to vacations as a break from restrictions and routines. Even during nonpandemic years, May and June are marked by improving weather and national holidays, resulting in a sort of "emergence" from dark winter months to sunny terraces and bike paths. Unfortunately, vacationers in May and June of 2021 were disappointed. These months were unusually cold and rainy, literally putting a damper on possible vacation activities. Making the situation worse, most indoor activities were still closed during the data collection period due to pandemic restrictions. Thus, it could be expected that the emotional profile of these vacations hewed rather close to that of working life. Perhaps there was little fadeout effect, and thus little impact from the perfume intervention, because the 'peak' in emotions associated with vacationing (Mitas, Yarnal, Adams, et al., 2012) never happened while vacationers sat in their bungalows, playing board games and watching the rainfall outside. Based on this possibility, we would like to stress the importance of measuring experiences and quality of life outcomes before, during, and after vacations. During-vacation measurements (Gillet et al., 2016) and retrospective postvacation measurements (Neal et al., 1999) are simply not enough, as they miss the *contextualization* of vacation experiences within daily life. This contextualization is possible using daily quantitative measurement during vacations, as well as daily life, but also using retrospective biographical methods, as advocated by Matteucci (2021).

12.6 Conclusion

The present chapter reviews existing research on the vacation fadeout effect, wherein subjective wellbeing effects of vacationing, specifically in terms of affect, seem to quickly disappear upon return home. We tested a scent-based intervention to reduce this fadeout effect among 45 visitors to Dutch vacation parks in the early summer of 2021. We found a very low fadeout effect in general, and that the intervention made only a very small difference. The intervention effect was in the hypothesized direction, but could not be detected statistically. The findings call into question the importance of modest interventions on postvacation experience, but also of the fadeout effect itself. We would like to close with several concluding thoughts for tourism-related businesses based on the literature and empirical findings presented here. We define tourism-related businesses broadly as including transport companies, tourism operators, as well as accommodations and destination management organizations.

First, we suggest that tourism-related businesses should consider the period after a vacation as part of the product they deliver, and the fadeout effect as a potentially unwelcome aspect. The importance of thinking about customers' vacations before and after the travel itself has entered the consciousness of tourism-related businesses. Delivery of marketing messages is carefully timed and tuned according to these considerations. The fadeout effect should be considered as well. It is known that the effects of tourism on wellbeing do reach beyond the vacation itself, and in fact accrue over a number of years (Mitas &

Kroesen, 2019). Thus, important outcomes of consuming tourism products occur well beyond the information-decision-consumption cycle. Second, we urge tourism-related businesses to then take the next step and apply experience design principles not only to transport, accommodation, and attractions, as is already the case, but also to the phase of recalling a vacation upon returning home. Instead of treating the fadeout effect as a reality to be accepted, tourism businesses should explore it as an experience design problem to be solved. Finally, we feel that potential solutions to tourism experience design problems should be tested experimentally, with random assignment to treatment and control groups, for appropriate decision making. If tourism-related businesses realize that the fadeout effect is part of their product, and approach it with experience design interventions, there is a risk that ideas based on "an inspiration" or "gut feeling" fail and are abandoned, further thinning margins in this competitive industry. If vacation experience design interventions are instead progressively tested and scaled up, perhaps even previously accepted "facts" of vacationing such as the fadeout effect can be positively changed in the future.

Funding Acknowledgement

The empirical research reported in this chapter was funded by a SIA HBO-postdoc grant of the Dutch government.

References

Bastiaansen, M., Lub, X., Mitas, O., Jung, T. H., Passos Acenção, M., Han, D., Moilanen, T., Smit, B., & Strijbosch, W. (2019). Emotions as core building blocks of an experience. *International Journal of Contemporary Hospitality Management, 31*(2), pp. 651–668. https://doi.org/10.1108/IJCHM-11-2017-0761.

Cahill, L., Babinsky, R., Markowitsch, H. J., & McGaugh, J. L. (1995). The amygdala and emotional memory. *Nature, 377*(6547), 295–296. https://doi.org/10.1038/377295a0.

Chen, C.-C., & Yoon, S. (2018). Tourism as a pathway to the good life: Comparing the top–down and bottom–up effects. *Journal of Travel Research, 58*(5), 866–876.

Chu, S., & Downes, J. J. (2002). Proust nose best: Odors are better cues of autobiographical memory. *Memory & Cognition, 30*(4), 511–518.

Dann, G., & Jacobsen, J. K. S. (2003). Tourism smellscapes. *Tourism Geographies, 5*(1), 3–25.

de Bloom, J., Geurts, S. A., Taris, T. W., Sonnentag, S., de Weerth, C., & Kompier, M. A. (2010). Effects of vacation from work on health and well-being: Lots of fun, quickly gone. *Work & Stress, 24*(2), 196–216.

Diener, E., & Seligman, M. E. (2002). Very happy people. *Psychological Science, 13*(1), 81–84.

Diener, E., Wirtz, D., Tov, W., Kim-Prieto, C., Choi, D.-w., Oishi, S., & Biswas-Diener, R. (2010). New well-being measures: Short scales to assess flourishing and positive and negative feelings. *Social Indicators Research, 97*(2), 143–156.

Duerden, M. D., Ward, P. J., & Freeman, P. A. (2015). Conceptualizing structured experiences: Seeking interdisciplinary integration. *Journal of Leisure Research, 47*(5), 601–620.

Eaker, E. D., Pinsky, J., & Castelli, W. P. (1992). Myocardial infarction and coronary death among women: psychosocial predictors from a 20-year follow-up of women in the Framingham Study. *American Journal of Epidemiology, 135*(8), 854–864.

Fredrickson, B. L. (2001). The role of positive emotions in positive psychology: The broaden-and-build theory of positive emotions. *American Psychologist, 56*(3), 218.

Fredrickson, B. L. (2010). *Positivity: Groundbreaking research to release your inner optimist and thrive*: Simon and Schuster.

Fredrickson, B. L., Cohn, M. A., Coffey, K. A., Pek, J., & Finkel, S. M. (2008). Open hearts build lives: Positive emotions, induced through loving-kindness meditation, build consequential personal resources. *Journal of Personality and Social Psychology, 95*(5), 1045.

Fritz, C., & Sonnentag, S. (2006). Recovery, well-being, and performance-related outcomes: The role of workload and vacation experiences. *Journal of Applied Psychology, 91*(4), 936.

Garland, E. L., Fredrickson, B., Kring, A. M., Johnson, D. P., Meyer, P. S., & Penn, D. L. (2010). Upward spirals of positive emotions counter downward spirals of negativity: Insights from the broaden-and-build theory and affective neuroscience on the treatment of emotion dysfunctions and deficits in psychopathology. *Clinical Psychology Review, 30*(7), 849–864.

Gillet, S., Schmitz, P., & Mitas, O. (2016). The snap-happy tourist: The effects of photographing behavior on tourists' happiness. *Journal of Hospitality & Tourism Research, 40*(1), 37–57.

Gump, B. B., & Matthews, K. A. (2000). Are vacations good for your health? The 9-year mortality experience after the multiple risk factor intervention trial. *Psychosomatic Medicine, 62*(5), 608–612.

Hair Jr., J. F., Black, W. C., Babin, B. J., & Anderson, R. E. (2009) *Multivariate data analysis*. 7th Edition, Upper Saddle River: Prentice Hall.

Herz, R. S. (2004). A naturalistic analysis of autobiographical memories triggered by olfactory visual and auditory stimuli. *Chemical Senses, 29*(3), 217–224.

Herz, R. S., & Schooler, J. W. (2002). A naturalistic study of autobiographical memories evoked by olfactory and visual cues: Testing the Proustian hypothesis. *American Journal of Psychology, 115*(1), 21–32.

Herz, R. S., Eliassen, J., Beland, S., & Souza, T. (2004). Neuroimaging evidence for the emotional potency of odor-evoked memory. *Neuropsychologia, 42*(3), 371–378.

Ito, E., Kono, S., & Gui, J. (2023). Psychological consequences of tourism ideal affect. *Current Issues in Tourism, 26*(3), 468–479. https://doi.org/10.1080/13683500.2021.2023479.

Kim, J.-H., & Jang, S. (2016). Memory retrieval of cultural event experiences: Examining internal and external influences. *Journal of Travel Research, 55*(3), 322–339.

Kim, J.-H., Ritchie, J. B., & McCormick, B. (2012). Development of a scale to measure memorable tourism experiences. *Journal of Travel Research, 51*(1), 12–25.

Kim, J. J., & Fesenmaier, D. R. (2015). Designing tourism places: Understanding the tourism experience through our senses. Travel and Tourism Research Association: Advancing Tourism Research Globally. 19. https:// scholarworks .umass .edu/ ttra/ ttra2015/Academic_Papers_Oral/19.

Kroesen, M., & Handy, S. (2014). The influence of holiday-taking on affect and contentment. *Annals of Tourism Research, 45*, 89–101.

Kühnel, J., & Sonnentag, S. (2011). How long do you benefit from vacation? A closer look at the fade-out of vacation effects. *Journal of Organizational Behavior, 32*(1), 125–143.

Lin, Y., Kerstetter, D., Nawijn, J., & Mitas, O. (2014). Changes in emotions and their interactions with personality in a vacation context. *Tourism Management, 40*, 416–424.

Lyubomirsky, S., King, L., & Diener, E. (2005). The benefits of frequent positive affect: Does happiness lead to success? Psychological Bulletin, 131(6), 803–855. https://doi .org/10.1037/0033-2909.131.6.803.

Magnini, V. P., & Karande, K. (2010). An experimental investigation into the use of written smell references in ecotourism advertisements. *Journal of Hospitality & Tourism Research, 34*(3), 279–293.

Matteucci, X. (2021). Existential hapax as tourist embodied transformation. *Tourism Recreation Research, 47*(5–6), 631–635.

Mitas, O. (2010). *Positive emotions in mature adults' leisure travel experiences.* (Doctoral dissertation). Pennsylvania State University.

Mitas, O., & Kroesen, M. (2019). Vacations over the years: A cross-lagged panel analysis of tourism experiences and subjective well-being in the Netherlands. *Journal of Happiness Studies, 21*, 2807–2826, https://doi.org/10.1007/s10902-019-00200-z.

Mitas, O., Cuenen, R., Bastiaansen, M., Chick, G., & van den Dungen, E. (2020). The war from both sides: How Dutch and German visitors experience an exhibit of Second World War stories. *International Journal of the Sociology of Leisure, 3*(3), 277–303.

Mitas, O., Hohn, A., & Nawijn, J. (2018). 'To mix with new people': The surprising day trips of mature Germans. In M. Uysal, M. J. Sirgy & S. Kruger (eds) *Managing quality of life in tourism and hospitality* (pp. 24–41). Wallingford: CABI.

Mitas, O., Nawijn, J., & Jongsma, B. (2017). Between tourists: Tourism and happiness. In M. K. Smith & L. Puczko (Eds), *The Routledge handbook of health tourism* (pp. 47–64). Abingdon: Routledge.

Mitas, O., Yarnal, C., & Chick, G. (2012). Jokes build community: Mature tourists' positive emotions. *Annals of Tourism Research, 39*(4), 1884–1905.

Mitas, O., Yarnal, C., Adams, R., & Ram, N. (2012). Taking a "peak" at leisure travelers' positive emotions. *Leisure Sciences, 34*(2), 115–135.

Nawijn, J., & Fricke, M. C. (2015). Visitor emotions and behavioral intentions: The case of concentration camp memorial Neuengamme. *International Journal of Tourism Research, 17*(3), 221–228.

Nawijn, J., Brüggemann, M., & Mitas, O. (2017). The effect of Sachsenhausen visitors' personality and emotions on meaning and word of mouth. *Tourism Analysis, 22*(3), 349–359.

Nawijn, J., Isaac, R. K., Liempt, A. v., & Gridnevskiy, K. (2016). Emotion clusters for concentration camp memorials. *Annals of Tourism Research, 61*, 244–247.

Nawijn, J., Marchand, M. A., Veenhoven, R., & Vingerhoets, A. J. (2010). Vacationers happier, but most not happier after a holiday. *Applied Research in Quality of Life, 5*(1), 35–47.

Nawijn, J., Mitas, O., Lin, Y., & Kerstetter, D. (2013). How do we feel on vacation? A closer look at how emotions change over the course of a trip. *Journal of Travel Research, 52*(2), 265–274.

Neal, J. D., Sirgy, M. J., & Uysal, M. (1999). The role of satisfaction with leisure travel/ tourism services and experience in satisfaction with leisure life and overall life. *Journal of Business Research, 44*(3), 153–163.

Pan, S., & Ryan, C. (2009). Tourism sense-making: The role of the senses and travel journalism. *Journal of Travel & Tourism Marketing, 26*(7), 625–639.

Proust, M. (1922 [1919]). Remembrance of things past: Swann's way (C. K. Scott-Moncrieff, Trans.). New York: Holt.

Rosenberg, E. L. (1998). Levels of analysis and the organization of affect. *Review of General Psychology, 2*(3), 247–270.

Rubin, D. C., Groth, E., & Goldsmith, D. J. (1984). Olfactory cuing of autobiographical memory. *The American Journal of Psychology*, 493–507.

Shahvali, M., Kerstetter, D. L., & Townsend, J. N. (2021). The contribution of vacationing together to couple functioning. *Journal of Travel Research, 60*(1), 133–148.

Smith, M. K., & Diekmann, A. (2017). Tourism and wellbeing. *Annals of Tourism Research, 66*, 1–13.

Strauss-Blasche, G., Muhry, F., Lehofer, M., Moser, M., & Marktl, W. (2004). Time course of well-being after a three-week resort-based respite from occupational and domestic demands: Carry-over, contrast and situation effects. *Journal of Leisure Research, 36*(3), 293.

Strauss-Blasche, G., Riedmann, B., Schobersberger, W., Ekmekcioglu, C., Riedmann, G., Waanders, R., Fries, D., Mittermayr, M., Marktl, W. & Humpeler, E. (2004). Vacation at moderate and low altitude improves perceived health in individuals with metabolic syndrome. *Journal of Travel Medicine, 11*(5), 300–306.

Strijbosch, W., Mitas, O., van Blaricum, T., Vugts, O., Govers, C., Hover, M., Gelissen, J., & Bastiaansen, M. (2021). When the parts of the sum are greater than the whole: Assessing the peak-and-end-theory for a heterogeneous, multi-episodic tourism experience. *Journal of Destination Marketing & Management, 20*, 100607.

Vada, S., Prentice, C., Scott, N., & Hsiao, A. (2020). Positive psychology and tourist well-being: A systematic literature review. *Tourism Management Perspectives, 33*, 100631.

Westman, M., & Etzion, D. (2001). The impact of vacation and job stress on burnout and absenteeism. *Psychology & Health, 16*(5), 595–606.

13 Future directions of tourism and wellbeing

Henna Konu and Melanie Kay Smith

13.1 Revisiting Research Perspectives of Tourism and Wellbeing

The preceding chapters illustrate well the broad perspective of tourism and wellbeing research. Starting from a wide approach on how wellbeing is discussed in tourism economics and continuing to the indicators and measurement of wellbeing in tourism, the authors go on to examine issues of individual wellbeing and how wellbeing experiences can be facilitated for diverse segments and what kinds of collaborative structures are needed. Finally, effects of tourism on wellbeing are explored from several perspectives starting from social tourism and continuing to smaller groups and finally exploring the fadeout effect with an experimental study.

This book revisits many of the important issues that have emerged from tourism and wellbeing studies in recent years, providing a deeper understanding of definitions, concepts, product and service development, motivation, segmentation, management and research methods. It does not claim to be comprehensive in scope, but it illustrates the interdisciplinary and multidimensional nature of the research linked to tourism and wellbeing. However, there are multiple research avenues still to be explored.

Most of the previous studies on wellbeing have focused on individual and economic wellbeing, while social and environmental wellbeing have received less attention. Studies of individual wellbeing have evolved to explore transformational experiences and their contribution to eudaimonia, engagement and meaningfulness. These aspects are also present in the discussion of idleness in tourism by Farkić et al. (Chapter 5) and what is important for Gen Zers on their way to meaningful life (Grenmán et al., Chapter 6). Both chapters also call for paradigm changes in tourism to a more meaningful and regenerative direction.

Diverse tourism types, such as nature-based, adventure or volunteer tourism are seen to have transformational opportunities and bring eudaimonic benefits (e.g., Coghlan, 2015; Saunders et al., 2017; Yang et al., 2023). Some of the most recent studies that have reconceptualised and measured tourist wellbeing include both social connections and connections to natural environments (Filep et al., 2022). For instance, it has also been argued that nature-based tourism is especially important for transformational wellbeing because it encourages people to reconnect with the natural world within a 'living systems' framework (Bellato, Frantzeskaki et al., 2022). Authors have also questioned how far tourism can become transformational (Reisinger, 2013; Fu et al., 2015; Knobloch et al., 2016; Sheldon, 2020), not only for the individual in terms of their own wellbeing, but also in terms of community and societal development and ecosystem protection because of a shift in consciousness (Sheldon, 2020).

Recently, more emphasis has been given to the connections between individual and environmental wellbeing at the same time when the broader discussions of planetary health, and the role of nature and biodiversity for human wellbeing have emerged (e.g., Horton et al., 2014; IPBES, 2019). In this book, both Grénman et al. (Chapter 6) and Kelly (Chapter 8) call for transformative nature-based tourism services that will positively affect nature conservation and biodiversity. Pope and Konu (Chapter 7) and Kelly (Chapter 8) also discuss the central role of nature in individual wellbeing experiences and they point out that meaningful experiences may contribute to environmentally friendly practices. The call for a more comprehensive approach in examining wellbeing in tourism has brought 'regenerative tourism' into the research discussions (e.g., Hussain, 2021). Regenerative tourism is regarded as 'a transformational approach that aims to fulfil the potential of tourism places to flourish and create net positive effects through increasing the regenerative capacity of human societies and ecosystems' (Bellato, Frantzeskaki & Nygaard, 2022, p. 9). Hence, this approach integrates the sustainability dimensions – ecological, social, cultural and economic – to wellbeing goals aiming to heal and even improve destinations. Inherent in this concept is the development of more respectful and caring relations between humans and nature (Dredge, 2022).

Recent literature calls for more research especially on social wellbeing and tourism (e.g., Filep et al., 2022) and examination should focus on relationships and interactions between communities, families and other tourists and what kind of influence they have on the subjective wellbeing of individuals. The importance of togetherness and social value in tourism are emphasised in diverse types of tourism (e.g., Sorakunnas, 2022), and in this book, Matteucci et al. (Chapter 11) brought forth the social benefits of diasporic tourism both for tourists and the host community.

Economic wellbeing also plays a central role in tourism discussions. As Dwyer (Chapter 2) pointed out, the economic measures have traditionally been the ones that have been used to measure the progress of societal advancement. This is also the case in many destinations where the main indicators of progress are overnight stays and tourism income. Recently, the discussion has moved more towards finding solutions about how to gain the same or more tourism income from smaller number of visitors. This is due to increased emphasis on sustainability aspects – how to maintain the economic wellbeing without compromising the social and ecological wellbeing of destinations. To measure the benefits of tourism for the destination, Dwyer (Chapter 2) recommends contextual indicators and suggests a broader Beyond GDP agenda to measure societal progress. He calls for identifying new concepts and systems of measures to support tourism policy making. In addition, Berbekova and Uysal (Chapter 3) call for indicators that include the sociocultural fabric of a place and integrate both demand and supply elements into the examination. Individual economic wellbeing can also be enhanced through tourism as shown in the case of diasporic tourism, where host communities benefit from financial donations and gifts (Chapter 11). Diverse structures can support tourism that advance social wellbeing, such as the Finnish social tourism system presented by Vento et al. (Chapter 10), which can bring economic benefits (financial support for holidays) for individuals, but at the same time provide income to tourism service providers at the destinations also during low seasons.

The role of tourism firms in providing wellbeing is manifold. They are responsible for creating a pleasant, welcoming and wellbeing-supportive environment both for their customers and employees. Gordon and Lehto (Chapter 4) present how a tourism firm can support wellbeing of employees through an employee wellness programme. They also suggest that the hospitality and tourism industry should take a more active role in contributing to a wellbeing-oriented society. This means integrating wellbeing-related goals into firms' strategies. Tourism firms also play a central role in facilitating tourist experiences that lead to experiences of wellbeing. Previous studies have identified, for instance the central role of guides and interaction in transformative tourist experiences and the importance of experience management and planning (e.g., Saunders et al., 2017; Soulard et al., 2021; Pope & Konu, Chapter 7). However, more insight is needed on how transformational components or triggers of transformation can be embedded into tourism services. Tourism firms could also focus on how to support tourists' feelings of wellbeing after the holiday. Mitas and Bastiaansen (Chapter 12) discuss the role of sensory cues on the vacation fadeout effect. This experimental study focused on one sense, smell, but as the tourist experience is multisensorial, it would be interesting to explore if certain sensorial stimuli can link to triggers of transformation and if the same stimuli can 'remind' someone of their transformational experiences after the holiday.

Collaboration practices, international cooperation and networking have received some attention in developing wellbeing and wellness tourism, related offerings and network products (Konu & Smith, 2017; Tuohino et al., 2013; Hjalager et al., 2016, Bočkus et al., Chapter 9). Additionally, some research has been conducted relating to collaboration structures between diverse industries and tourism, for example, between tourism firms and cosmeceutical providers (Hjalager & Konu, 2011). Collaboration between diverse industries and public–private partnerships may be critical in future to provide multiple wellbeing benefits at destination level. This need for interindustrial collaboration is also called for by Kelly (Chapter 8) who emphasizes coproduction as a key mode of operation at local and destination levels.

Communicating and marketing wellbeing-related services are topical issues in wellness tourism. Challenges have been faced related to the understanding of the concepts used in marketing messages especially when the offerings are targeted at diverse international customer groups. Bočkus et al. (Chapter 9) points out the importance of adjusting the marketing messages and offerings for specific target groups. It is recommended that future studies should investigate the marketing and communication strategies used also in relation to transformative travel (Soulard et al., 2021). Communication also plays an important role in stakeholder collaboration.

It is important to link tourism and wellbeing discussions more closely to development goals that have been identified in a wide range of strategies. Tourism is a very resource-intensive industry that relies on diverse natural elements in different destinations. Hence, the utilisation of natural resources by other industries can influence the operational environments of tourism (e.g., agriculture, forestry and mining). Some strategies may also enhance ecosystem services that are essential for tourism. This is especially true in the context of natural landscapes, such as protected areas or national parks. It is worth noting that the human wellbeing dimension in cultural ecosystem services research has come to the fore in recent years (Willis, 2015; Ram & Smith, 2019; Csurgó & Smith, 2021). Consequently, the tourism industry should take a more active role in maintaining their operational environment to be able to provide wellbeing benefits for tourists, residents and for destinations as a whole. Grenmán et al. (Chapter 6) and Kelly (Chapter 8) call for transformational change in the tourism industry and highlight the role of the tourism sector in safeguarding ecosystems and biodiversity. New indicators are also needed to follow development and strategy implementations and to support new policies. Here, it is important to link tourism and wellbeing research and development to the latest discussions about sustainable development, regenerative tourism, resilience, smart governance and so forth.

13.2 Future Research Agenda

Most research on wellbeing in tourism appears to adopt a demand-led focus concentrating on individual wellbeing perspectives and hence, leaving many research gaps related to a host community perspective and their experience of wellbeing. Moreover, new phenomena emerging due to the COVID-19 crisis provide new avenues for research (e.g., resilient and regenerative tourism). The study of *social wellbeing* should critically examine how to maximize benefits for local communities in destinations (e.g., Soulard et al., 2021). To support and follow the realization of social wellbeing in destinations, resident wellbeing should be seen as one of the main tourism industry performance variables and it should be prioritised as one of the main goals in policy discussions (Dwyer, Chapter 2). Studies have often focused on the negative perspectives of tourism on residents' wellbeing, especially in the early days of tourism research (Sharpley, 2014). Some tourism and quality of life studies did measure the positive benefits of tourism for both tourists and residents alike (Uysal et al., 2012). Many researchers use the term quality of life in preference to wellbeing, but they are sometimes used interchangeably, for example, by Berbekova and Uysal in Chapter 3. Definitions can become important when indicators are developed for measurement and broader debates about host–guest relations have typically included sociocultural impacts of tourism too. More recent studies also focus on individual and community support for tourism incorporating attitudes, impacts and personal benefits (Šegota et al., 2022). It is perhaps worth considering in more depth how far social wellbeing is individual, subjective and personal rather than collective or community-based. Certainly, this book differentiates between individual wellbeing and group wellbeing (e.g., of diasporic tourists or social tourists).

Future research should examine how self-empowerment of host communities can be enhanced, and how meaningful encounters between hosts and guests as well as civic engagement can be encouraged (e.g., Soulard et al., 2021). This is especially important in destinations in which the experiences rely on a social context where local communities play a central role in facilitating experiences that are meaningful for visitors (e.g., Lehto et al., 2020; Nandasena et al., 2022).

COVID-19 has caused changes in travelling and length of stay at the destination. The combination of work and leisure has increased and visitors may travel to work abroad for longer periods of time as distant working has become easier and more approved. For example, digital nomadism is combining features of both tourists and locals (Hannonen et al., 2023), which blurs the line between everyday life and tourism. This phenomenon brings new research topics when the role of digital nomads in host communities and their wellbeing is studied.

Even if *individual wellbeing* in tourism has been explored extensively from diverse perspectives, there are several research gaps that are linked to transformational and eudaimonia-generating experiences. Less research has been conducted on examining the possible accumulation of or longitudinal eudaimonic benefits of tourists during travel careers (Yang et al. 2023). Studies could also focus on investigating the triggers of transformation during both general and specific tourism experiences – what kind of settings, offerings and interactions are more likely to bring eudaimonic benefits and how to augment them (e.g., Yang et al. 2023, Grenmán et al. Chapter 6, Pope & Konu, Chapter 7). In addition, more insight is needed on the effect of diverse landscapes, cultural background and role of authenticity on wellbeing experiences (Teoh et al., 2021). In addition, studies could explore how transformation or eudaimonic benefits are experienced by tourists that have diverse motivations for doing the same tourist activities. Are tourists intentionally seeking wellbeing and transformation or not, and how much does this affects the perceptions of the experience, satisfaction and permanence of the experienced wellbeing benefits?

From a tourism firm's perspective, it is important to examine how practitioners can *facilitate experiences of wellbeing and inner transformation* for tourists. Service providers would benefit from information about how they could best respond to their customers' needs in enabling opportunities for inner transformations. Research could focus on and collaborate with service providers to conduct experiments to examine how transformational and eudaimonia-cultivating practices can be incorporated into design of regular and specific tourism services (e.g., Yang et al., 2023) and look at how to involve customers in the design of wellbeing enhancing tourism services (e.g., Konu, 2015). Insight is needed both from the viewpoints of diverse target groups (e.g., different nationalities and generations, such as Gen Zers mentioned in Chapter 6), as well as from diverse tourism settings. More insight is needed also from the less studied fields of tourism with eudaimonia-creating potential, such as nature-based science tourism (Räikkönen et al., 2021) or modern-day nature pilgrimage tourism (cf. Sheldon, 2020), as specific settings might bring new insights on wellbeing and transformation-creating practices (e.g., the pathways to nature connection mentioned in Chapter 7). It is worth reiterating here that different kinds of landscape can afford different benefits (e.g., blue spaces, forests, deserts). In this book, very little attention has been paid to cities and urban tourism, but it is worth noting the growing studies that relate to smart cities and quality of life (e.g., De Guimarães et al., 2020; Chen & Chan, 2022), the importance of urban green spaces (Du & Zhao, 2022; Jabbar et al., 2021), as well as urban wellness tourism (Saari, 2022).

The role of tourism professionals and facilitators of experiences is essential in the provision of wellbeing enhancing services for tourists. Hence, their own wellbeing deserves attention. There is a need for further studies to understand how the emotional and socially interactive nature of the tourism profession influences employees' wellbeing, especially if their role is to support transformational experiences for customers. Such situations may also have some kind of influence on the guides and facilitators of the experience themselves. For example, Teoh et al. (2021) called for studies that aim to understand the dual role of facilitators as providers of transformative experiences for customers and at the same time as a transformed participant. Tourism firms should also take responsibility for the wellbeing of their employees and as Gordon and Lehto (Chapter 4) highlight, a strategy of supporting employees' wellbeing is crucial to an organization's success. The new types of tourism offerings may also bring new challenges for employee wellbeing. Hence, more insight is needed about how tourism firms integrate the evaluation of employee wellbeing and support it in human resources management in different types of tourism companies.

Tourism firms are also expected to take a more active role and leadership in making tourism better (e.g., Grenmán et al., Chapter 6; Gordon & Lehto, Chapter 4), which is one of the promises of regenerative tourism. This includes supporting practices that enhance wellbeing for tourists, employees and their operational environment. For instance, nature-based tourism firms can develop their experiential services in a way that they could trigger and support appreciation of nature and possibly also positively affect the maintenance of natural environments. This would impact on the wellbeing of the destination in addition to the wellbeing of the customers. However, more insight about these kinds of holistic wellbeing impacts is needed. This links to the research needs identified in the field of regenerative tourism that focuses on the wellbeing of social-ecological systems. The regenerative tourism concept challenges the paradigm of constant economic growth that is still dominant in tourism and instead focuses on regenerating whole systems and highlights mutually beneficial and reciprocal relationships (e.g., Ateljevic, 2020; Bellato, Frantzeskaki & Nygaard, 2022). In order to develop regenerative tourism as a transformational approach aiming to create flourishing tourism destinations and increasing the wellbeing of humans and ecosystems, a system-based approach is needed. For example, Bellato, Frantzeskaki et al. (2022) called for exploring 'tourism living systems' by using regenerative tourism approaches in case studies and coproduction processes and examining the roles of diverse stakeholders, collaborative patterns and their potential for creating sustainable and flourishing destinations.

The role of *technology* and the opportunities it brings to promote wellbeing in the context of tourism have so far been little studied. Most often, discussions focus on the negative effects of technology on wellbeing, such as spending excessive time on using social media, online services or games which can lead to negative psychological outcomes (e.g., Tanouri et al., 2022). From this point of view, tourism has been seen as one of the ways to break away from busy everyday life and constant stimuli. Recent studies have also noted the importance of digital detoxification for wellbeing or at the very least, switching off one's gadgets for at least part of a holiday and positively embracing JOMO or the 'joy of missing out' (Ayeh, 2018; Egger & Wassler, 2020; Floros et al., 2021; Farkić et al., Chapter 5). However, using different technological solutions or applications as part of tourism can bring new opportunities to increase wellbeing for tourists, residents, and destinations. Virtual solutions may also enable wellbeing-creating experiences for diverse target groups that do not necessarily have the chance to visit certain places and destinations or take part in some services due to certain disabilities. Technology may enable experience of wellbeing with immersive experiential services, for instance, interactive virtual nature is developing to the point in which it is possible to simulate contact with actual nature (e.g., Litleskare et al., 2020). However, more research is needed about how virtual solutions or virtual nature influence the wellbeing experiences of tourists and residents in diverse settings (e.g., at airports, hotels, restaurants or diverse public places in a destination). It should also be noted that in the growing body of knowledge about smart cities, research has recently started to focus on residents' quality of life and wellbeing with many authors arguing that technology and innovation must incorporate and be responsive to citizens' needs (Del-Real et al., 2023). This can include the development of digital participation platforms which allow citizens to comment on issues that affect their wellbeing (Braga et al., 2021; Leung & Lee, 2022) as well as the enhancement of infrastructure and public services like transport (Bielinska-Dusza et al., 2021) which also benefits tourists.

It is also noted that, for instance, transformative gamification services can enable practitioners to uncover the association and explore the link between particular mental wellbeing issues and diverse places (Tanouri et al., 2022). In some areas, technological applications are already used to map places in which the visitors feel that they experience wellbeing benefits, like the case of

Nordic Health Hub (Almén, 2021). This understanding could help planners and policy makers to develop public spaces, as well as tourism facilities (e.g., MacIntyre et al. 2019), and can help to guide visitors to places that are seen to bring wellbeing benefits. However, technological solutions can help to channel visitor flows from fragile and crowded areas to less vulnerable places, which may improve wellbeing of residents and the environment. It is acknowledged that the usage of diverse applications and location-based games in promoting wellbeing is an emerging and promising field of study that requires further research and exploratory studies (Tanouri et al., 2022; Lee et al., 2019).

Technology enables also new possibilities and *tools to research wellbeing* in tourism. It can be used to examine visitors' experiences of wellbeing in diverse environments and situations, help to increase understanding of what kinds of environments can bring wellbeing benefits for individuals, what kinds of elements in diverse travel environments or sites can bring wellbeing and influence stress levels or mood, for example. *Experimental studies* have not yet been very common in studying wellbeing in tourism. However, recently, some experiential studies have started to emerge in this context (e.g., Yang et al., 2023, Baldwin et al., 2021). The experiments have focused either on some specific type of tourism experience, such as rural tourism experiences in bungalow parks (the Mitas & Bastiaansen study presented in Chapter 12) or looking at how eudaimonia can be potentially generated in general tourism experiences (Yang et al., 2023). Some studies, such as Baldwin et al. (2021), have focused on developing virtual settings and laboratories to simulate tourism environments for studying (hedonic) wellbeing. Many studies call for more experimental studies (e.g., related to sensory experiments) and looking at both general and specific tourism experiences that have wellbeing-generating potential (e.g., Baldwin et al. 2021; Yang et al. 2023; Mitas & Bastiaansen, Chapter 12). New technology and built laboratories can bring new kinds of opportunities to conduct experiments. The laboratory environment can help to test different variables and stimuli (individually or simultaneously) that can impact the experiences of wellbeing.

Other methodologies are called for to study wellbeing and transformational experiences in tourism. For example, transformational tourist experiences should be studied with explorative and longitudinal studies that could map transformational elements before, during and after the trip (e.g., Teoh et al. 2021; Yang et al., 2023). This is an important perspective also when designing transformational tourism experiences that are evaluated over time, as this influences the self-reflection processes of individuals (Nandasena et al., 2022).

The research on tourism and wellbeing is becoming more and more attractive among tourism scholars. This wide topic provides numerous research opportunities and this book provides only a glimpse from the surface. The research topics of the theme have evolved over the years and the authors aimed to present some topical issues and research agendas for forthcoming years. We would like to encourage scholars to explore wellbeing in tourism from diverse disciplinary perspectives and from different points of views and we hope that this book inspires future researchers to explore the opportunities to enhance wellbeing through tourism and find solutions how to make tourism better by increasing wellbeing of individuals, communities and destinations.

References

Almén, L. (2021). En hälsofrämjande skog är en gammal skog: Ett arbete om att finna och identifiera vad som utmärker hälsofrämjande miljöer i Västerbottens län. Examensarbete, SLU, Institutionen för skogens ekologi och skötsel nr 2021:5.

Ateljevic, I. (2020). Transforming the (tourism) world for good and (re)generating the potential 'new normal. *Tourism Geographies, 22*(3), 467–475. https://doi.org/10.1080/14616688.2020.1759134.

Ayeh, J. K. (2018). Distracted gaze: Problematic use of mobile technologies in vacation contexts. *Tourism Management Perspectives, 26,* 31–38. https://doi.org/10.1016/j.tmp.2018.01.002.

Baldwin, J., Haven-Tang, C., Gill, S., Morgan, N., & Pritchard A. (2021). Using the Perceptual Experience Laboratory (PEL) to simulate tourism environments for hedonic wellbeing. *Information Technology & Tourism, 23*, 45–67.

Bellato, L., Frantzeskaki, N., Briceño Fiebig, C., Pollock, A., Dens, E., & Reed, B. (2022). Transformative roles in tourism: adopting living systems' thinking for regenerative futures. *Journal of Tourism Futures, 8*(3), 312–329. https://doi.org/10.1108/JTF-11-2021-0256.

Bellato, L., Frantzeskaki, N. and Nygaard, C. A. (2022). Regenerative tourism: A conceptual framework leveraging theory and practice. *Tourism Geographies, 25*(4), 1026–1046. https://doi.org/10.1080/14616688.2022.2044376.

Bielinska-Dusza, E., Hamerska, M., & Zak, A. (2021). Sustainable mobility and the smart city: A vision of the city of the future: The case study of Cracow (Poland). *Energies, 14*(23), 7936. https://doi.org/10.3390/en14237936.

Braga, I., Ferreira, F., Ferreira, J., Correia, R., Pereira, L., & Falcao, P. (2021). A DEMATEL analysis of smart city determinants. *Technology in Society, 66*, 101687. https://doi.org/10.1016/j.techsoc.2021.101687.

Coghlan, A., & Weiler, B. (2018). Examining transformative processes in volunteer tourism. *Current Issues in Tourism, 21*(5), 567–82.

Chen, Z., & Chan, I. C. C. (2023). Smart cities and quality of life: A quantitative analysis of citizens' support for smart city development. *Information, Technology & People, 36*(1), 263–285. https://doi.org/10.1108/ITP-07-2021-0577.

Csurgó, B., & Smith, M. K. (2021). The value of cultural ecosystem services in a rural landscape context. *Journal of Rural Studies, 86,* 76–86. https:// doi.org/ 10.1016/ j .jrurstud.2021.05.030.

De Guimarães, J. C. F., Severo, E. A., Felix Júnior, L. A., Da Costa, W. P. L. B., & Salmoria, F. T. (2020). Governance and quality of life in smart cities: Towards sustainable development goals. *Journal of Cleaner Production, 253,* 119926. https://doi .org/10.1016/j.jclepro.2019.119926.

Del-Real, C., Ward, C., and Sartipi, M. (2023). What do people want in a smart city? Exploring stakeholders' opinions, priorities and perceived barriers in a medium-sized city in the United States, *International Journal of Urban Sciences, 27*(S1), 50–74. https://doi.org/10.1080/12265934.2021.1968939.

Dredge, D. (2022). Regenerative tourism: Transforming mindsets, systems and practices. *Journal of Tourism Futures. 8*(3), 269–281. https:// doi .org/ 10 .1108/ JTF -01 -2022-0015.

Du, Y., & Zhao, R. (2022). Research on the development of urban parks based on the perception of tourists: A case study of Taihu Park in Beijing. *International Journal of Environmental Research and Public Health, 19,* 5287. https:// doi .org/ 10 .3390/ ijerph19095287.

Egger, I., Lei, S. I., & Wassler, P. (2020). Digital free tourism–An exploratory study of tourist motivations. *Tourism Management, 79,* Article 104098. https:// doi .org/ 10 .1016/j.tourman.2020.104098.

Filep, S., Moyle, B. D., & Skavronskaya, L. (2022). Tourist wellbeing: Re-thinking hedonic and eudaimonic dimensions. *Journal of Hospitality and Tourism Research,* https://doi.org/10.1177/10963480221087964.

Floros, C., Cai, W., McKenna, B., & Ajeeb, D. (2021). Imagine being off-the-grid: Millennials' perceptions of digital-free travel. *Journal of Sustainable Tourism, 29*(5), 751–766. https://doi.org/10.1080/09669582.2019.1675676.

Fu, X., Tanyatanaboon, M., & Lehto, X. Y. (2015). Conceptualizing transformative guest experience at retreat centres. *International Journal of Hospitality Management, 49,* 83–92. https://doi.org/10.1016/j.ijhm.2015.06.004.

Hannonen, O., Aguiar Quintana, T., & Lehto, X. Y. (2023). A supplier side view of digital nomadism: The case of destination Gran Canaria. *Tourism Management, 97,* 104744. https://doi.org/10.1016/j.tourman.2023.104744.

Hjalager, A.-M., & Konu, H. (2011). Co-branding and co-creation in wellness tourism: The role of cosmeceuticals. *Journal of Hospitality Marketing and Management, 20*(8), 879–901.

Hjalager, A.-M., Tervo-Kankare, K., Tuohino, A., & Konu, H. (2016). Robust innovation anchors in rural wellbeing tourism. In N. Pappas and I. Bregoli (eds). *Global dynamics in travel, tourism, and hospitality* (pp. 148–162). IGI Global.

Horton, R., Beaglehole, R., Bonita, R., Raeburn, J., McKee, M., & Wall, S. (2014). From public to planetary health: A manifesto. *The Lancet, 383*(9920), 847. https://doi.org/ 10.1016/S0140–6736(14)60409–8.

Hussain, A. (2021). A future of tourism industry: Conscious travel, destination recovery and regenerative tourism. *Journal of Sustainability and Resilience, 1*(1), 5.

IPBES. (2019). Global assessment report on biodiversity and ecosystem services of the Intergovernmental Science-Policy Platform on Biodiversity and Ecosystem Services. *Zenodo.* https://doi.org/10.5281/zenodo.3831673.

Jabbar, M., Yusoff, M. M., & Shafie, A. (2021). Assessing the role of urban green spaces for human well-being: A systematic review. *GeoJournal, 87,* 4405–4423. https://doi .org/10.1007/s10708–021–10474–7.

Knobloch, U., Robertson, K., & Aitken, R. (2016). Experience, emotion and eudaimonia: A consideration of tourist experiences and well-being. *Journal of Travel Research*, 56(5), 651–662. https://doi.org/10.1177/0047287516650937.

Konu, H. (2015). Developing a forest-based wellbeing tourism product together with customers – an ethnographic approach. *Tourism Management, 49*, 1–16. http://dx.doi.org/10.1016/j.tourman.2015.02.006.

Konu, H., & Smith M. (2017). Cross-border health tourism collaborations: Opportunities and challenges. In M. K. Smith & L. Puczko (eds). The Routledge handbook of health tourism (pp. 298–314). Routledge.

Lehto, X., Davari, D., & Park, S. (2020). Transforming the guest–host relationship: A convivial tourism approach. *International Journal of Tourism Cities, 6*(4), 1069–1088.

Leung, K. Y. K., & Lee, H. Y. (2021). Implementing the smart city: who has a say? Some insights from Hong Kong. *International Journal of Urban Sciences, 27*(1), 124–148. https://doi.org/10.1080/12265934.2021.1997634.

Litleskare, S., MacIntyre, T. E., & Calogiuri, G. (2020). Enable, reconnect and augment: A new ERA of virtual nature research and application. *International Journal of Environmental Research and Public Health, 17*(5), 1738. https://doi.org/10.3390/ijerph17051738.

MacIntyre, T.E., Gidlow, C., Baronian, M., Nieuwen-huijsen, M., Collier, M., Gritzka, S., & Warrington, G. (2019). Nature-based solutions and interventions in cities: A look ahead. In A. A. Donnelly & T. E. MacIntyre (eds), Physical activity in natural settings: Green and blue exercise (pp. 335–348). Routledge.

Nandasena, R., Morrison, A. M., & Coca-Stefaniak, J. A. (2022). Transformational tourism – a systematic literature review and research agenda, *Journal of Tourism Futures, 8*(3), 282–297. https://doi.org/10.1108/JTF-02-2022-0038.

Ram, Y., & Smith, M. K. (2019): An assessment of visited landscapes using a cultural ecosystem services framework. *Tourism Geographies*, 523–548. https://doi.org/10.1080/14616688.2018.1522545.

Reisinger, Y. (2013). *Transformational tourism: Tourist perspectives.* Wallingford: CABI.

Räikkönen, J., Grénman, M., Rouhiainen, H., Honkanen, A., & Sääksjärvi, I. E. (2021) Conceptualizing nature-based science tourism: A case study of Seili Island, Finland. *Journal of Sustainable Tourism, 31*(5), 1214–1232. https://doi.org/10.1080/09669582.2021.1948553.

Saari, S. (2022). In search for new urban tourism niche. Could European cities be destinations for urban wellness providing food for body, mind and spirit? *Tourism and Hospitality Research, 23*(2), 1–13. https://doi.org/10.1177/14673584221086888.

Sheldon, P. J. (2020). Designing tourism experiences for inner transformation. *Annals of Tourism Research 83*, 102935. https://doi.org/10.1016/j.annals.2020.102935.

Saunders, R., Weiler, B., & Laing, J. (2017). Transformative guiding and long-distance walking. In S. Filep, J. Laing, & M. Csikszentimihalyi (eds), *Positive tourism* (pp. 167–184). Routledge.

Šegota, T., Mihalič, T., & Perdue, R. R. (2022). Resident perceptions and responses to tourism: Individual vs community level impacts, *Journal of Sustainable Tourism.* https://doi.org/10.1080/09669582.2022.2149759.

Sharpley, R. (2014). Host perceptions of tourism: A review of the research. *Tourism Management, 42*, 37–49. https://doi.org/10.1016/j.tourman.2013.10.007.

Sorakunnas, E. (2022). 'It's more than just status!' An extended view of social value in tourism. *Tourism Recreation Research*, 1–15. https://doi.org/10.1080/02508281.2022.2103251.

Soulard, J., McGehee, N., & Knollenberg, W. (2021). Developing and Testing the Transformative Travel Experience Scale (TTES). *Journal of Travel Research, 60*(5), 923–946. https://doi.org/10.1177/0047287520919511.

Tanouri, A., Kennedy, A.-M., & Veer, E. (2022). A conceptual framework for transformative gamification services. *Journal of Services Marketing, 36*(2), 185–200. https://doi.org/10.1108/JSM-12-2020-0527.

Teoh, M. W., Wang, Y., & Kwek, A. (2021). Conceptualising co-created transformative tourism experiences: A systematic narrative review. *Journal of Hospitality and Tourism Management, 47*, 176–189. https://doi.org/10.1016/j.jhtm.2021.03.013.

Tuohino, A., Konu, H., Hjalager A.-M., & Huijbens, E. (2013). Practical examples of service development and innovations in the Nordic wellbeing industry. In J. Kandampully (ed). *Service management in health and wellness services* (pp. 325–346). Kendall Hunt.

Uysal, M., Perdue, R., & Sirgy, M.J. (2012). (eds). *Handbook of tourism and quality-of-life research. Enhancing the lives of tourists and residents of host communities*. Springer.

Willis, C. (2015). The contribution of cultural ecosystem services to understanding the tourism–nature–wellbeing nexus. *Journal of Outdoor Recreation and Tourism, 10*, 38–43. https://doi.org/10.1016/j.jort.2015.06.002.

Yang, W., Zhang, Y., & Wang, Y.-C. (2023). Would travel experiences or possessions make people happier? *Journal of Travel Research, 62*(2), 412–431. https://doi.org/10.1177/00472875211064631.

Index